With Friends in High Places

BOOKS BY THE SAME AUTHOR

Not by Money Alone – Economics as Nature Intended
(with Jane King), Jon Carpenter, 2002
The Management of Greed, RUI Publishing, 1997
Dictionary of Energy (2nd edition), Macmillan, 1988
Biological Energy Resources, Spon Press, 1979
Energy in the Economy, Macmillan, 1978
The Island of Skye, Scottish Mountaineering Trust, 1975
The Politics of the Environment, Allen & Unwin, 1972
Scottish Mountains on Ski, West Col, 1970
The Discovery of South America, Hamlyn, 1970
Brazil: Land Without Limit, Allen & Unwin, 1969
The Andes Are Prickly, Gollancz, 1966
Red Peak, Hodder, 1965

With Friends in High Places

An Anatomy of Those Who Take to the Hills

Malcolm Slesser

Foreword by Hamish MacInnes

MAINSTREAM
PUBLISHING

EDINBURGH AND LONDON

Cover photographs: front – April in the Roscoe Bjaerg in north-east Greenland with Tvillinggerne, the highest peak, in profile, 1996; back – Malcolm Slesser during the attempt on Uummannaq Peak, north-west Greenland, 1950 (photo by Norman Tennent)

Copyright © Malcolm Slesser, 2004
All rights reserved
The moral right of the author has been asserted

First published in Great Britain in 2004 by
MAINSTREAM PUBLISHING (EDINBURGH) LTD
7 Albany Street
Edinburgh EH1 3UG

ISBN 1 84018 848 0

The Bare Abundance © G.F. Dutton reproduced courtesy of Bloodaxe Books, 2002

A catalogue record for this book is available from the British Library

Typeset in Baskerville and Myriad

Printed in Great Britain by
Antony Rowe, Chippenham, Wiltshire

To those who cherish the freedom of high places

Acknowledgements

Though climbing on your own is perhaps the most intense way to appreciate a mountain and its environment, you would not get far in this game without companions. Those with whom I have shared days on the hill are too many and too diverse to name here, but if they happen to read this book they will surely know and understand that I acknowledge my debt to them.

As it happens I have outlasted many of my former companions: a few have died on the mountain, some in the lottery of life itself; others have settled into their armchairs. I reflect on my climbs with them with more than just nostalgia. The potential of a climbing 'rope' of two is greater than that of either mountaineer. Without these companions and the umbilical cord that linked us together, my life would have been much the poorer and my experiences sorely diminished. This book, in a way, is a thank you, an acknowledgement, of the important part they played in my life. Without them there would have been no book to write.

I am grateful to the Scottish Mountaineering Club for the camaraderie that I have found there and for permission to quote extensively from its journal. In an effort to bring a sense of balance to the history of events I have quoted from many other mountaineering authors, and I greatly appreciate their permission to quote from their own published stories. These are acknowledged in the text and bibliography. I should like to express my especial thanks to John Howell for rendering maps and photos into a form suitable for publication.

This book started out as a discourse on risk as appreciated through the experiences of a mountaineer. Gradually it was steered in another direction, and for this I am grateful to Jane King and David Fletcher. When I had reached the point of wondering whether the component parts had enough coherence to merit publication it was Leslie Hills who gave me the necessary confidence to continue and Bill Campbell of Mainstream who took on the risk of publication. I am enormously grateful to Deborah Warner, whose meticulous editing has shaped the book so well. Any remaining errors are mine alone.

I should also thank the mountains for letting me into some of their secrets, but they are well able to speak for themselves.

Contents

Foreword

When Malcolm Slesser sent me the manuscript of *With Friends in High Places* I was prepared for a quantum leap back in time; I never thought I could get seduced by a book which had a high percentage of Arctic ice in it. As I read I discovered that there are other compensations in the wilderness; for example, Malcolm was invited by an Inuit to sleep with his daughter as he pointed to the communal family bed in the small room of the hut. Scottish genes were apparently in short supply. My respect for Malcolm grew.

I first met Malcolm in the late 1940s when on weekdays we both lived in Greenock and at weekends escaped to the hills. Though we never did climb together we had numerous mutual friends. One was Major Mike Banks, a Marine Commando. Mike, like Malcolm, doesn't suffer fools gladly. They were on the Greenland ice cap together for three long months, a place where even a saint would suffer cabin fever, especially when subjected to constant irritating prattle from their leader.

Despite some personal observations on the late Dougal Haston, which should have been long forgotten, the book is an excellent read. It spans a golden period when there were still *unknown* places to go. The Staunings Alps of Greenland are a good example.

When Malcolm and his friends ascended the Bersaerker Brae it proved to be the entrance to a wonderland of virgin peaks. This book is diverse with accounts of international peregrinations from a climber/explorer who knows his own mind and who has left his imprint on previously unclimbed and untrodden places.

Hamish MacInnes,
Glencoe, 2004

Preface

Familiar pleasures, like the taste of freshly made jam or reclining in your bed after a long absence from home, are agreeable episodes in your life. But they are no substitute for a taste of the unknown. This is an affliction that settles upon many of us – the urge to explore, to know what lies beyond the next bump and over the next hump, or in the next chapter.

In 1937 I was one of a bunch of boys camping under the auspices of the Scripture Union on the shores of Loch Tay, Scotland, by the little village of Ardtalnaig. Across the loch, unbelievably high to an 11-year-old boy, soared Ben Lawers, its ethereal summit fading into the purple haze of an August heatwave. I instantly knew I wanted to climb it and to my surprise, for I was a puny youth, I was the first to reach the top. From there, crest after unknown crest greeted my eyes. It was my first taste of the unknown. It left me with a compelling desire to explore. In the years that followed I was lucky enough to meet others of a similar disposition. And no matter where I travelled – and I travelled a lot – there was always someone to be found with whom to share this deep desire to penetrate beyond the immediate skyline.

However on my very first serious mountaineering outing, while still a teenager, my companion died through an unbelievably trivial accident – he pulled up onto a large detached block of rock on Sgurr Dearg in the Cuillins. This slid down on top of his thigh and crushed it. By the time we ran down the hill and called the police in Portree, then got a stretcher up the hill, his condition had become fatal. The lesson for me from that tragic incident was that safety lay not in avoiding risk, but in being aware of all the factors in play: to stay alive, imagination had to ride shotgun at all times. Mothers of young children exhibit this awareness to an uncanny degree, in some cases so much so as to inhibit the development of their offspring. It's a difficult choice to let the emerging child find out for him or herself that safety lies in awareness of danger. This theme links the narrative of this book. It is not the story of my life as a mountain explorer, but of discovery shared with friends in high places. Mountaineering may be the sole remaining pastime that is not regulated by overzealous authorities. Long may we continue to enjoy this freedom: the nanny state must be kept in its place.

Edinburgh, 2004

List of Maps

of only a single poem

above the plains
mountains flourish,
white, distracting eyes
from lower compulsions.

they are cold, frequently
dangerous, always
exhausting and when you come down
are still there.

then why climb them?
ask your constituents
ask the headbellies ask
the paunchbrains. not knowing

what it is to represent them
what it is to be the guest
dirty unapologetic

of even a minor pinnacle.

The Bare Abundance, G.F. Dutton

CHAPTER 1

Constructive Boldness or Destructive Folly?

We were two not particularly gifted climbers struggling up an ice-girt cliff face in the dead of winter. I was a salvationist, committed to staying alive and well, whereas my companion was a fatalist. And little wonder. He had been in submarines during the Second World War and, I imagine, without a streak of fatalism day-to-day living would have been insupportable.

Picture the setting. The great north face of Ben Nevis was cloaked in snow, every crevice filled with ice, every overhang fringed with dagger-sharp icicles poised like a portcullis ready to drop upon the unwary. The uncanny silence was disturbed only by the distant roar of the gale that swept the summit ridge, sounding for all the world like distant motorway traffic, except that it was punctuated by an occasional howl, as if some anguished being was pleading for mercy. And then, for the climber, there was another, more ominous sound. The gentle sifting of powder snow as it coursed down the cliff in a never-ending cascade. These fine grains were blown off the summit in a plume 100 or more feet into space before gravity took over and let them parachute gently onto the mountainside, at which point they rolled on downwards. Occasionally they would be stopped in their tracks by an upward eddy of the wind, and so would rest awhile, nourished from above, growing into a modest pile which, eventually becoming unstable, would release itself as a small avalanche.

We had already been hit by several of these. They had little force, but even so the powder snow wormed its way into every gap in our clothing where, as it penetrated, it softened and then thawed, wetting our wrists and necks, adding to our general physical discomfort.

Our progress was slow, each of us moving in turn, alternating the lead, while the other, belayed to the cliff face, paid out the rope that linked us. Here our recognition of each other's style and attitude affected the play. I, the salvationist, made elaborate attempts to secure myself firmly to the cliff face so as to be able to hold my companion should he fall. The mountain was not very cooperative. No spikes or cracks offered themselves. All was cloaked with ice. Our wrought-iron pitons driven into the ice seemed a frail security. But my fatalist companion scarcely cared. He was indulgent of my concern for his safety and waited patiently on the occasions that I led, stamping his feet to keep warm. Then off he went to forge the route anew.

At the time of this tale – over 40 years ago – we were climbing in an era that must seem primitive to today's hi-tech ice climber. Up to 1950 it was considered unsporting to use crampons on the relatively small mountains of Scotland. Brought up on the writings of W.H. Murray, a man we both knew and had climbed with, we had been trained to hack the ice into steps, both for feet and hands, a physically exhausting process, but one which called for skill and rhythm. We two, however, had moved on a little and wore heavy wrought-iron crampons made by a blacksmith in Grindelwald, Switzerland; crude compared with the lightweight models available today. We had yet to learn the present-day two-pick technique. It was about this time that the rubber-soled climbing boot, known at that time as Itshide, had taken over from nailed boots. At first we could scarcely credit the idea of using rubber in winter on snow and ice. Clinker nails were the thing, and for the more affluent, tricounis. Unlike the earlier hobnail, the clinker was made of soft metal attached around the welt of the boot. They held well on wet rock, but required huge welts, making precision footwork impossible. The tricouni was made of tough, hard metal with teeth which, though able to hook onto a tiny protuberance, provided no great feeling of security. They also wore down quickly. Some inventor had come up with replaceable nails, but the idea never took on. Anyway, like most mountaineers of the day, we eventually transferred our affections to Itshide soles, a synthetic plastic product developed for the SAS commandos during the Second World War. They were positively dangerous on wet rock. In due course along came the far superior Vibram.

So, ice axe in hand, Norman scraped and cut and wormed his way along the narrow ledge on the rock wall, occasionally enveloped by dumps of powder snow. It melted on his tan-coloured breeches, garnishing them with lumps of ice. The backside of his breeches was heavily patched with rough stitching and the threads stretched as he bent forwards, reminding me of a mandolin. Only his green Ventile anorak showed any signs of water resistance. Snow, too, had accumulated around his ankles as a result of wearing a second pair of socks that curled over the lip of his boots. It was a common combination in those days and gave a rather smart appearance in the car park or hotel foyer. In fact, it acted like a gutter, draining water into the boot.

His movements were not those of a man nervous of his situation. He moved easily, balancing his body comfortably on the narrow steps, quite at home in his surroundings. The climb was Cousin's Buttress, now a winter Grade III, which means it's pretty easy with today's equipment. A 30-foot traverse and he paused. The summer route, we believed, went up vertically at this point, a pitch that would have been straightforward, but was now covered by a thin carapace of ice. For many minutes there was little movement from my companion. My view of him came and went as eddies of spindrift cavorted around me like some *corps de ballet* and then, as the wind relented, left me an opportunity to see again. My eyebrows were iced up. Every now and then, while still guarding the rope, I would run my wrists against my face to improve my vision and in so doing add a little more snow to the accumulation around my arms. I jumped about to keep warm, for the cold was penetrating fast. Speed equalled warmth. I wished he would get on with it. It appeared that all he had to do was cut a line of holds up the near-vertical ice above him, gain a commodious ledge and call me to follow. I concentrated on sending him strong telepathic messages. Meanwhile the snowfall increased, blotting out all view of the Allt a'Mhuillin glen below. Our world was restricted to the few feet between the two of us. Don't imagine we were in distress. We were there because we wanted to be. A little cold and a bit of dampness was a trivial price to pay for being in such awesome surroundings. Our senses were keenly honed. In the intense concentration that climbing demands, all other thoughts and worries were discarded. We asked for nothing more.

More time passed. He was fiddling about on the rock face, presumably seeking a running belay before pressing on. Then came a shout and the rope was pulled from me. Unclipping from my belay, I followed, grateful for the steps he had cut. Norman was wedged into a corner, his red nose framed by his anorak hood, resembling a puffin peaking out of its burrow. In his languid voice he told me that he had decided it best to belay here as I would make a faster job of the rest of the pitch. This did not surprise me, for though he was the stronger climber and a fatalist to boot, he regarded the opportunity to lead a hard pitch as a privilege, one which, in politeness, he now handed to me. After careful examination of his unsatisfactory belay and various unsuccessful attempts to make it more secure, I took the lead. I cut steps in the 70° ice facing me but as quickly as I did so, they filled with snow: 70° is not vertical, and so with hack and cut and chip, hack, cut and chip, I slowly made height. The spindrift accumulated around my waist, and every now and then I would ease back and let it slide away, whereupon it would engulf Norman. He would shake himself like a dog emerging from the water and mutter familiar but unprintable imprecations.

Eventually I was most of the way up the icy corner. It was not technically hard, and with today's front-pointing technique it would barely invoke a mention down in the pub afterwards, but it was hard physical work with the methods of those days. My arms were tired, my neck was ringed with melting snow, and I needed a third hand to clear off the matted ice on my eyebrows which was restricting my vision. So I cut a good foothold and a decent handhold, wiped the ice from my eyes with my free hand, and for the first time got a good view of the rest of the world. There was not much to see. Just vague outlines, with snow in the air and particles sifting down the cliff face. There were no coordinates to place one in that totally white world. I could have been anywhere: Greenland, the Antarctic, the Alps, even the north wall of the Eiger. The only thing that mentally stood between me and disorientation was that I had arrived here by my own effort and by my own skill I knew I could find my way back down if necessary.

The wind was now stronger, the flow of spindrift more violent, the void below apparently bottomless. It was certainly no place to fall off, especially as I was painfully aware that my companion's approach to belaying was that it was a ritual he engaged in only to please me.

Perched on the points of my crampons, with aching calf muscles and with my frozen fingers clinging onto a snow-filled pocket in the ice, I now gave some thought to what would follow after I completed this pitch. I knew from summer exploration that I would reach a commodious ledge and that beyond was gentler terrain leading to a steep final slope. Access to the summit plateau would be guarded by a cornice that might easily be sticking out many feet into space – we would probably have to tunnel through it. My concern was whether it would have grown to the point where, like snow on the end of a branch, it would eventually break off. A falling cornice can be lumpy enough to cause injury and can also trigger an avalanche. As the current Scottish Mountaineering Club (SMC) guidebook to Ben Nevis remarks, 'this is a fine and remote part of the mountain in winter, but the corrie [*sic*] is prone to avalanche and should be avoided in heavy snowfall'. But it would be another 40 years before these informative words were on sale to the public. I had never been seriously avalanched and considered it a particularly unattractive way to go. From my tenuous perch I could not see the upper mountain, but I could work out for myself that what with the summit gale, the heavy snowfall and the endless spindrift, an avalanche from above was now on the cards.

Now climbing is an activity that favours the bold. But being bold, then dead, was not on my agenda. I was not to know it then, but I was to survive to have at least another 50-odd years of such adventures. On the other hand, the fact that I was within ten feet of the end of the hardest part of the climb was a spur to stop havering and get on with it. Once on the ledge I could make a judgement about whether it was wise to continue. I cut another step and moved onto it. Then I stepped back down again and reconsidered my position. I repeated this manoeuvre several times. Each time I stepped up my intuition told me to retreat. When I retreated I told myself not to be a wimp. Norman was nothing more than a cone of powder snow below and unavailable for advice. Anyway he was a fatalist. Well, I eventually concluded, best to run away and fight another day, and so I climbed back down. I had almost reached Norman, with perhaps two feet to go, when there was a sound of a light crump followed by a swishing sound and suddenly I was embraced by a mass of snow, pulled off my feet and falling. I hoped Norman was firmly holding the rope. He was. The avalanche continued for what seemed like minutes, though it may only have been a few seconds, but it was big. We watched it clear the rocks below and hit a gully, which in turn avalanched, the entire mass disappearing into the snowy void beyond our vision.

'That was a bit close,' opined Norman, not a man given to hyperbole. Our hopes had dissipated like sand before the desert wind. I suggested retreat and he agreed.

Now, is there a moral to this tale? Had I reached the commodious shelf I would have been hit by the full force of the avalanche and would undoubtedly have been swept off, with Norman yanked away after me. As it was we were sheltered by the wall above so that the greater mass of the snow shot over our heads, and Norman's meagre belay sufficed to hold me and him. The question is this: was our presence on the mountain in these conditions a matter of ambition overriding good sense? Did I turn back out of fear, cowardice, wisdom, or some sixth sense of danger? A mountaineering friend of mine, Iain Smart, is fond of saying of himself that the only reason he is alive (he is 70) is because he is a coward. He does himself an injustice, for to my certain knowledge he has taken many a finely judged risk, but he was not above turning back or changing his mind. His was an intellectual assessment, not cowardliness. As he put it himself: 'Where is the boundary between constructive boldness and destructive folly?' This is the eternal question for all adventurers.

What if Norman, the fatalist, had led the pitch instead of me? Would he have discounted the avalanche risk and pressed on? I believe he would, though he was every bit as experienced as I was in judging these things. It would not have mattered if he were the finest climber in the world, avalanches make no exceptions for mere talent.

Many will wonder why we chose to be there in the first place. That morning as we walked up the Allt a'Mhuillin track we were much in that dreamy mood induced by a hot bath, where pleasant fantasies of all sorts cross the mind, dwell for a moment and move on. Once dressed and out and about, sadly, they seem less probable. Our fantasies faded as the shrouded cliffs came more into view. It was clearly not a day for ambition, so we settled for exploration, one of the more satisfying aspects of mountaineering. We were not in search of glory or fame, but out for a bit of fun, that peculiar mountaineers' way of enjoyment. Even my fatalist friend had no death wish. We enjoyed each other's company. A tussle on the mountain was a great way to spend a day and bond with a pal. In the evening a hefty meal and good dram would be the final reward for sustained physical effort and having exercised skill and fine judgement. Perhaps it's a little more subtle than that. Wilfred Noyce, a well-known British mountaineer and author, once put it very well: 'In leaving behind the transitory hopes and fears of pathetic humanity, does one, perhaps, come closer to the things that abide, to forces which endure?'

The idea of being at risk never entered our minds. Of course we knew that a careless move could have serious consequences. But that's what makes climbing interesting and such a passion for its devotees. Mountaineers consider that precise, careful climbing and attention to detail virtually remove any risk. One wouldn't choose to be there with a novice or a manic-depressive. Perhaps it is this need for adventure that drives some young people to vandalise property? Without the element of risk, where is the fun? Life without risk, we believed, was not only impossible but boring. Perhaps the vandals too feel that way, but lack our means of satisfying it. A considered element of risk was the essence of our day out. The adventure and fun was in outwitting risk, just as the vandal likes to outwit the police. For us, however, we had the bonus of an aesthetic experience and physical well-being.

The trick is to know when to give in. Though young, I was no greenhorn. My escape from annihilation was not just luck. My safe arrival up to the high point of this climb had several years of experience behind it. I had learnt the hard way. I had already done a lot of the stupid things a novice does and in so doing I had learnt faster and better than if I had been shepherded by some expert. I had experienced all sorts of snow conditions. My final decision to retreat was an intellectual judgement based on some experience and an understanding of the physics of snowfall. I might have been wrong, and so missed the satisfaction of completing the climb. Had we been able to complete it I believe it would have been the first winter ascent of the buttress. Tennent later wrote a piece entitled 'The primitive approach', which describes our day out in rather colourful language. Ken Crocket in his book *Ben Nevis* interpreted it to imply that we did make the first winter ascent and thus is it recorded in subsequent guidebooks. As it happens I made the right decision. No notices, no injunctions to be careful, no avalanche warnings posted in the valley were offered or wanted. To live well one has to make one's own decisions and abide and learn by them. But the dismal conclusion is that you do need a bit of luck in those early days in this craft of mountaineering – indeed, in life itself.

But luck keeps no one alive for long. The key factor is the need for an awareness of danger. Safety lies in awareness. Whatever your calling, whatever your recreation, this is an essential ingredient of a happy and fulfilling life and, as in mountaineering, the crucial element is appreciating and understanding the nature of the risk you are exposed to. It may be objective risk like avalanche, weather, loose rock, stonefall or melting ice. It may be subjective risk, like losing your nerve, poor route-finding, a weak companion, overconfidence, being out of your depth or being unfit in relation to the climb's demands.

The golden rule is that if your mind is in neutral make sure your armchair is well away from the fire. Alas, from time to time I have ignored my own advice and almost paid the penalty. On one occasion I was at the foot of a climb on the Bonnaidh Dhonn in the north-west

Highlands of Scotland. As I was third on the rope I felt no need to be involved in the doings of my two companions above – Richard Bott and Jane King – so my mind was in neutral, absorbed in the magic sparks of sunlight darting out of the waters of Loch Maree, wondering which of the many islands was the holy island with a well whose waters allegedly cure insanity. I wondered if it could cure my passion for climbing. Thus I was totally oblivious to impending disaster, to the fact that a rock about a foot in diameter had been dislodged 100 feet higher and was noiselessly spinning through the void heading for me. It clipped my ear! Had it been a fraction closer it would surely have killed me, for I had not donned my helmet. It is possible that more mountaineers have died out of carelessness than have ever fallen negotiating some challenging pitch. Thus did Herman Buhl perish on Chogolisa. How absurd that this climber, perhaps the best mountaineer in the world in his time, so self-confident that he climbed the 2,600-foot north-east wall of the Piz Badile before lunch after a late start and who, incredibly, survived 41 hours at 26,000 feet without bivouac equipment, should perish from sheer carelessness. Unroped, he dropped through a cornice. It is a reminder that none of us can be perfect or on-the-ball all of the time. Everyone will sooner or later make a mistake, perhaps at the wheel of a car, in the care of a baby, or as an air-traffic controller. How many of us have cursed our own stupidity at one time or another? And how often has good luck kept us whole? But never bank on it.

I don't go along with the notion of karma. Sherpas will string prayer flags – Lung-ta, or windhorses – on the high mountains of Nepal, and with each flap of the flag, the horse depicted lops off into the wind carrying wish-fulfilling gems needed for survival. It represents positive spiritual energy and awareness. Sherpas say that if their Lung-ta is high, they can survive almost any difficult situation and if it is low, they can die while resting on a grassy slope.[1] I do not believe in confusing karma with fate. Those who insist they are masters of their fate and captains of their soul are deluding themselves. Fate laughs at probabilities. One man who escaped from the Twin Towers horror in New York on 11 September 2001 died 6 weeks later in an air crash. In neither situation was he taking a risk in the ordinary sense of the word. On 26 May 2002, a car was crossing a bridge in Ohio at the very moment when a barge bumped into the support pillar. The bridge collapsed and the car plunged into the river. The driver drowned. Statistical analysis informs us that even if your lifestyle is as cautious as that of a turtle seeking out a beach to lay its eggs, each one of us still runs the risk of extinction in an unforeseen, unforeseeable manner.

There is no such thing as a risk-free existence. This alone is good grounds for making the best of every continuing moment of life. But it is no excuse for fatalism. That has no proper role in mountaineering, which, incidentally, is by no means the most dangerous of activities, even though insurance companies disagree (see appendices).

It is extraordinary how we compartmentalise our lives. On the occasion of this climb on Cousin's Buttress we had driven up from the city. Not for one moment did we consider ourselves to be at risk on that drive, yet statistically we certainly were. According to Smeed's Rule[2] you have roughly a one-in-five million chance of extinction if you are in a car on British roads. Because it would make life very inconvenient if one refused to travel on the roads whether by bus or by car, virtually all of us do. We instinctively discount the risk. I have driven over 600,000 miles in over 50 countries in all sorts of conditions and never hit or been hit by anything more substantial than a snowdrift or a wandering sheep, whereas my fatalist friend had written off several cars by the time of his final demise in 1995 – he inadvertently backed off a pier into the sea. What does that tell us? That I am lucky or that he was unlucky? More likely that my imagination, and hence my sense of awareness, was more vivid than his.

Climbing would not be interesting were it not for gravity. The pull of gravity is a factor, not a risk. A free-falling body drops 16 feet in the first second, a further 48 in the next second and an additional 80 feet by the third – 144 feet in all. If you haven't come to rest by then your prospects are poor. During those three seconds the racing mind will have covered considerable ground. Today the art of belaying has been brought to an advanced level. When Norman Tennent and I were climbing Cousin's Buttress our equipment amounted to three thin nylon slings with laughably low breaking strain plus three wrought-iron pitons – today's climber is girt with so much gear that even carrying it to the bottom of the climb can be an effort. However this has not always made climbing safer. In many cases it has merely allowed the adventurous climber to push out the envelope that little bit further. An example is given in Chapter 5, 'The Tigers of Yesterday'. In Hollywood films falling climbers (even those supervised by Hamish MacInnes) fill their final moments with screams of anguish: in reality this is not what happens. I love this description of a fall off one route on Nevis taken from the pages of the *SMC Journal*:

> Eli streaks out of the groove head down like a 225-lb torpedo,
> my eyes are on stalks as he smashes a crater from the ledge and

bounces into orbit. I wrap the rope tight and think of the 500-foot drop below.

The belay held.

Heinrich Harrer records his thoughts as he and his companions were hit by an avalanche on the White Spider section of the Eiger Nordwand and the pressure of snow increased:

> My thoughts were quite clear and logical, although I felt certain that this avalanche must hurl us off the 'Spider' and down to the bottom of the mighty wall . . . All these thoughts were calm, without any sense of fear or desperation . . . No important thoughts moved me . . . nor did scenes from my whole life go chasing in front of my eyes . . .

I suspect it is the increasingly cloying nature of modern life that is driving more and more people to seek solace in harmless adventure. Mountaineering is one of the more mature of these pastimes, perhaps the only remaining activity that is not regulated by law or rules. The climber is motivated by a complex amalgam of aestheticism, the joy of isolation, self-sufficiency, applying technical skill, the feel of rock on one's fingers as if touching a sculpture, freedom from the restrictions of modern life, but above all, the pursuit of adventure. Chris Bonnington, whose *Quest for Adventure* is one of the best anthologies of its type, remarks in his foreword:

> To me, adventure involves a journey, or a sustained endeavour, in which there are the elements of risk and of the unknown, which have to be overcome by the physical skills of the individual.

I would put it even more simply: for an enterprise to be called adventurous all that is needed is for the outcome to be unknowable. This is why downhill skiing, while fun, is hardly adventurous. Many so-called adventure holidays are a fraud. Before leaving the hotel or hostel you are told what will happen during the day and when supper will be served. My definition, on the other hand, could even include taking up the offer of a blind date.

Mountaineering fits the bill perfectly, offering adventure through a whole panoply of uncertainties, which in turn engage a subtle range of risks and skills. Hillwalking is a delightful pastime, nominally without risk, yet there is always the possibility of a sprained ankle, a thunderstorm, or of losing one's way in the mist. Searches for lost walkers are common. Some perish through hypothermia. The mountain accident statistics are full of such events. Rock climbing, an adjunct of mountaineering, is theoretically more dangerous since if you fall off the consequences can be very serious. But the statistics hardly bear this out, presumably because if you're driven to rock climb you're also minded to take elaborate precautions to minimise the consequences of a fall. It is when we fully commit ourselves to the mountain, especially a big mountain, that the risk widens to embrace many possibilities. Indeed so many factors have to be taken into account that mountaineering truly becomes an intellectual as well as a physical activity. The bigger the mountain, the wider the space, the greater the mental involvement.

NOTES

1 A detailed description of Lung-ta and what they represent is given in the book *Touching My Father's Soul*, written by Jamling Norgay, Sherpa Tenzing Norgay's son.

2 R.J. Smeed, who examined motor vehicle statistics for many countries over a period of time, found that all the data could be cohered into one equation and that the deaths per 1,000 vehicles asymptoted to one death per 1,000 when the car ownership reached 0.7 per adult in the population!

CHAPTER 2

Falling in Love

Once you fall in love with the hills, they become a commanding directive in your life. Many a wife knows this only too well. This is not all bad. Mountains provide an exceptional environmental quality of life for the urban dweller, a source of mental and physical renewal. Husbands and wives can return refreshed to the domestic battlefield. To get in amongst the folds of a mountain is to acquire new knowledge of nature and of oneself. There is solace there. There is beauty. And there is adventure. More particularly it is adventure on a one-to-one basis, which makes it so much more rewarding and lasting than competitive sport. The mountaineer tends to be his or her own person and this holds even for those who do not achieve great recognition.

In short, once hooked on the hills, our careers are dominated by the need to be on or near mountains. And those acolytes whose circumstances place them far from the hills are known to make superhuman efforts in order to spend time in the mountains. Mick Fowler, who has made so many notable winter ascents in the north-west Highlands of Scotland, did so from a base in London, making weekend round-trips of 1,300 miles, travelling by car through the night. Some become so obsessed with the hills that they treat them as a collector's item, ticking off all the 4,000 m peaks in the Alps irrespective of their character, or climbing all the Munros in Scotland irrespective of their quality. Known as Munrosis, over 2,000 people have succumbed to this incurable affliction, with occasional severe cases of Polymunrosis.

In the period when I emerged well enough educated to make a living, a fortnight's holiday a year was the norm – and working Saturday mornings. After the freedom of university this was an unbearable prospect, so I took a job in the West Indies which offered three months leave every three years. Imagine, then, the temptation I faced when after only ten months in the job I received an invitation to climb in Greenland. Pocketing the letter I went off to do my nightshift at the Pointe-a-Pierre oil refinery in Trinidad.

The 35°C heat of the day had given way to a cooler evening, but in the control room the radiation from the thermal cracking unit still had me sweating. The drip from my nose told me that the humidity was not far off 100 per cent. I made a routine examination of the furnace, peering through the inspection ports at the tubes glowing dull red in the flames. This was a vital aspect of control, because if a tube coked up it would soon blister and then burst like an abscess, creating an almighty blaze that would have the fire crew on site in a trice followed by the shift manager. My neck would be on the block and my nascent career as a refinery engineer at an end. All was well. The recording instruments traced their meticulous history with barely a squiggle. I left Harry, my Trinidadian assistant, in charge and went out into the cool night air for a drink. I pulled Norman's letter out of my pocket and read it again for the umpteenth time.

Harold Drever, a geologist at the University of St Andrews, was organising a three-month expedition to west Greenland to measure glaciers. There would be an opportunity to explore unclimbed mountains and he was looking for a competent mountaineer to assist. Bill Murray had been asked but was off to the Himalaya. Was I interested?

What a stupid question! And what an outrageous temptation. Well, as Oscar Wilde said, 'The only way to get rid of a temptation is to yield to it'! Very undecided and to take my mind off this potential disruption to my professional career, I hooked up my bagpipes (to explain: the refinery's automatic control systems worked off a supply of compressed air – when I attached my pipes to this supply I could play lying back in a chair with my feet up without using my own lungs, and at the same time keep an eye on the instrument panel). In the roaring din of the cracking unit Harry raised no objections. I passed an agreeable half hour diluting my thoughts with the pibroch of Donuil Dubh, particularly practising the tricky fingering of the *crunluath a'mach*. I went off shift at daybreak and when I awoke about lunchtime I found myself agreeing with Oscar Wilde.

Three months later I was on a tanker negotiating the muddy waters of the Humber estuary. And within a fortnight I was on the deck of the MV *Disko*, a ship belonging to the Royal Greenland Trading Company, as she punched through the standing waves between Orkney and Fair Isle. Farewell Scotland. At a stately seven knots she plodded across the north Atlantic towards that other Farewell, Kap Farvel (now named Uummannarsuaq), the southern tip of Greenland.

Drever had mustered four young men around him. Pete Wyllie was a graduate student of geology, there to help Drever. His handsome features could have been a model for a sculpture of Adonis. He was a serious scientist with no time for the insanity of mountaineering. Trevor Ransley, a civil engineer, was a chubby, placid individual and a member of the Scottish Mountaineering Club. He was expected to carry out a geodetic survey. Norman Tennent, whom I introduced in Chapter 1, and myself were supporting cast. Our fellow passengers were Danish officials going out to relieve their counterparts and Inuit students returning home. All 20 of us ate at the Captain's table, where we went through a very Danish ritual. The steward would fill small glasses with a vitriol known as akvavit, a foul-tasting spirit which starts life as a potato mash. The Captain would raise his glass. We in turn would raise ours. It was considered de rigueur to catch the eye of each person at table and give the merest nod of acknowledgement. Then on a cue from the Captain we simultaneously threw the vile stuff down our throats in one gulp. Fortunately this seared the taste buds, so that the unpleasantness was transient and was followed by an agreeable glow suffusing our bodies.

It was after an exceptionally good meal with much liquor, for the Captain was celebrating the rounding of Uummannarsuaq, that I gazed in considerable awe at the precipitous snow-flecked mountains rising straight out of the sea on the starboard quarter, and in sheer wonder at the luminous beauty of the icebergs we were now encountering on all sides. This was 1950. Virtually all the peaks were unclimbed. They were to become a fabulous playground in the later years of the twentieth century, accessible from the nearby airfield at Nassarsuaq served from Reykjavik. That very ship, the *Disko*, on that very spot, was to founder in a winter gale many years later with the loss of almost the entire crew and passengers. But on this occasion we glided along on a glass-like surface through patches of fog and amongst an ever-enlarging flotilla of icebergs. Norman, at my side, idly wondered which collective noun would be most appropriate. Flock? No! Bevy? No! Covey? Closer. Procession? Good, almost perfect!

Kap Farvel is at latitude 60°N, the same as Fair Isle. Our first port of call was to be the administrative capital Godthåb (now known as Nuuk), 250 miles to the north. I barely slept on that voyage, and had to be called down to meals, so absorbed was I in the magic of endless mountains, deep inlets, and more and bigger icebergs as the latitude increased. By now the collective noun had evolved from 'procession' to 'armada'. The bergs have seven eighths of their bulk below the water line, so are scarcely influenced by the wind. They are brought south by the current known as the Atlantic Conveyor that passes northwards up the Baffin Island east coast and then veers south on the west Greenland side. For a young mountaineer whose experience was limited to Britain and the Alps, this was an opening of the mind to hitherto unimaginable possibilities.

It came as a surprise to me to learn how much European settlement had once existed on these coasts. According to the sagas, around AD 930 the Viking Gunnbjorn, on his way from Norway to Iceland, lost his way and found himself confronted by the east Greenland pack ice, backed by distant snow-capped mountains. Actually these may also be seen from a high point above Akureyri in north-west Iceland. This is the southern part of the Blosseville Kyst (coast) to be visited in Chapter 11.

The Viking Erik, known as Erik the Red, is credited with establishing the first Norse settlement in Greenland. He had been forced to leave Norway because of a criminal charge and had tried to make a living in Iceland, where he again got into trouble. He was forbidden to return to Iceland for three years. Naturally, he went westwards and reached the west coast of Greenland just north of Uummannarsuaq, where he found lush valleys with better pasture than in Iceland. There were small birch trees and willows, and plenty of seawrack to feed sheep. The moors, or tundra as they are called in the Arctic, were well populated by reindeer and the seas were brimming with seals and cod. Erik resolved to remain. Back in Iceland he told them of a green land. This spin successfully lured other adventurers. In the fullness of time the settlements expanded to such an extent that a Bishop was appointed, Christianity having penetrated the Norse fastnesses. Recent excavations have shown that some indigenous Inuit people had also occupied this region, but were long gone when the Norse arrived.

Trouble was not long in coming – actually it took about a century. At that time up north – north of Melville Bugt (bay), north even of Kap York, right up at latitude 80°N – in an area known as Thule (now

Qaanaaq) lived the indigenous inhabitants of Greenland, the palaeo-Eskimos, whose existence depended entirely on hunting. In 1950 Qaanaaq became the setting for a huge American missile early-warning base. When these hunters first arrived cannot be known with any certainty, but there is evidence from tent rings and charcoal residues to suggest it was about 900 years ago, that is to say a century before the Vikings occupied south-west Greenland. What does seem certain is that they migrated from what is today the Canadian Arctic, driven no doubt in a search for new hunting grounds. To make a living in a climate where for four months of the year it is total darkness; where the temperature can dip to -60°C; where apart from rocks there is no building material save a little driftwood; and where such a thing as a metal knife did not exist, implies an incredibly ingenious and self-sufficient culture. Some of them migrated north and then east around the top of Greenland. Evidence of their passing can be found at Independence Fjord in the very north-east corner. Some went south. Their population numbers must have been determined precisely by the amount of game to be found. One might wonder how such people with such primitive tools could hunt so large a creature as a whale or narwhal, far less catch a seal or hook a fish. The answer, of course, lies in the imaginative use of every single bit of every animal from the intestine to the skin, from the bone to the blubber, from which the means of survival are fashioned. At the time of my visit these skills were still very much in evidence.

Their southward migration on the west coast was inhibited by Melville Bugt, a 200-mile stretch of coast where the ice cap, like an over-iced cake, flows directly into the sea. A few skerries are all the land to be seen until you reach the Devil's Thumb at 73°N, a 600-foot-high obelisk of rock climbed by Tom Longstaff and Pat Baird in 1928, probably the first 'very severe' route on rock ever made this far north. The Thumb was a marker for the Scottish whalers – time to turn back!

The fact of the matter is that some bold hunters and their families took the risk and made that long journey across the sea ice of Melville Bugt. And worthwhile it was. For there, south of latitude 73°N, the Nugsuaq peninsula was a Garden of Eden in comparison to the arid steppe of Qaanaaq: with a land base, plenty of seal, walrus and narwhal, and cod so abundant that they could be caught by foul hooking, the word must have got around. Soon population pressure forced a further migration south, where the sun was higher in the sky and things, in principle, could only get better. Inevitably the two cultures, Norse and Inuit, bumped into each other. Two such different cultures! The one warlike, modern, equipped with fine boats and sophisticated armaments against the peaceful Inuit, whose sole weapons were wooden harpoons tipped with bone.

Then, as so often happens in the affairs of men, the climate took a hand. Winters became harder, summers wetter. The Great Plague in Europe had cut off trade. By the sixteenth century the Norse settlements had withered, while the Inuit, better adapted to harsh environments, had the last laugh. One emigration wave even rounded Uummannarsuaq onto the much less hospitable east coast, where two groups got a toehold, in particular at Angmaggsalik (now Tasiilaq) at latitude 66°N. For centuries the east- and west-coast Inuit were completely isolated from each other. In due course the eastern Inuit were to meet the white man again, in the shape of the Norwegian explorer Nansen, when he penetrated the coastal ice pack in search of an appropriate starting point for his bold journey across the Greenland ice cap in 1882 – a journey later emulated by the physiological research expedition of Hugh Simpson with his wife Myrtle, Bill Wallace and Roger Tuft in 1962. Like Nansen's party, they hauled their own sledges.

Amazing, too, is the migration of the reindeer. What could have impelled these herds grazing the tundras of Canadian north-west territories to make their way north to the vast and empty Ellesmere Island, cross the frozen waters of Smith Sound to Qaanaaq and then further migrate south over 200 miles of the winter sea ice of Melville Bugt? There could have been so little food for them during that passage. But they flourished on the tundras of west Greenland and, as we discovered in 1969, seem also to have made their way as far north as latitude 70°N on the east coast.

Anyway, of all this we were avidly reading as our boat cruised slowly northwards. Several European vessels had long traded with the west-coast Inuit. In this period of history, when European nations were busy expropriating lands throughout the globe, traders from Norway and Denmark were active in west Greenland, each claiming a monopoly. The issue was put to the International Court in the Hague for arbitration and judgement was handed down in Denmark's favour, but with Norwegian rights to hunting on the east coast. With the access to Greenland's resources also came the obligation to manage them in the interests of the Inuit. It has to be said that the Danes have done an excellent job as colonial rulers. They organised schools, built harbours, introduced regular communication and brought a legal system to bear upon a society that was based on harsh traditions that arose from the

Inuit's remorseless fight for survival in a hostile environment. They provided houses, coal, fuel for lamps, built stores to help out during time of scarcity, and organised a market for the hunters' furs. Today Greenland is an independent country, yet the Danes continue to subsidise it to the tune of £6,000 per head per year.

By 11 July the *Disko* was off Sukkertoppen, named after the sugar-loaf peaks behind the settlement now known as Maniitsoq, spires as crenellated as the Dolomites; another paradise for climbers in the years to come. The three mountaineers amongst us were at fever pitch. The *Disko* finally ended her northward voyage at a lively settlement then called Jacobshavn. We visited the nearby fjord into which debouched a truly living glacier flowing down from the inland ice. Every few minutes there was a calving – a process in which the ice front moves into the sea, becomes buoyant and breaks off from the parent mass, pushing out a powerful tidal wave. Carried by the Atlantic Conveyor, these icebergs then float slowly and majestically out into the Atlantic.

Our journey north continued onboard a 1,000-tonne icebreaker, the *Tikeraq*. Under cloudless skies and in utter calm the boat headed for Disko Island (now Qeqertarsuatsiaq). By now it was continuous daylight. That night the red orb of the sun hovered just a couple of degrees above the horizon for hours on end. Surrounding us were icebergs of every imaginable shape, from the size of super tankers to lumps of brash ice, which the boat knocked aside with a dunt that sent a shiver through its hull. But it was a pleasing euphony. The bergs were so deeply sculpted that parts acted like a lens, both concentrating and diffusing the sunlight into a kaleidoscope of colours from yellow to rose to gold to red. We were transfixed by the ethereal beauty of the scene. Nothing could be heard except the swish of water as the bow cleaved the silent sea. Time stood still.

First we dropped into Kudliqsaq on Qeqertarsuatsiaq, Greenland's only coal mine, where the coal seams are openly visible. This, too, had briefly had a Norse settlement. After an exchange of passengers and goods the boat headed north and east for Uummannaq Fjord and Island at latitude 72°N, home to a large and ancient settlement of Inuit, and incidentally in recent times, a venue for an annual Arctic golf tournament – on the ice! It was cancelled in 2003 for lack of ice: a harbinger of global warming? On all sides rose ice-capped precipices, separated by glaciers that plunged straight into the sea. We were approaching the finest peak of all, the 3,800-foot tower of red granite that forms the east side of Uummannaq Island. For Norman and I, its ascent was a must.

Uummannaq Island is an Arctic desert to the extent that the main source of water is from passing icebergs. We found the inhabitants busily engaged in flensing a huge whale, whose blood stained the sea on the south-east side of the island. I was disturbed to see an eight-foot foetus. The locals regarded it as a delicacy, but it was one less whale in a declining population. Today there are hardly any whales left and very little cod. This would not have happened in historic times, as the Inuit would not have had the technology with which to plunder the sea's bounty. Sadly Greenland has gone the way of the rest of the world in over-fishing and over-hunting. A recent BBC wildlife programme renamed it 'Grimland'. According to Kjeld Hansen, in a piece entitled 'A Farewell to Greenland's Nature', polar bear, walrus, narwhal, common seal and harbour porpoises are all under threat from over-hunting. The eider duck is in danger of extinction. If you have an eiderdown sleeping bag, cherish it. It is irreplaceable.

We were informed that two members of the German 1932 expedition led by Alfred Wegener, of continental-drift fame, had climbed Uummannaq Peak, but no one could tell us their route. Norman and I examined the face with binoculars and picked out a way to the col between the two summits. It proved a straightforward rock climb and within four hours we were on the col. From here the only feasible route appeared to be by a commodious ledge, or *vire au bicyclette* as it might be described in a French guidebook, that led upwards and out of sight. As we followed it the exposure became ever more dramatic, until eventually we had a sheer drop below us of over 3,250 feet. Above was a near-vertical wall defending the route to the summit. Though climbing this wall was technically possible, subsequent descent would have had to be *en rappel*. Norman pointed out that we had only 100 feet of climbing rope, which meant at most a rappel of 50 feet each time. We had no gear with which to fix more than one rappel. Regretfully, we returned to base.

Next day we boarded a small schooner, the *Hvid Fisken*, which led us back out of Uummannaq Fjord to our destination further north and west at Karret's Fjord. This four-mile-wide channel had been carved out over millennia by the Rinks Glacier, which is nourished from the inland ice cap. It was one of Drever's scientific objectives. We were to measure its rate of flow.

It was at this stage that the expedition started to fall apart – and very educational it was for my future role as an expedition organiser. Drever's efforts had secured the necessary funds. He had arranged the food and materials and had organised the travel. He thus had leader's rights. As he was much older and more knowledgeable than the rest of us about the Arctic, we accepted him as our leader and guide. Unfortunately he had no leadership qualities. An academic by occupation and nature, he was indecisive and, being unsure of himself, compounded the problem by failing to include us in his thinking. We acolytes, finding ourselves in this stunning environment, were anxious to make the most of every moment. We were like tethered huskies bursting to be off. But Drever played a slow hand and to our gestures of impatience kept muttering 'titti galore' – a corruption of a Gaelic phrase, *tide gu lèor*, meaning 'no hurry'. He would explain it in his ponderous way through a story of an Englishman who had bought a plot of land in Lewis and had organised workmen to build a house. They came, laid a foundation and then departed. Days turned into weeks with no sign of their return. Whenever he telephoned his builder he was fobbed off with 'tide gu lèor'. In search of enlightenment he called on his Gaelic-speaking neighbour who lit his pipe and took a deep breath.

'Well,' he said, 'you will know the Spanish word *mañana?*'

He nodded.

'Well, tide gu lèor doesn't have quite the same sense of urgency.'

From then on we referred to our leader as Titti Galore. Rebellion was now in the air, quelled only by his departure to Ubekenjdt Island to conduct his geological enquiries. He offered no advice on the next stage of our journey, which was to head up Karret's Fjord to a point where we could reach the Rinks Glacier, whose speed and other properties would be measured. Nonetheless it was his duty as leader to see that we beginners in Arctic matters were properly apprised of any dangers we might face.

Our final voyage was in a 16-foot dory with outboard to a point 4 miles short of where the Rinks entered the sea. If I had known then what I know now about such fast-moving glaciers, I would have demanded a wetsuit and a life jacket. Such is the speed of this glacier that when it calves, the subsequent tidal wave generates a literal tsunami that sweeps down the fjord, tossing aside anything in its way, from boats to icebergs. It was totally irresponsible of Drever to send us off ignorant of these dangers without the means of survival. Good leadership is essential to safe travel. We needed to be aware of the danger. However, ignorant of our peril, we boated to within four miles of the snout of the Rinks Glacier and made camp on the moraine of a side glacier. It was then we became aware of the risks we had run. Huge lumps of ice were stranded on the shore 20 feet above the high water line, clearly left there from the last calving. We wisely pulled our boat 30 feet up from the shore. I was relearning the old rule of survival: always be aware of what could happen even if it's unlikely.

It was a messy struggle to get all the scientific equipment to the upper Rinks Glacier via some subsidiary glaciers. We stayed there a week in poor weather. It even rained. We were as wretched as a cat in a bath. We set up markers at various points on the four-mile-wide glacier and then observed their movement with a theodolite. To our amazement the glacier was found to be moving downhill at 40 feet a day, making it one of the fastest in the northern hemisphere. As we lay silently in our damp sleeping bags at night we could hear its arthritic creaks and groans.

By the end of August we had evacuated our base at Karret's Fjord and rejoined Drever at the settlement of Igdlorsuit on Ubekenjdt Island. Archaeologists had found remains of an old Norse cooking pot there. Ten miles across the fjord was Upernavik Island, a forest of shapely peaks rising 6,000 feet out of the sea, seemingly unexplored.

So, at last liberated from scientific duties, we headed for some mountaineering fun. Drever allocated an Inuit named Joseph to accompany us to Upernavik Island. He was a tiny fellow, whose Mongol features were perpetually creased in a smile. He wore sealskin trousers and a dun-coloured cotton anorak. We had no common language beyond a few Danish phrases. He paddled over in his kayak while Trevor and I used the dory. Norman, who had damaged his leg on the foray to the Rinks, had been carted off to Uummannaq to have his leg X-rayed. We camped on a strip of tundra by the shore just beside a glacier that flowed into the sea. It had everything a camp should – it was dry underfoot, with a little burn for water, tundra to loll in, a view of the sea and ice-clad mountains, and scarcely a breath of wind. The incipient autumnal night frost had killed off the mosquitoes. Joseph supplied us with endless cod. It was heaven. It was here that a Runic inscription by three Norsemen dated 1135 had been found. They must have settled here, if only briefly.

The glacier led us into a snow basin from which rose four superb peaks, all virgin. Two were of no great difficulty, but revealed 4,000-foot precipices on their north side, meat for some future escapades. The jewel in the crown lay at the head of the glacier, a triangle of ice topped by a rock tower – Hvidfjell, 6,800 ft, on our Danish geodetic survey map. OK, it *was* a white peak, but it deserved something grander. Danish place names in Greenland are generally pretty boring, if mildly descriptive. Many are named after visitors and especially after people who have funded expeditions, hence Rinks Glacier.

Trevor and I were fit and aided by Joseph for a couple of hours soon reached the point where the mountain rose in a sweep of snow that narrowed to a fine arête. In late August the snow was well consolidated and we cramponed up the 50° slope moving together and soon found ourselves at the base of the final 200-foot granite tower. Happily its north side proved amenable to climbing, and within the hour we had claimed our third virgin peak, one to be proud of.

We asked Joseph what it was called: 'Kakortoq Napasadleraq,' he replied. Much more authentic than 'white mountain', we thought. Unfortunately it means the same thing.

Back at Igdlorsuit the night before heading home we partied at Joseph's house. His domain consisted of a wooden shack comprising a single room about 20 sq. ft. One side was given over to domestic arrangements and the other had a large raised area covered with seal skins upon which the entire family slept. Bodily functions were performed outside in the open. When so engaged I found I had to bring with me a pile of stones with which to ward off loose and starving husky dogs anxious for my faeces.

We danced to the music of my bagpipe chanter and drank copiously of the Inuit beer, *imiaq*. Then came the embarrassing moment. Joseph presented me with his daughter and indicated the bed. I was in no doubt that I was being invited to deflower his daughter. I should have known this would happen. We had noticed several red-headed people about, which was strange in a race that naturally had black hair. On enquiry it seemed that a certain Scottish whaling captain had spent a winter here several decades ago. He had distributed his favours and they were much appreciated in a society suffering from inbreeding. But whatever my value to the local gene pool or my attraction to the young lady, I was certainly not about to exercise them in public. I feigned incomprehension. Joseph exhibited puzzlement and then anger. The party died on its feet. It was a good thing we left next day for home.

I was now totally seduced by the Arctic. This was no land of black and white, but of both subtle and vivid colours, of textured landscape, of a million shades of green and brown, of great people, of fabulous weather, of continuous daylight and, need I say it, of innumerable virgin peaks. I couldn't wait to get back. I was addicted for life.

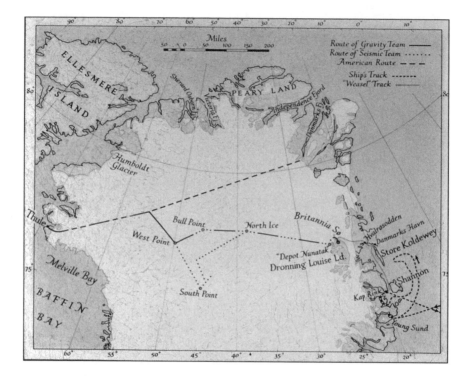

CHAPTER 3

Where There's a Will, There's a Way

One of the ruses adopted by mountaineers to get away from their gainful employment and onto the hills is to embrace scientific exploration. Carefully thought out this can create an aura of respectability and even advance your career. Who knows how many restless husbands have adopted this stratagem. Perhaps Pytheas, pining to get away from the domesticity of his Marseilles home around 330 BC offered map-making for the benefit of mariners as his excuse. It was a splendid effort. He probed the very edges of the Arctic sea and produced a most creditable map of northern Europe. Columbus spent years trying to persuade Spanish and Portuguese monarchs to support his crazy notion that the best way to Japan was to sail west. Queen Isabella eventually backed him and the rest is history. What you need to pull off this sort of trick is a good idea and the help of influential people. Wally Herbert, who had won his spurs in Antarctica, hit on the bold idea of crossing the polar basin from side to side. He got support and in 1968 made this very adventurous journey over 18 months, the first in the world to do so. It earned him a knighthood as well as a profitable way of life.

Naval Commander and mountaineer C.J.W. (Jim) Simpson got his inspiration while flying on a mission over north-east Greenland. The seemingly endless ice cap below suddenly gave way to land, a dramatic mountainscape entirely surrounded by ice, for it was separated from the east coast by 2 gigantic 20-mile-wide glaciers. Could it really be, he asked himself, that in the year of grace 1949 there was still virgin territory in the northern hemisphere? That delicious word 'unexplored' registered in his mind. What good reason could he think up to persuade their lordships of the Admiralty to let him take time off and explore it?

Nursing such things to fruition is a long and arduous task and requires four essential things: along with an idea and influential contacts, you need persistence and money. Back home he scoured the maps and found it had a name: Dronning Louise Land, named after a Danish Queen. Situated at 77°N it had never felt the foot of Man. What red-blooded mountaineer could resist such a temptation? He had observed that there was, of all things, an ice-free loch lying between two subsidiary glaciers. Could a flying boat land there? If so, access would be so easy. The following year he tested his theory, persuading the RAF to land a Sunderland flying boat on the loch. Understanding that national pride is a great lever, he named the loch Britannia Lake and added an Admiralty Glacier for good measure. Thus was an expedition born.

He still lacked one ingredient: a respectable reason for going there. There is so much we still do not know about the world and its origins that it took him very little time to find a suitable scientific peg. An unresolved issue amongst geologists and glaciologists was whether Greenland's ice cap was a layer of ice overlying a plateau or, as some thought, a huge store of ice as deep as it was high surrounded by a ring of mountains. To resolve this issue, he was told, it would be necessary to transit the ice cap measuring its height above sea level and the depth of the ice. What started as a summer jolly for a few climbers finally turned into a 24-man expedition costing £80,000, which in today's money is little short of £1 million. Considerable organisation was called for. It would require tracked vehicles, sophisticated equipment, a winter base and all the paraphernalia of survival in a remote region, together with the right people to man the scientific programme. As the idea was examined in detail it became clear that two summers on the ice cap would be needed. This meant two winters as well.

Simpson realised that everything could be supplied by the British armed forces and that by engaging all three arms of the services, but with leadership resting with the senior service, he might better capture the minds of the top brass. First he set out to acquire influence. He put the jingoist idea of 'once again raising the flag of British Naval Arctic Exploration' to the Admiral of the Fleet, A.U. Willis. Admiralty Glacier went down well, while the significance of Britannia Lake (Britannia Sø) was not lost on the Queen, who agreed to be a patron, as did the then Prime Minister, Winston Churchill. The Air Force offered the services of their Sunderland flying boats and the War Office threw in the sappers, mechanics and radio facilities. Scientific respectability came when he got the support of the Scott Polar Research Institute in Cambridge. This was followed by the Royal Society. By early 1952 all was set except for the appointment of the manpower. In the services men were queuing up to join, but scientists had to be recruited and this was when I got my call.

It being a naval expedition, all activities would have their officer in charge. Mike Banks, a Major in the Marines and author of *Commando Climber,* was to be in charge of the ice-cap team measuring the surface height of the ice from the east to west coast. Satellites and global positioning systems did not yet exist. The height and distance would be measured by the laborious method of observing angles on a subtense bar. This is a horizontal rod with two marks exactly two metres apart. The bar is carried forward a mile or two and levelled. With a theodolite the angle subtended by the two marks is noted. Thus the distance can be calculated by trigonometry. Once this was done the height difference could also be computed. Pretty simple, really. In fact, it requires many corrections and took Stan Paterson, who took over the post of surveyor in the second year, six months to do all the calculations. Stan later wrote the seminal book on glaciology which was published by the Russians. Each year he goes to the Siberian Arctic to spend his royalties in non-transferable roubles.

Mike, with whom I had often climbed, suggested I apply for the post of surveyor. I pointed out that surveying was not part of my chemical engineering training. He countered that all I needed was an elementary knowledge of trigonometry and that the important thing was to have mountaineering skills and a desire to go to the Arctic. I applied and found myself being vetted by one of the expedition trustees, the Bishop of Portsmouth, an old Antarctic hand. We had a nice chat over afternoon tea and then I was asked the killer question: as a last expedient, would I be willing to eat the dogs? To someone desperately wanting to go to Greenland there could be only one answer. I was selected. As a lover of dogs, I am happy to say I was never called upon to eat any of my dog team and I have a picture of my favourite husky in my study to this day. My salary was to be £265 per year all found.

At the expedition HQ in London it was explained that each of us had to be a master of several trades. I was told to organise photography, learn about boot repair, the use and care of a theodolite and subtense bar, and take a course in institutional cooking. This latter experience I describe in Chapter 14. I was briefly apprenticed to Robert Lawrie at Marble Arch, at that time *the* mountain boot maker in the UK. We each had enormous custom-made boots that required two socks and a furry liner. These were of the *weltschoen* type and I was initiated into how to repair and re-sole them with Vibram soles. I knew nothing of photography beyond snapping the shutter, but I never mentioned this to anyone and somehow gained and retained a totally undeserved reputation as an expert. In a steep learning curve I ordered chemicals and enlarging equipment, and bought myself a decent camera. Meanwhile I was introduced to a theodolite, with which I was at once captivated. It was so incredibly precise, measuring angles to a mere second of an arc. I read up all about compensation for parallax, dip and other corrections. As a numerate person none of these were abstruse and I felt quite confident about this part of my duties.

The Army issued us with its Arctic warfare clothing and thus attired we stood to attention, dripping with sweat, on a sweltering June day in London, while the Queen inspected us. Finally we were off in a chartered Norwegian sealer called MV *Tottan*. It chugged slowly up the east coast of England at a speed somewhat slower than a punt powered by out-of-condition dons, rounded the Butt of Lewis and slid and slewed and rolled its course to the west Greenland port of Ivittuut. They say sailing is a grand way to get to know your companions. Some, overcome by sickness, never appeared at all. No wonder! We were allowed the use of the galley only after the three-man crew had eaten. My recollection is of a floor coated in fat and of an irredeemable odour of rotting seal.

On our already crowded vessel were now housed 24 huskies with whose melancholy howling one could sympathise. They were miserable, seasick and disinclined to eat the loathsome dried fish we offered them daily. Its rancid smell penetrated the entire vessel and accounted for the even smaller number of expedition members up and about.

We sailed north up the Denmark Strait between Greenland and Iceland, alongside the edge of the pack ice. Our objective was Young Sound on Greenland's east coast at latitude 74°N. Here we would be met by Sunderland flying boats and be flown into Britannia Lake. There is a strong southerly current down the coast bearing icebergs and polar pack, which can extend as far as 100 miles out into the Denmark Strait. With the ice belt becoming ever wider as we sailed north, the Captain finally put the bow into the ice at 75°N and headed landwards. Slowly the boat cleaved a passage, eventually to become ice-fast. It was remarkable how swiftly our erstwhile bedridden companions rushed to leave the ship and scamper about on the ice floes. However, land was in sight and, from a perch in the crow's nest, the Captain manoeuvred the boat from one lead to another, reaching Young Sound at 74°N on 29 July 1952. Just east of our anchorage stood the Danish Sledge Patrol base at Daneborg which was later to prove so valuable to us. Two days later the Sunderlands flew in. There followed a 16-hour working day unloading the ship, transferring food and equipment to the flying boats, and then unloading them again at Britannia Lake. There a party started assembling our prefabricated base hut under the direction of Sapper Jim Walker.

Considering the size and complexity of the enterprise it is to the credit of Simpson, Major Mike Banks, Lt.-Commander Angus Erskine and Captain Jim Walker that everything went as well as it did. The summer weather was brilliant, the tundra warm and accommodating. We cooled off in the sea. It was 2°C.

Britannia Lake was disappointing. It had none of the allure of the west Greenland Arctic. Hemmed in by a glacier at each end, its waters were muddied by glacial silt and continually battered by a katabatic wind flowing down from the ice cap. Tendrils of rock dust forever spinnied into the air penetrating our clothes, ears and eyes. We would just have to make the best of it. Our base hut was to be perched on a moraine above a sandy beach. The 2,000-foot hillside above was bare of vegetation, striated into varicoloured bands of rock. By comparison the Red Cuillin or the Tatra would be considered verdant. We were splendidly isolated, but the important thing was that we had easy access to the inland ice which was to be the essential focus of our endeavours.

As we were all virtually strangers this was the interesting period where human relationships were being freshly formed and tested. If you are going to spend 2 years in the sole company of 23 other individuals, shorn of female contact, you are wary of setting precedents. Careless talk can cause rumours – and rumours or criticism can cause lasting harm in such a small community. Our leader did himself no good by constantly issuing orders to people who already knew what they were doing, and chiding us for not working hard enough and not getting out of our sleeping bags sooner. We were working flat out, giving our best. He suffered from a grievous malady: undifferentiated enthusiasm.

Once established in our base hut we dossed in four-man cubicles. It was very much officers and other ranks, plus scientists, though all had

47

the same standard of quarters. The biggest problem was for the three officers who had to share with Jim Simpson. He turned out to be a most irritating individual, with an idiotic laugh used with unnecessary frequency, for he had no real sense of humour. During the subsequent summer, after the teams had been on the ice cap for three months, Mike Banks reminded us of an ancient navy regulation, to wit that buggery was permitted after three continuous months at sea. To tease Simpson a radio signal was sent asking for permission. Unfortunately, unbeknown to us, our radio communications were being listened to by radio hams all over the world. Commander Simpson was rightly furious. The poor man! Throughout the winter everyone avoided him at meals so that only the latest arrival at table sat next to him. Yet he was a decent soul, though no Shackleton. Fortunately he was not called upon to face decisions of the magnitude facing those crossing the Weddel Sea in an open boat. If any one person can take the credit for keeping the expedition together that winter it was Richard Hamilton, our chief scientist – a marvellous man. In his job back home he was responsible for the Scottish weather forecast. He used to say that had he been allowed to look out of the window he might have got it right. *Plus ça change, plus c'est la même chose?*

So there we were, all of us trying to be nice and accommodating, compressed into a space of 50 x 24 feet and suddenly with nothing much to do except whinge. Britannia Lake quickly became Camus Cac. North-east Greenland is an Arctic desert, with low snowfall and a very brief period in summer when the temperature rises above freezing point. The big task was to get six men off by dog team out into the middle of the ice cap. The RAF would drop them a hut and supplies to set up an ice-cap base to be manned by three of them through the winter. The trouble was that though it was now freezing, the glaciers had been stripped of snow, leaving bald ice. The dogs could not get a grip. Moreover the summer's melt had eroded the ice into channels as deep as 6 feet and between 10 and 20 feet wide. Sledges had to be man-handled across these obstacles, difficulties that would disappear, it was thought, once the winter snows filled them in. In fact winter gales scoured the ice clean of snow, polishing the surface like jeweller's rouge. Eventually we got the dog teams onto snow at the 4,000-foot contour on the edge of the ice cap and bade them farewell in their 250-mile dash to the crown of the ice cap. I return to this story in Chapter 8.

This initiative dealt with, the next problem was how to bring our tracked vehicles (weasels) to Queen Louise Land (QLL). It had been intended that in the late summer the *Tottan* would sail to Dove Bay at latitude 78°N, more or less on the other side of the 20-mile-wide Storströmmen (big stream) glacier and deposit the weasels at the mouth of the Seal River, where there was a disused trappers' hut called Hvalrusodden. In the spring the weasels would be collected and driven to base. But the pack ice had been too dense for the *Tottan* – the crew were stranded 200 miles to the south. The entire expedition's raison d'être depended on getting them here in time for the spring exploration of the ice cap. Mike Banks with three others had gone with the *Tottan* to Reykjavik to pick up the weasels. He recorded their efforts in *High Arctic*:

> The ice kept forcing us further and further south . . . until we found ourselves in the middle of Hochstetter's Bay . . . The factor that gave me most concern was our shortage of fuel. It would be impossible to drive all eight vehicles to QLL. We asked the Captain to steer as far north as he could . . . To our delight as we approached Kap Hamburg, we saw open water ahead . . . We reached Kap Rink on Hochstetter's Foreland.

There they unloaded the vehicles and Banks and his companions, Sergeant Taffy Oakley, Hans Jensen (a captain in the Danish Army and our liaison officer) and Lt. Richard Brookes (RN) settled down to await a team from base, also interestingly recounted in Mike Banks' book.

The plan, illustrated in Map 1, was for 4 men to walk across the 20-mile-wide Storströmmen, then 30 miles down frozen Seal Lake in Germania Land to the Hvalrusodden hut where sledges from the Danish weather station at Danmarks Havn, 40 miles to the east, would pick them up. They would stay there until the sea was sufficiently frozen, and then dog-sledge 180 miles south to Kap Rink. They would then drive the vehicles to Hvalrusodden. Sounded easy, simple: certainly interesting. I was one of the four selected as we set forth on 19 September. It was almost the equinox and at this latitude daylight diminishes perceptibly day by day and is gone by late October. The logistics of this trip were no easy matter, for not only had we to make a 70-mile trip to the coast, but we would be returning in the dark in November, when we could expect temperatures of -40°C with a possibility of long-lasting gales which would have to be sat out. So we burdened ourselves with double sleeping bags and a double skin pyramid tent. Even dry, these monsters weigh 25 lb. They have no groundsheet but if properly erected can be very snug. We carried sheepskins as mattresses. These served the dual purpose of insulation and absorbing moisture. The tents had four corners of which two were reserved for snow to be melted for food and drink, one for slops and one for defecation and urination, it often being impossible to carry out these functions outside. As we moved every day, or most days, and as the cold snow acts like a sponge, these intimate activities resulted in no smell or hygenic risk. All this together with food and fuel added up to a considerable weight – 65 lb each.

As befits a naval expedition, an officer had to be in charge. This was Jim Walker. He finished his Army career as a general, but at this time he was a captain, and an active hillwalker. The other two were Spike Boardman (a REME sergeant), whose views on glacier walking were unprintable, and naval officer and radio expert Brett-Knowles, a beanpole of quite extraordinary height. We never knew his christian name. He was always referred to as BK. Though Winston Churchill had sent the expedition a valedictory exhortation about our 'daring mission', I at no time experienced any great sense of daring or indeed real danger. This was not so for many of the non-mountaineers. I also think that we mountaineers were better able to make ourselves more comfortable in the often primitive situations.

The first day we made about 12 miles, but not in a straight line. We were searching for a route that could be used by our vehicles on the return journey. The Storströmmen was well named. Crossing the huge, but now frozen, meltwater channels called for ice-climbing techniques. The glacier surface was rough and easy to walk on, whereas the meltwater channels were smooth and slippery, and since each one would end up in a *moulin*, a slip was not to be contemplated. A moulin is where a summer meltwater stream disappears down a crevasse – never to reappear! By the third day the eastern wall of mountains, Germania Land, at last seemed attainable. The sheer boredom of that walk would take some beating. Up, down, up, down. No change of scene, yet every step to be carefully considered; shoulders aching. Eventually we agreed on a stop every half hour.

The last and fourth day on the glacier filled us with gloom: the terrain made us zigzag; a light mist cloaked the far hillside, our goal; we had disagreements about the best route. Sufficient fresh snow had blown into hollows so that the trailbreaker would sink to his knees. We had never imagined it taking so long to cross and we were now eking out our food supplies. Abruptly the glacier ended and there, facing us, were two musk oxen. BK whipped out his revolver but the beasts were more frightened of us than we were of them. It was bliss to walk on tundra again. We completed the last six miles to Seal Lake in the remainder of the day's pale light and camped on sand; a joy after snow and ice. My diary recalls, though, that we could not agree on a camping site. Well, that's why we had an officer in charge.

To our astonishment and enormous disappointment, freshwater Seal Lake was not frozen! Its sides consisted of steep scree running straight into the water, hellish to walk on, especially with a light covering of snow. Our only recourse was to go by the 3,000-foot mountain plateau above the lake. Now on half rations and with little fuel, we slogged up the brae. The plateau consisted of boulders and breakable snow crust, yet because of the fine weather we enjoyed a tremendous sense of exhilaration. The bright sun at midday, barely 5° above the horizon, cast long shadows from the icebergs in Dove Bay, already partially frozen in for the winter. One had to remind oneself that they were the residues of the ice cap, from snow that would have fallen centuries before.

Then BK sprained an ankle. His hobble reduced our speed so much that we were forced to take stock. Most of his load was distributed between the rest of us, who would now be carrying coolie-type loads of 90 lb. We adopted the camel's approach to getting to our feet: as you knelt, someone would ease your rucksack onto your back, then first on all fours, followed by a helping hand we stood up. The fourth person's sack was lifted onto his shoulders by the others. This was so much safer than swinging the sack onto your shoulders in the traditional way. Such a manoeuvre can give rise to a strained back or even catch a nerve in a vertebrae. This was no place to suffer from back problems. As it was we all had piles from the stress of our heavy packs. That night we ran out of fuel.

Next day our immediate destination, Hvalrusodden hut, came into distant view nestling in a corner of Dove Bay, like some remote Highland bothy. A brutal scree descent brought us onto lovely tundra. BK was hobbling slower and slower. The only thing to do was to leave him, with Spike in support, in the tent, while Jim and I pressed on to the hut, which we gained in darkness after a day of 20 miles. What bliss! This fine old hut was stocked with food and fuel and there were bunks to sleep in. We lit the fire, soaked in the heat, rehydrated our bodies and ate and ate and ate. Next day we returned for BK and shepherded him to a nearby old expedition hut, leaving him and Spike with food and fuel for a week. I often wondered what they talked about between them. They were such disparate characters.

Plans, of course, never quite work out. The Danmarks Havn people were supposed to be there to sledge us to their base. Why they were not was at once clear. The sea surface, though frozen (it was 27 September), could not yet support a sledge. Jim and I, now more lightly laden, set off for the 40-mile traverse of the coast of Dove Bay to Danmarks Havn. The temperature was somewhere close to -20°, but the day was windless, so we felt no discomfort. The sun, though a bare 5° above the horizon at midday, still provided a touch of warmth. This was a tribute to the clarity of the Arctic atmosphere; in, say, the Alps, the sun's rays would have been attenuated by air pollution. Our bodies cast shadows 40 or more feet long. The sun hung like a lantern, apparently unmoving until imperceptibly the light turned from gold to orange and finally to the steel grey of dusk. Not a sound was to be heard, neither bird, nor beast, nor Man. Our footsteps were hushed by the lemon-tinted powder snow. I cannot ever wish for a more moving experience. This was textured country, each rise and fall a delight to behold. Such moments are what those of us who leave the crowd hope to find: rare experiences of intellectual ecstasy.

Our journey was not without its concerns. We had two days' food, but no fuel, no stove, no tent. Dove Bay is notable for its polar bears and we had no weapon. Both Jim and I were skinny, so hopefully unappealing to a bear, but with the sea not yet fully frozen, seals would be in short supply and a forage on land for musk oxen would be the bears' obvious strategy. These primeval beasts, the musk oxen, were also a problem for us. We kept sighting small herds of them and knew they would not chase us, but if they felt threatened, then what? So we were forced into long detours. Just as well, for later at Danmarks Havn I witnessed an adult husky that dared to challenge a musk ox being gored and tossed into the air like a sack of garbage. When danger looms these engaging beasts form a crescent facing the enemy, presenting a schiltron of horns that no polar bear is willing to risk.

We were lucky that night to come across a tiny trapper's refuge: a box of a hut measuring 6 x 4 feet, but with a coal stove – and coal! How we roasted ourselves that evening! Every mountaineer will know the overwhelming seduction of warmth and comfort after privation. Jim had an awful job next morning getting me out of my sack and on the move. A sea mist had crept in and the sun was a mere halo above us. Our journey did not go well: Jim had pulled a thigh muscle; his pace became slower and slower; the prospect of reaching Danmarks Havn that day slipped away. We plodded on, with myself in the rear. I had fantasies recalling Ejnar Mikkelsen's incredible struggle for survival told in *Two Against the Ice* when he and his companion were so hungry that the man behind dared not carry a gun lest he was tempted to shoot his partner for food. We had no gun, and anyway we were far from desperate. What with the mist and avoiding musk oxen, our route-finding was difficult. The Danes had left a sketch map at Hvalrusodden which indicated another hut at Storm Bay, but in this light who could tell one bay from the next? At one stage Jim was so lame I resorted to relaying his pack.

In the gathering dusk and fog we lost contact with the coast. A compass at this latitude has a huge declination, for the magnetic North Pole is to the west in northern Canada. We were not at all sure we were heading in the right direction. Our situation had all the uncertainty associated with being on the snow-covered Cairngorm plateau in a white-out. Then I stumbled across a fox trap. Beyond was a frozen river. Could this be Storm Bay? I scouted up and down while Jim nursed his leg and smoked a pipe. Out of the gloom emerged a huge square structure. I was so taken aback I retreated. Then as I approached again it took form and eventually revealed itself as another 6- x 4-foot hut. Within was fuel and food. We tossed for the use of the bunk. I won – and added to Jim's miseries by falling onto him during the night.

Abandoning most of his gear, Jim hirpled bravely on next day and, within a few hours, tracks led us to the Danish base. Two figures rushed out to greet us. They treated us royally. Fed, watered, bathed and duly intoxicated on that vile, but on this occasion thoroughly acceptable, Danish spirit akvavit, we slept the sleep of a lifetime. We, and in due course Spike and BK, enjoyed the wonderful camaraderie of these Danish weathermen living in the lap of luxury in this Arctic wilderness. We sat down at every meal to tables groaning with the finest products of Europe's delicatessen. There was beer and wine, and akvavit to follow. Most spoke some English and a few very good English. We restricted our language development to the key phrase at table: '*Vaer så gud ad ryke mÿ . . .*' (please pass me the . . .) and of course '*Skal*'. I could scarcely believe it when Jim produced a bottle of malt whisky. He had carried it all the way from our base – 100-plus miles – and never said a word! Whereupon the station leader, Neergaard, produced a Dufftown malt! We taught them to say '*Slainte Mhath*' and drained it dry.

We were now in radio communication with all parts of the expedition and indeed with the world beyond. Mike and his crew were at Kap Rink awaiting our arrival. The ice-cap station had been fully established and named 'North Ice', 78°04.3'N, 38°29.3'W. The support party had got back to base in the teeth of blizzards and a further plan had been formulated – three Danmarks Havn men had volunteered to sledge us south with three dog teams to a point 60 miles short of Kap Rink, where we would be met by sledge teams of the Danish Sledge Patrol coming north from Daneborg. The sea ice was finally declared safe on 24 October. Next day was set for departure: BK had to remain behind, his ankle still troubling him; Jim and I were to drive our own team of dogs. 'Don't worry,' said the Danes, 'you will go third team, and the dogs will just follow us.' Oh yeah! The dogs were trained to Danish commands, the equivalents of right, left, go, slow, stop. We polished up on our Danish, but it's a language rife with glottal stops which, even when we imagined ourselves denizens of Glasgow, we never quite managed adequately.

By now the sun had set, though a glorious rose sky filled the southern horizon for several hours each day. It was coming up to full moon, but this also meant high tides, which weaken the ice at headlands. There would be light enough for a few hours each day. I rose that morning with all the sense of anticipation that one has on the eve of a big alpine climb. Our first day's run would be 55 miles! All went well except that our team went slower than the others. Shortly after midday they stopped to let us catch up. We lunched beside bear tracks. A few words of advice and we were off again. The sun set. The moon had yet to appear. Our companions vanished, but the dogs smelt the way. The trouble was that they seemed in no hurry: now and again they would stop and grin at us, tongues lolling, steam escaping from their massive jaws; sometimes they would go in for a little friendly rough and tumble which always ended in a fight. Separating fighting husky dogs is no task for inexperienced dog handlers. And once separated, the dogs, again grinning impishly, were disinclined to move. Exhortation proved little use: we had no carrots. At this point I decided to use the whip. A good driver can wield a whip to sting the rump of any chosen animal, but my first attempts almost removed my eye. Slowly we gathered skill, making the whip sail over the team with a fearsome crack. It was a choreographed performance. Out would sail the whip, down would sink the tails, back would come the whip, up would rise the tails, and off we'd go.

In an effort to get moving faster, Jim and I took turns to run behind the sledge; it kept us warm anyway. What concerned us was what would happen if one of us slipped and the sledge charged onwards – we knew fine that the dogs would pay no attention to a stop command – so we left a 20-foot rope trailing behind the sledge to act as a safety line: 'If you fall, grab it.'

Whatever faint trail left by the sledges ahead that might have been visible in daylight, could not be found now, even in torchlight. The dogs however seemed quite confident. Ahead was the just-discernible outline of a massive hill – Suilen (the needle) – our sole signpost. The sky clouded, so that the promised moon did not appear. By 7 p.m. we had been going 10 hours, unsure whether we were past our objective or not. The dogs were now tired and became uncertain of their direction. They had to be goaded – but to where? We urged the dogs towards the faint outline of Suilen and then to our immense relief a pinpoint of yellow light suddenly appeared as we rounded a rocky point. It guided us to our haven: the large trapper's hut of Alberghus on Godfred Hansen Ø (island). The 55 miles, 35 of which we had run between us, had taken 12 ½ hours. We chained and fed the dogs. I was rapidly falling in love with them, particularly a gorgeous bitch called Jeda, whose striped facial markings gave the impression that she used mascara. Though these dogs could have bitten off my hand in a single snap, I never felt in the least afraid of them. We caressed and nuzzled each other. We rested here for two days to hunt musk oxen for dogfood and to build a cairn on the summit of Teufel Kap for the following summer's survey work. It turned out to be just a super mountaineer's day out. Using Knuth Enroe's team, he and I sledged ten miles to its base. We reached the top of the peak two hours after sundown, but it was still light enough to enjoy the fabulous view of endless mountains, glaciers and frozen fjords. We built a six-foot cairn, sweating the while.

Husky dogs love exercise and pulling sledges, but they do not necessarily want to go where you want to go. The Danes had adopted the Greenland fan trace, not the Alaskan tandem system. Next day Jim and I elected to be first off in order to show who was boss: the dogs won. Tirania, the lead dog, was not happy with his new human companions and our patently un-Danish accents, and kept turning to see if the other teams were closing in, which eventually they did. We had a superb run east and then south through Bessel Fjord: a motorway-smooth passage between mountain walls towering into the black void of the night. The Danes had some difficulty finding the Bessel hut in the darkness but finally succeeded. One dog had a sore foot; Jeda was as loving as ever; Tirania could scarcely stop wagging his tail.

The next day a blizzard forced us to stay put. I was worried about the welfare of the dogs, but was told they were perfectly OK – when I went out to inspect all I could see were gently pulsating mounds of snow. These huts are the wonder of the Greenland scene. Trapping had by then died off somewhat, but for a full century past single men came up to east Greenland where they wintered, trapping and shooting fox and bear and living off the value of their skins. It was accepted that anyone could use any hut at any time. If you left a hut empty you made sure that the fire was laid and two matches already pulled out of the box, so that no matter how near the end of his or her tether a visitor might be, frozen fingers could light the fire. Some huts that had been abandoned were in poor condition, but the Sledge Patrol saw to it that they had dumps of coal and dry sticks to set the fire going. Ancient tins of canned food shared space on the shelves with bags of rice, tins of tea and coffee, and often a bottle of akvavit or rum. Every hut had its tiny population of mice, so grateful when someone lit the fire they would pop out to tell us.

My 26th birthday, on 30 October, started auspiciously with a hefty dram of Ballantines before breakfast and a rousing chorus of 'Happy Birthday' in two languages. Then off we sledged. Things then went rapidly downhill as we encountered the most diabolical surface. A previous gale must have broken up the sea ice. When it refroze it left a terrain of jagged spikes, often three or more feet long, resembling anti-tank defences. It was sheer hell for both dogs and men. There was talk of stopping and camping. The wind was up and it was cold, cold. Moreover the moon was almost full and hence tides were high. This had weakened the sea ice by the shore and particularly at headlands where currents ran faster. Haystack was one such and for a while it seemed as if our objective, Munster Hus on Hochstetter's Foreland, could not be reached. The Danes seemed somewhat defeatist, but we had to remind ourselves that they were scientists at a weather station, not seasoned mountaineers. They had volunteered to help us. They had no training that fitted them to be out in the Arctic winter night fighting bad ice and testing dangerous waters. I was adamantly opposed to camping and persuaded them, by making a reconnaissance on foot, that we could cross a strip of snow-free land and thus gain Munster Hus. In the end they followed and I was able to complete my birthday party. It was the sort of riotous boozy night that naturally follows when one has successfully overcome a difficult situation. But not before we tended the dogs. Kwik had collapsed earlier that day and had to be put on the sledge for the last few miles. Tirania had lost command and Kassan had appointed himself lead dog.

Going south 2° had gained us some daylight, but eventually the last sun of 1952 ebbed away on 2 November, to be compensated for by a week of 24-hour moonlight, so bright that one could almost read newsprint. The Sledge Patrol arrived, large athletic men with well-fed dogs fat on walrus meat. Competition to join the Greenland Sledge Patrol is intense. Those who make it have the most wonderful opportunities for adventure and companionship: a most likeable bunch. I said a long and soulful farewell to my dog team, tears in my eyes, and thanked the Danmarks Havn men. The Sledge Patrol whisked us off first to Ottostrand, another hut. Odd Bogholm, the Norwegian occupant, looked for all the world like an RAF officer with smooth hair, wiry moustache and manners appropriate to the dress. He had planned to leave that summer after two winters, but the relief boat failed to reach him. So another winter.

On our last day's journey to Kap Rink, our sledge fell through new ice. It is not pleasant removing socks and boots and changing into dry ones in the open air at -20° in a brisk wind! Frostbite was an ever-present danger and we all took precautions, such as examining each other's noses and warning the owner if it went white.

The journey home to base had all the atmosphere of what today we call virtual reality. At the helm of a tracked vehicle speeding at 15 mph over the ice, headlights stabbing the night, roasted by a heater, the stark hills washed in the white light of the full moon, you felt as impregnable as a typical BMW driver does at 110 mph on the motorway. But it was an illusion. One moment the ice was solid and white, the next the headlights showed a grey rolling surface of barely frozen sea. I waited for the sickening moment when we would fall through. Nothing for it but to press on, gently. Solid ice again. Breathe again.

We left the vehicles at the edge of Storströmmen, where we were met by four companions who had come by dog team from base. They had taken 11 days to cross, 7 more than we walkers. The sledges were damaged, the dogs and men exhausted. It had been a bad, if well-intentioned decision aimed at making our return journey easier. In fact it made it much worse: the sledges were a burden to be humped and heaved up and down the ice hillocks of the glacier; the cold was intense; we could only travel during moonlit periods, about six hours each day. Everyone was at the limit of his strength. One day we made only two miles. When we were five miles from the edge we dumped most of the gear, freed the dogs, left the sledges and took to our feet. The final episode found us at the southern edge of the Storströmmen with the screes of Queen Louise Land 300 feet off, but separated by a 60-foot vertical ice cliff. This is typical of glaciers in this Arctic desert. In summer the reflected heat from the mountainside melts the edge of the glaciers, leaving a canyon between it and rocks. Using mountaineering techniques we arranged an abseil for the men and lowered the dogs. It was 5 December; the temperature was -38°C. Mission accomplished.

QLL was thoroughly surveyed topographically, botanically and geologically and recorded by Hamilton in the *Geographical Journal*. It turned out that the ice cap was a deep layer of ice on top of a low plateau of rock, which due to the weight of accumulated ice, had sunk below sea level at several points, a phenomenon known as isostasy. Greenland was not an iced cake, but a huge reservoir of ice surrounded by mountains. Scientifically the expedition justified the huge investment in time and money engaged. We were not just boys enjoying ourselves. Simpson got a CBE and the rest of us a Polar Medal.

CHAPTER 4

Serendipity – Finding the
Staunings Alps of Greenland

Serendipity is defined as unexpected good fortune. I find it gets more common as I get older. On this occasion it was the consequence of someone else's bad luck. It was the middle of August 1953 and I had my bags packed for my return home from the British North Greenland Expedition, first by Sunderland to Young Sound, then by boat to the UK. As the flying boat taxied towards us we got word to the pilot that there were some rather big lumps of glacier ice floating in his path. He let the plane drift backwards on the wind, and then as he powered the starboard engines to circle round, wind caught the wing and drove the plane ashore. The hull was breached. The story of its repair and recovery makes good reading.[1] In the end a whole tonne of cement was poured inside to hold down the roughly caulked hull and I was told to get aboard pronto. The pilot, Squadron-Leader McCready, decided to fly direct to Reykjavik and then head for his base at Loch Ryan in south-west Scotland. By chance my mother lived just a few miles away and it took little to persuade him to let me to stay aboard, so that I was home in Scotland within ten hours of leaving Greenland!

As we flew south from Young Sound I had my head in the viewing dome, goggling at the huge fjords penetrating into the interior and at mountain range after mountain range. And not just any old mountains, but peaks and precipices such as to make any mountaineer salivate. Then, just when I thought there could be nothing more dramatic, the plane crossed to the south side of Kong Oscars Fjord revealing below

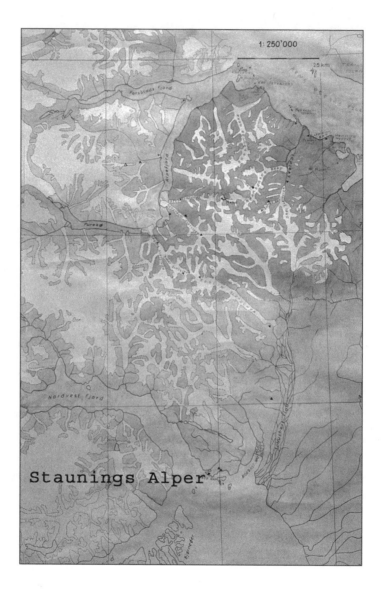

1: 250'000

25 km

Forsblads Fjord

Nordvest Fjord

Staunings Alper

a range of truly Alpine peaks girt with impressive icefalls. Whereas many of the hills further north were composed of sedimentary rocks, here were granite aiguilles to rival Chamonix-Mt-Blanc and cliffs high enough to match the Eiger. I had to know more. I had to get there.

My research revealed they had been named the Staunings Alps (after some expedition benefactor), first viewed at close quarters by an American millionairess, Louise Boyd, whose boat had penetrated a deep fjord on their north-west side, which she aptly named Alpe Fjord. Towards its head two fast-flowing glaciers, the Sefstrøm and the Gully, join forces and plunge into the sea. You can see from old shoreline marks that at one time they extended to the mountain wall opposite, plugging the waters to the south and thereby forming a huge freshwater lake that stretched far inland. Now, with glacier recession, their retreat has left a dramatic passage between the ice cliffs of the glaciers' snouts and the steep precipices of the Berzelius Bjaerg to the west. All that is left of the huge lake is a lagoon called Dammen. Seen from aerial photos, this appeared to be an ideal site for an exploratory base camp. Thus was a plan gestated. From the 1953 edition of *Mountain World* I read that Peter Braun, a Swiss geologist, had skipped away from his scientific duties to ascend an 8,560-foot virgin peak, which he named Frihets Tinde. His party also attempted, unsuccessfully, the second-highest peak, which they called Hjørnespids – Horn Peak. Their pictures were enough to make my pulse beat faster. And apparently there were still innumerable virgin peaks awaiting the exploratory climber. I just had to get there. It took me five years, as meanwhile I had a living to earn.

The first serious mountaineering expedition in the region was an Austro–Danish party in 1954 led by the Danish lawyer and Alpinist Erik Hoff. They attacked these hills from Viking Brae, a glacier that ran westwards into the outer part of Alpe Fjord. They picked off Norske Tinde, which at 9,315 ft (2,840 m) was the third-highest peak. When one considers that these hills rise almost straight out of the sea, it gives some idea of their grandeur. There is barely a mountain in the Alps that rises that much above its adjacent valley. At this period a fresh wave of east Greenland scientific exploration was under way under the leadership of Dr Lauge Koch. He had little time for mountaineering and his Swiss assistants had to steal away when he wasn't looking. John Haller and Wolfgang Diehl penetrated the three icefalls of the Gully Glacier to pick off the highest peak, which they named Danske Tinde, 9,610 ft (2,930 m). Between then and when we arrived in 1958 there had been no further exploration.

I adopted Simpson's approach: seek a source of finance and

influence, while offering some plausible scientific objective. In search of influence I called on Jim Wordie, who was an old polar hand, having been on Bruce's Antarctic expedition of 1910, as well as on geological trips to north-east Greenland, where Wordie's Glacier and Jordanhill on the then current maps indicated marks of his passing. Wordie was Master of St John's College in Cambridge and on the Council of the Royal Geographical Society. Like me, he was a member of the Scottish Mountaineering Club. He told me who to see in Copenhagen and how to lay my plans before the Danish Ministry for Greenland in such a way that they would not oppose them. I cadged a tenner from each of my putative expedition colleagues and flew over. The Greenland Ministry dislikes mountaineering parties and understandably so. If anyone gets into trouble the rescue effort is a severe dislocation to their activities during the very short Arctic summer when ships, stores and people can be moved around. On one occasion, many years later when Keith Millar had to be rescued, the helicopter which had just been dismantled for carriage to Denmark, had to be reassembled. Much tooth-sucking!

Anyway I got permission subject to several caveats, one of which was that we would carry a radio (Morse code!) transmitter. They put me in touch with the shipping magnate Knut Lauritzen, whose icebreakers serve east Greenland. He proved to be a wonderfully eccentric old man who at once agreed to convey our goods to Greenland for free and to lend us a boat to get to the head of Alpe Fjord. I also learnt that a lead mine had opened up on the fringe of the Staunings and was served by an airfield called Mesters Vig. I visited Herr Brinch, head of Nord Minen, and elicited from him a reluctant offer of transport from the airfield to the mine, which would then be our launching point. The Mount Everest Foundation assisted us financially. Thus was the Scottish East Greenland Expedition of 1958 finally born.

Our chartered DC4 landed at Mesters Vig on a crisp, brilliantly sunny dawn at 2 a.m. on 8 July. We were all goggle-eyed from peering out of the windows as the plane grazed the mountain tops while we feverishly picked out feasible routes and possible camp sites, and judged the ferocity of the glacier torrents. The air was like wine, the temperature a little below freezing. We experienced an incredible sense of vitality. It was good to be here at last.

Serendipity was still active. No sooner had we set up camp on the tundra above the mine offices than a charming middle-aged American lady arrived in a jeep. She invited us back to her house where, with her geologist husband Linc Washburn and her children, she held sway as the chatelaine of a tiny little red timber house with a panoramic view of Kong Oscars Fjord and hills beyond. Linc, who specialised in the quaternary era, puzzled us by talking about 'erotics', which we later divined to be 'erratics', those huge boulders perched randomly on top of moraines. They fed us and poured so much fine drink down us that I have no recollection of the party's end. *Det Lille Røde Hus* became our home from home, and the Washburns lifelong friends. Many expeditions have subsequently been welcomed there. After Professor Washburn had completed his research he gifted the house to the Danish Arktisk Institut. It is available for visiting parties.

The 1958 expedition was a party of old friends: five were one-time members of Edinburgh University Mountaineering Club; seven were members of the SMC. The new man was Roddy Cameron, an engineering apprentice from Glasgow, who was later in life to become the world's most sought-after baroque flute maker and no mean folk singer. He found a natural talent as an impresario which he cultivated to great effect. We had a light scientific programme – nothing that would impede a resolute attack on the virgin peaks awaiting us. As there was no record of an exploration of the Bersaerker Brae, which dropped northwards from the heart of the range, its exploration became our immediate objective. But there was one impediment. First we had to cross the torrent of the Skel River. Lauge Koch told me it was impossible to cross during the melt season. He was almost right. These icy waters, an impenetrable grey from glacial silt, sweep down in a series of standing waves. We could actually hear boulders trundling along under the water. Our first attempt was abandoned within seconds. Our legs immediately lost all feeling. As you moved your foot forward you could not tell whether it was solidly grounded and certainly you had no idea whether there was a round boulder or a deep hollow beneath your foot. With this total lack of feeling, it was easy to trip and fall. Too many have drowned this way. We tried again at 4 a.m., when the stream was at its lowest due to night frost. Still the crossing was impossible. Then we hit on a solution which is worth passing on: we replaced our socks with plastic bags, put our boots back on and then immersed them in water. We then leapt around until our feet and our bodies were again warm. Then in pairs, clutching an ice axe between us, we bent ourselves against the formidable current – because our feet exchanged no water with the river, we were able to feel our feet all the way across, and so place them carefully and safely on the rolling rocks below.

Within a few days we had 80 man-days of food and a modest assortment of climbing gear on the west side of the Skel. This was long before the days of chalk bags, banana-shaped picks, friends and kevlar slings. I think the entire party's gear was a dozen karabiners of doubtful provenance, some light nylon slings, a few pitons and four 100-foot ropes. I doubt if we could have carried more and still made it up the glacier anyway. The weather, as we had been led to expect, was peerless day after exquisite day. After all, this was the Arctic Riviera. Future parties were to find that the expected 'East Greenland High' occasionally slips away – one high-powered expedition in 1996 actually retreated back to Iceland deterred by endless drizzle, sleet and soggy glaciers. The downside of the brilliant weather was that there was little wind and at midday temperatures were in the low 20s. This brought out that Greenland plague: mosquitoes. Mozzies don't like glaciers, so we lost no time in heading for the ice. Our first virgin peak on the periphery of the range was composed of terrible rock – the mountain was probably about three feet lower by the time we hauled off loose debris and claimed the summit. Nonetheless we gave it a name: Glamis Tinde. This name arose from a policy that we thought up that might be followed by later parties from other countries, namely to call our first ascents after castles in the home country of the expedition. Later parties, including those from continental Europe, followed suit. One Cambridge expedition couldn't resist the witty temptation to call a virgin glacier 'Verte Brae'. Such names have to be submitted to the Greenland authorities for approval. Ours were accepted, but today, with Greenland semi-autonomous, all new names have to be Greenlandic.

Bersaerker Brae proved to be far from berserk. In its lower reaches it was a high road of smooth ice, barely crevassed. At its head it was protected by a tumultous maze of crevasses. Here soared the 4,000-foot face of the Bersaerker Tinde. Its north face rebuffed all attempts for 40 years. We camped just below the summer snowline on a grassy bank speckled with yellow hyracium, more worn out by heat than cold. During a few days of riotous exploratory climbing we had christened Dunnotar, Dunvegan, Stirling, Merchiston, Carrick, Achnacarry and Kismul. Later parties added Harlech, Elsinore, Tintagel and Beaumaris. Much later a London-based expedition with a less romantic soul added Vauxhall, Poplar, Blackwall, Kensington, Pimlico and, needless to say, Elephant & Castle.

Our plan was to boat to Alpe Fjord as soon as the break-up of the pack ice allowed. On 23 July we were at the little harbour of Ny Havn on the south shore of Kong Oscars Fjord where true to Lauritzen's promise a red 12-foot dory lay awaiting us. Frankly it was a little on the small side, somewhat like our boating competence. By now we had taken up residence in a tiny, squalid and dilapidated trapper's refuge on the southern shores of Kong Oscars Fjord, where the hot sun by day and golden, lingering light and long shadows by night had totally undermined the party's resolve to do anything more than just drink in the unparalleled beauty of the high Arctic. Sloth reigned supreme.

Finally we girded our loins and placed Len Lovat, Douglas Scott and Roddy Cameron into the dory, which bore the ominous name *Tippa Dan*, and sent them on their way to establish a base at Dammen at the head of Alpe Fjord. The hawk-faced Len was a lawyer and towering wit. Douglas Scott, small and wiry, was and is a superb mountain photographer. He had recently set himself up as a freelancer. And of course Roddy, the talented folk musician. Why I chose these three complete landlubbers for this first vital exploration I cannot now recall. Maybe they volunteered – Scott averred he had once had a sailing boat. Such was the load of food, fuel and gear that the boat had barely eight inches of freeboard, but the sea seemed calm as a millpond day after day. This was their undoing. A short, sardonic rendering of 'For those in peril on the sea' soon turned out to be by no means inappropriate. In Lovat's words, 'we had been cast loose upon the fjord'. To our amazement, an hour later we observed them climbing out of the boat half a mile from the shore! They appeared to be frantically bailing. We later learnt they had gone aground on silt banks at the outlet of the Skel River and thus stranded were quickly swamped by waves. We watched helplessly. Eventually they got the boat afloat and unloaded some gear onshore. When they returned five days later it was with tales of terrifying katabatic winds, wild waves and the sinister ice canal that led past the snouts of the two glaciers into Dammen. Douglas considered it should be nominated as the eighth wonder of the world.

To while away the time we set up our pedal generator and attempted to communicate by Morse code with the radio station three miles away. Our call sign was acknowledged and back came a stream of dots and dashes whose grouping was beyond our ability to interpret. We sent back a signal in 'Q-code' saying 'please send slower'. The signal got slower and slower but we could never distinguish the groupings. By common consent communication by radio was declared pointless. What a relief!

Since our tiny dory could not convey us all to Alpe Fjord, 7 of the party set off to walk the 65 miles along the shore. Many said it was the finest part of the trip. As I later sailed through the ice canal I had to agree with Douglas. The fissured ice front of the combined Gully and Sefstrøm glaciers presented cliffs 100 feet high, the ice was seamed with the deep green stripes of pure water ice and discoloured by flecks of rock debris. It was splitting and falling into the sea continuously, and I prayed that a major surge would not occur until we were through. The base-camp site beyond was ideal: flat, dry tundra to camp on and a stream nearby. The fjord ran a further half-mile inland. Opposite us the Berzelius Bjerg was a textbook example of sedimentary rock, with bold black-and-coloured twisted bands, the entire cliff face rising sheer over 3,000 feet. The head of the loch was filled with high mountains in a wild tangle of ice-filled gullies and rock pinnacles. Immediately above us was a 6,000-foot wall whose summit was later climbed, while to its side was the tundra-girt moraine of Sefstrøm Brae. The only sounds were the distant roar of meltwater and the eerie keening of red-throated divers and the squawks of glaucous gulls.

The lower Sefstrøm Brae was easy enough and led to the heart of the range. At its head were peaks of Alpine stature whose ascent took 24 hours or more from a high camp. One naturally tackles a virgin peak by the easiest line. None were exceptionally challenging by Alpine standards. One of the nice things about climbing in the high Arctic is continuous daylight so that one can choose to bivouac at midday – when the sun's warmth makes the experience quite painless – then climb through the night, which offers an aesthetic experience without equal. We added Tantallon, Inverarnan, Eilean Donan, Lennox, Beaufort, and Tioram to our list of first ascents. We failed on Sefstrøm Tinde and Attilaborgen, the latter because the final 200 feet was a 'very severe' crack for which we lacked any decent gear.

The expedition made two notable geographic explorations. From aerial photos it looked as if from the head of Dammen there was a glacier route south leading to the Schuichert Valley, a southward-tending strath of 40 miles that debouched into the inner reaches of the vast Scoresby Sund, east Greenland's biggest fjord. A party went to explore the route and came back with the news that the glacier was hopelessly crevassed. This news came at a low point for the expedition because what we had thought to be two bags of flour turned out to be sugar and, moreover, it was now discovered that the pemmican (the age-old standby of nineteenth-century explorers) ordered from Copenhagen had never arrived. Food calories were at a premium. A boat would have to return to Ny Havn for fresh supplies.

In spite of the poor report, Iain Smart and I were keen to try the southern passage. Smart is a man who travels light. His eating utensils consisted of one large plastic cup which served both as bowl and cup, and his only cutlery was a spoon attached to a string that hung perpetually round his neck. It was as much a part of him as the ring around Saturn. We presumed this method of attachment was because he was rather prone to lose things. He claimed that it was only to stop others nicking it. He etched the handle with an 'S'. This seemed like a good idea until I did likewise, also an 'S'. When, later, one of these spoons went adrift it raised an argument that lasted three decades and spilled into the pages of the *SMC Journal* where Smart alleged that I was a disreputable collector of spoons.

With minimal rations that we hoped would last us 11 days, Iain and I slowly and carefully threaded the tortuous labyrinth of the crevasses of the Spørre Brae. It was a dismal day of low cloud and rain. There is nothing so dreich as a 'dry' glacier coated grey with the debris of rock dust. It was washed by a steady drizzle. Roped, we made just a couple of miles the first day. Once onto the snow-covered glacier, the danger of hidden crevasses increased and we moved with almost morbid care but covered more ground. Finally, on the third day, we reached the crowning snowfield that linked it to the glacier running south-east to the Schuichert. Here we climbed an easy snow peak and left the traditional sardine can with names and date. Ten years later I got a note from a German climber who had made the second ascent. We called the peak Roslin Tinde and applied the same name to the glacier running east to the Schuichert. It turned out to be so free of crevasses that one could have driven a truck along it. And it went on forever and ever. To relieve the tedium we arranged to walk close, one behind the other, the rear person reading aloud from Rachel Carson's *Silent Spring* which had just been published.

As we slithered off the final moraine onto the tundra we smelt wood smoke, and there was Douglas Scott, last seen five days before in Alpe Fjord, ensconced in front of a fire of willow twigs! This wily old campaigner had gone with the boat to Mesters Vig, jumped ship and persuaded a bush pilot to land him at the head of the Schuichert. There he was with tent, fuel and ample food. A bit miffed, we extracted several bars of chocolate from him, since in our view he seemed a trifle over-provided. Scott is a naturalist and so prefers his own company. We left him to travel at his own speed. This Douglas was incidentally *the* Scott, not the more recent accession to fame, Doug Scott.

Smart and I, stimulated by the scent of warm sun on the tundra, strode forth upon the waving fields of cotton grass and brilliant autumn-coloured dwarf birch and willow-herb, leaving behind a food dump, a tent and a stove. There would be ample fuel in the form of dry willow herb. On the second day we were amazed to see a forest of peaks lining the southern horizon, peaks which did not appear on any map. Slowly it dawned on us that they were enormous icebergs. That night, as we dozed in our sleeping bags cosseted by the soft dry tundra, a snort awoke us. There, not 20 feet away, was a musk ox gently pawing at the ground. Iain chucked some sticks on the fire and blew them into a flame on the principle that animals are afraid of fire, while I let out eldritch screeches, as much a natural reaction of terror as an attempt to frighten the beast. Blinking at us with lowered head it seemed uncertain of the best course of action. After a while it ambled off, snorting. Next day we hit the little summer Inuit settlement of Syd Kap, an experience I relate in Chapter 14.

Back at Alpe Fjord after a round trip of 11 days we found the expedition slowly starving. Retreat was called for. One exploration remained to be done – finding a route across the range to the Bersaerker Brae. Donald Bennet was to have been in the party but had been hit on the head by a falling rock, needing stitching. Smart, our doctor (though he had abandoned medicine some time before), advised him not to stress himself. I replaced him in what was to be the finest of all the trips I made that year. It involved ascending the Gully Glacier. Here is an extract from my article 'The Staunings Alps of East Greenland' published in *Mountain World*:

> Around us rose a bewildering mass of unclimbed peaks, Grepons, Ravenels, Réquins, their frail snow crests and serrated granite arêtes untouched and unnamed. At this time we did not know how Haller had handled the third icefall, and though we were impressed with it as he was, we sought out and made a route up its chaotic centre, and were almost stopped by an enormous crevasse splitting the glacier in two.

My two companions were Kenny Bryan, a young climber of great ability with whom I had made new routes in Scotland. I used to tell him I was his perambulating belay, for he always forced the crux. The other was Charlie Rose, who gave up a lucrative career in advertising in London to run a bed and breakfast business in the Highlands. He couldn't bear to be far from the mountains.

At one point we were only able to make progress by using a lip of old winter snow that clung to the rock wall on the north side. Two days later we were camped on a snow col overlooking the Bersaerker Brae. Beyond lay Kong Oscars Fjord and the distant gleam of the outer pack ice highlighting the blue of the fjord. The slender trumpet of the Hjørnespids soared 3,300 feet above us. Side glaciers harboured peak after delectable peak, summits and walls that would provide fun and excitement for an increasing number of climbers in the years to come. Little did we think then that in those later explorations the sweat of man-packing into the mountains would be relieved by helicopters. In the 14 years that separated our 1958 trip from the publication of Donald Bennet's guidebook, *Staunings Alps*, no less than 240 virgin peaks were to be ascended by parties from all over the world. As the virgin summits were overcome more emphasis was put on faces than on peaks, searching for difficulty and interesting climbing.

Back in the summer of 1958 we three pioneers were peering down upon the upper Bersaerker Brae, not a little intimidated by the steepness of slope below and the crevasse-strewn glacier beyond. But there was no turning back. Our Alpe Fjord base had been evacuated. We called it Col Major, for it was the main breach in the northern part of the Staunings. The descent was about 1,800 feet on ice. Charlie enlivened the proceedings by falling, but was held.

In the winter of 1959 I received a letter asking me for information on the Staunings. It was written on Alpine Club notepaper and bore an illegible signature. Not knowing to whom my reply should be addressed, I cut out the signature and pasted it on the envelope. Sir John Hunt, for it was he, then invited me to join him as deputy leader on an expedition to the Staunings, planned for 1960. Its purpose was to take 20 lads who had achieved the Duke of Edinburgh's Gold Award and give them a taste of the wild. There would be some climbers as leaders, to wit, Ian McNaught-Davis, George Lowe (of Everest fame), John Jackson (Warden at Plas-y-Brenin) and Alan Blackshaw, the author of the then definitive book on climbing technique. An advance party composed of the naturalist and writer Tom Weir, Roddy Cameron, Iain Smart and I were to go ahead to prepare a base camp at Menanders Bay, on the west side of the Skel River. This was a superb spot. A sandy tundra ran down to a beach worthy of the Outer Hebrides, with a view of the Lion Crag on the far shore of the fjord. One entertaining event was when our motorboat rode up onto an ice floe as we were forcing our way through the pack, thus placing the boat partly in dry dock. In an effort to extract ourselves I put the engine in reverse, whereupon the prop shaft slipped out. While Roddy, as the party's engineer, sorted this the rest of us weakened the ice by sawing through it with a carpenter's saw.

A great time was had by all, especially the lads. Inevitably with such a large party a certain rigour and order was called for, quite foreign to the habits of mountaineers. Lady Hunt's stentorian tones could be heard urging the lads to clean their mess tins properly. Anyone presenting a particularly polished example received a fulsome accolade: 'What a gorgeous mess tin!' She was nicknamed 'Gorgeous Mess Tin'.

Smart assumed his protective colouring of sybarite and aesthete and withdrew from the scene. Sorties were made up the Bersaerker Brae and to Alpe Fjord. Hunt, while climbing a snow arête on Harlech, fell through a cornice, to be saved by Blackshaw who, having read his own book, threw himself off the other side of the ridge. That year there were periods of poor weather: I recall sitting in a tent with McNaught-Davis, Jackson and Lowe playing bridge for two days – since the only currency of any value was weight carried by another, we played for 1 kg per 100 points. McNaught was by far the best player, and ended up with a credit of two tonnes! It looked as if we would have to carry him up the glacier in a litter. Fortunately he didn't push his luck.

In the Bersaerker area there were three outstanding mountaineering challenges remaining: the north wall of the Bersaerker Tinde, for which we lacked equipment; the Bersaerker spire which I climbed with McNaught-Davis – it was a blade of immaculate granite akin to the Salbitschen in the Urner Alps in Switzerland, which I had once climbed with Ken Bryan; and the third and most challenging was the second-highest peak in the Staunings, the Hjørnespids. With Mac, John Hunt and John Jackson I once again found myself on Col Major looking up at the trumpet stem of this superb summit. The two Johns went off to explore a distant col. Mac and I went for the peak. It was noon on a windless, cloudless day. The east ridge rose directly from the col. Since it looked as if the climb would be entirely on rock, we decided to leave behind our axes and crampons to lighten our sacks and speed our way. What folly! As Mac put it: 'It was a siren luring us to its bosom.'[2] Severe rock climbing brought us to the first summit of the east ridge by early afternoon, 7,900 ft on Mac's aneroid. There followed a level gendarmed ridge, 14 gendarmes in all as it turned out. There was little opportunity to move together. On a couple of the pinnacles we were able to climb round, but the rest had to be climbed over. This traverse took eleven hours, with one 'very severe' pitch and one perilous pendulum, followed by an ascent of a holdless slab on friction. It had been a mistake not to take at least one ice axe. This is how Mac described the slab pitch:

A thin coating of 'Black Death', an indigenous frictionless slime, maintained the interest, and little skill would have been required to fall a long way. The first set-back to our plans was after an abseil down the flank of one unclimbable spike onto the steep bare ice at its foot. The long horizontal traverse, without crampons, bent double chipping steps with a piton hammer, made us feel foolish . . . Four hours brought us to the final barrier (of the E ridge); a tetrahedron of granite set squarely in our path.

When we finally left the 14th gendarme it was an hour and a half to midnight. The sun was almost due north. We hungered for it. The wind was up. A touch of moisture in the air drained the feeling from our fingers. The final 1,650 feet of Hjørnespids soared above us, its red granite smooth and speckled with black lichen. There seemed no way to get to the north face and into the blessed sun. Anyway without crampons and axe we would soon be in trouble. Everything pointed to the shadowed south-east side. It would be six hours before the sun came round to warm us. We traversed across the south-east face for a bit, only to be stopped by an utterly smooth slab topped by an equally holdless wall. Quite suddenly we lost all impetus, both of us feeling bone weary. Mac proposed sleep: I demurred, it was too cold. But he was already asleep, slumped on a ledge, limp as a Salvador Dali watch. As Mac put it: 'While Malcolm was looking at his shattered dream I slipped off my boots, thrust my feet into my rucksack, lay down on a small square of plastic foam and went to sleep.'

However, that hour of sleep revived us. We abseiled to the centre of the south-east face, where we found a chimney, then a series of ice-filled cracks that somehow led us up and up to a brêche. By now it was 3 a.m. The sun was slowly coming round, but had yet to hit us. Opposite us, peak upon peak was glistening with a creamy yellow sheen, brightening by the second. Forty more minutes of climbing and we were on the top, and in the sun – but out of film! Though quite exhausted we were revived by the magnificent scene around us. Only the nearby Danske Tinde was higher. We could see far, far to the north, even to Peterman's Bjaerg, 10,000 feet beyond Kejser Franz Josephs Fjord. Years later I was to be in a party that attempted this peak. We could see Royal Geographical Society Island, and Vega Sund, the huge southern cliff of Ella Island, rising 4,000 feet straight out of the sea. The inland ice stretched to the horizon, looking as infinite as it seemed when I was crossing it back in 1953. Across to the south-east we could see the serrated granite peaks of the Liverpool coast and I made a mental note to go there one day. We nibbled the last of our chocolate.

It was now that we truly regretted the lack of axe and crampons. The easiest descent would have been down a couloir, one which was later to be the route of the first winter ascent by a Scottish party comprising Ian Angell, Tim Pettifer, John Morrison, David Ritchie and others. So without proper gear there was nothing for it but to rope down the south-east face. By mistake we had left our second rope on Col Major, so not only would the abseils be short, there was no possibility of a safety line. Of our original 14 pitons, 3 had been left in place on the gendarme traverse.

The sun came round into the east and grew stronger and as it did so we became sleepier and sleepier. Rappel followed rappel, most of them forcing us to leave some gear behind. Sleepwalking is one thing; sleepclimbing is extremely dangerous. At 9.30 a.m., I fell asleep on my stance. Mac allowed me two hours. With several hundred feet still to go, we were obliged to be ultra-mean with our gear. Whereas normally we would have put two loops round a spike, now we put one. The tension was rising, especially for me. I have a deep and abiding dislike of abseiling, having lost two friends whose belays failed. Towards the col we could see figures moving: the two Johns were coming to welcome us. Finally we needed only one last abseil to reach beyond the rimaye, the final crevasse. We had no gear left – no pitons, no slings, no pieces of rucksack cord or straps, nothing. We had even used the cord on the piton hammer.

'Well,' said Mac, 'it's time for bootlaces.' And so it was. Mine.

Our companions greeted us with water, food and our skis. We slid contentedly down to our camp. It was 5 p.m. We had been on the go for 28 ½ hours. I reckon it to be the best climb I have ever experienced and made with an excellent companion.

Today the Staunings Alps are witness to the doings of many parties. Access is so easy. They are, for example, as near to Glasgow as is Vienna. A flight to Iceland and charter to Mesters Vig may be had for a price that is a fraction of a Himalayan or Andean expedition. The presence of a helicopter at Mesters Vig has opened up many possibilities allowing parties to set up camp with loads of hi-tech gear. During the Hunt expedition and the years following, the south Staunings were heavily explored. In 1961 a party led by Jim Clarkson explored the southern Staunings peaks. In a magnificent tour de force they climbed every peak (with one exception) in an area of 50 square miles. Theirs was the last of the hardy backpacking parties. The whole area is now a holiday destination. Greenland Air now operates a scheduled service that includes Mesters Vig.

One other tour de force which opened up a lot of terrain was the first ski traverse from inner Scoresby Sund in the south to Kong Oscars Fjord in the north in 1992 by an international party. This was the initiative of John Peden, a dynamic Scottish engineer, mountaineer and skier, and Pierre Flamand from France. It was a mixed party in several senses. The French used Alpine equipment; the others Nordic heel lift. There were five men and two women: three French, one Australian, one Englishman and two Scots. This was an extremely tough and adventurous undertaking, in which they covered over 120 miles, crossed 8 cols, several of them for the first time, climbed 3 peaks, 2 of which were virgin. The Icelandic pilots favoured them with a glacier landing, leaving one dump of food and fuel at their halfway point. It took them 16 days starting on 9 May. They were lucky in that the cold weather was sustained: there is nothing worse than camping on melting snow.

As I left Greenland in the autumn of 1958 I thought back to that serendipitous flight with Squadron-Leader McCready. I had been able to do him a good turn. We had been flying blind for some hours out of Reykjavik with ten-tenths cloud below us. My head was in the viewing dome eager to get my first glimpse of my homeland. In a brief gap in the cloud I recognised the Paps of Jura. Dropping down into the cockpit I remarked that it would not be long now.

'Are you sure it's Jura?' McCready asked. 'I hope you're right!' and with that he pushed the stick forwards and down we went into the clouds to emerge with Arran ahead.

NOTES

[1] The story of the repair of the hull is told by McCready in 'Salvage of "Charlie"', in C.J.W. Simpson's *North Ice* (Hodder & Stoughton, 1957) pp.255–65.

[2] A very detailed account of this climb was written up in the *Alpine Journal* (66, No. 303, 1961) entitled 'Hjørnespids'.

CHAPTER 5

The Tigers of Yesterday

Although the climber who executes bold and possibly dangerous climbs will be much admired within the climbing fraternity, descriptions like 'idol' or 'hero' would generally be out of place. And there is little the public likes more than to destroy an idol when he or she is found to have feet of clay. The drive to climb is understood by all to be the solution to a personal equation. Unlike the soldier, no external force, physical or moral, obliges the climber to expose him or herself to risk or danger; one can always turn back. Idolatry needs a mass market like football or pop songs, where mountains and climbers, thankfully, don't figure. You can't feel special in a vacuum. You would have to go to an Alpine country to find a mountaineer or skier attracting even a tenth of the adulation accorded to footballers, pop singers or Formula 1 drivers. Heinrich Harrer, who made the first ascent of the Eiger Nordwand, was probably the first Alpinist to receive national adulation, but that was in Hitler's Germany.

However, there are those whose exceptional talent turns them into icons in the more limited world of mountaineering – the English climber Joe Brown, whom I discuss in Chapter 9, was an icon in his milieu. He has survived to maturity and I have never heard a bad word of him. His contemporary, also an icon of English mountaineering, was Don Whillans, a man of few words, and those few extremely blunt. He died in his bed.

Like all great achievers, their personal weaknesses and peccadilloes are glossed over when looking at the broad canvas of their achievements. In this chapter I reflect on three such icons whose personae flourished in Scotland in the late 1950s. Their undoubted skills allowed two of them to behave very badly indeed. I refer to Dougal Haston and Robin Smith. I add a third icon, a very different character altogether, namely Tom Patey. If they share anything it is that they all died young and needlessly through a trivial error of judgement.

Back in the 1940s, when I was first placing boot on rock, our mountaineering icons were the legendary figures we encountered only in books, such as Frank Smythe and Graham Brown with their first ascents on the Brenva face of Mont Blanc. Copying Smythe, we wore trilby hats even when rock climbing. We devoured Ashly Abraham's *Rock Climbing in Skye,* and with great difficulty got ourselves there. Far beyond our reach seemed the exploits of A.F. Mummery as described in *My Travels and Climbs in the Alps and the Caucasus.* Oh, to have a private income! How we wished that we had been alive in that golden age of mountain exploration, when every ascent was upon untrodden rock and led to virgin summits. We revelled in an almost masochistic way in Heinrich Harrer's *White Spider*, with its vivid descriptions of the competition to be the first to climb the north face of the Eiger, or 'Mordwand' as the German press called it. There was undoubtedly a certain voyeurism in reading about the 'death bivouac' and of the fatal fall of Tony Kurz. We could recite almost every page of the retreat from Annapurna in Maurice Herzog's *The Ascent of Annapurna* or Lionel Terray's *Conquistadores of the Useless.* Of all those legendary figures of my youth only one remains alive: Harrer's companion on the 1938 Eiger climb, Andreas Heckmair, 92, still climbing and still enjoying his malt whisky, according to Jim Wilkie, who supplies his tipple. Closer to home veterans like Norman Collie, Jim Bell and Bill Murray were respected but not held in awe. Collie had led the development of the Cuillins as a rock-climbing paradise. Bell, whose chiselled face reminded me of granite, had pioneered many routes, but was particularly remembered for his exploration of what he called the 'Orion face' of Ben Nevis. Murray's talents were not widely appreciated until he published his highly acclaimed *Undiscovered Scotland.*

Haston became an icon even before he left school. He and two pals, Jimmy Stenhouse and Elie Moriarty, were collectively known as the 'Currie boys', after their village just outside Edinburgh. Initially Stenhouse was the better climber of the three, but Haston had the aura. Elie was a genial, corrupted giant who, as things evolved, became Haston's protector, with fists when necessary. During 1958, a highly regarded active climber in Scotland, Jimmy Marshall, an architect and member of the SMC, educated the Currie boys by the simple expedient of pointing them towards harder and harder climbs, which they lapped up like starving wolves. In fact they would soon overtake 'the old man', as they called Marshall. This was in deference to his great age – he had already turned 30 would you believe it!

In the summer of 1958, Haston, then 18 years old, joined Robin Smith (of whom more later) in a raid on the hardest routes in north Wales and returned triumphant. English climbers had just introduced a new standard of 'extremely severe', whereas in Scotland 'very severe' was nominally the hardest grading. Smith disliked Haston, but recognised his phenomenal ability.

I was barely familiar with all this. Schoolboy climbers just don't impinge on 30 year olds. But they soon would. Of course tales of the Currie boys penetrated to the west where I was living: we heard that they honed their skills on railway walls, but were ignorant of the mountains and were a source of endless trouble. We were wrong on the first count, but not the second. Haston had planned to enter physical education, but a motorbike accident left him with a dislocated shoulder and damaged arm, so he opted to read philosophy at Edinburgh University. One suspects that his thinking was that such a course didn't require much attendance at classes, so he would be able to spend his time climbing, with the added advantage that the State was paying his keep. He never graduated.

It was in Glencoe that our paths eventually crossed – and cross they verily did. I was the custodian of the SMC's Glencoe hut, Laggangarbh, just across the river from the keeper's cottage on the main Glasgow–Fort William road at Allt-na-Feidh. I arrived one evening to find Haston and friends illegally in occupation. The mess was appalling, added to which they had daubed the walls with splashes of paint of various colours. The hut had originally been a shepherd's bothy and when Percy Unna and others gifted Glencoe to The National Trust for Scotland, part of the deal was that this bothy, then unused, would be let to the SMC for use as a club hut. There was not a lot of money around in 1958 and the facilities in the hut were pretty minimal. Indeed sordid might be a better description. With the help of club work-parties I had been trying at minimal cost to tart up the place and make it more agreeable. One contribution to the world at large was to improve the track up to the Buachaille Etive Mor, so that people could reach the mountain with dry feet.[1] So I deeply cared about what happened to the hut and the efforts put in by many people to make it more habitable. And here was this tousy-haired insouciant loon undoing all that good work.

Consider the personalities here: I was a young academic at Strathclyde University, Haston was a tearaway on the verge of studenthood; some 14 years separated our ages – we were at the dawn of the era when age no longer brought a measure of respect. Even greater differences separated us however: I was middle-class, he came from a working-class background; I had a good income, he was an acknowledged scrounger, reputed to steal when he couldn't afford to buy. Worst of all I was a member of the SMC, which meant that by definition I was a reactionary fuddy-duddy and a fit subject for ridicule.

I was furious. He was indifferent. I booted them out. As far as I was concerned the devil would be ice-skating to hell before I let Haston into Laggangarbh again. Now it so happened that I was currently on the SMC committee and when at the next meeting his application for membership came up, I opposed it. The committee admitted him and I resigned as custodian.

Once you have crossed swords with someone you tend to keep in touch with their frailties rather than their achievements, so in spite of the fact that Haston went on to do great things in the mountains, my dislike of him was sustained. I was not alone in this antipathy. When he was later invited by the American John Harlin to come to Leysin in Switzerland to help run an international mountain school he more or less shook off his Scottish roots. At least, I reflected, one's gear would now be safe from pillage.

My next physical encounter with Haston was shortly before his death. I had arrived at the top of a ski-lift in Verbier and there he was; lean, intellectual-looking, usual hooded eyes, well-attired, sporting the best skis that money could buy. Quintessential Haston. Anyway, many years had passed since the hut episode, and it was time to bury the hatchet. So I gave a friendly shout of recognition. But it was not to be. Haston's menacing eyes reminded me of a mongoose about to strike a cobra. Growling like a coffee pot coming to the boil he strode past me and then, propelled by his sticks, hurtled over a steep bank and disappeared at frightening speed down the piste. We learnt later that he was there to be filmed skiing steep narrow couloirs with Davie Agnew, a long-standing member of the Creag Dhu.

Haston had become a brilliant mountaineer, winning international recognition for his ability not merely to climb the most taxing routes, like the 'direct' on the north wall of the Eiger, but to make sound mountaineering judgements. Chris Bonnington, who had teamed up with Dougal for the Eiger climb, found him a gentle and agreeable companion, demonstrating that people do evolve out of their odious past. On Himalayan climbs it was not uncommon for older and more experienced climbers to defer to his wisdom. He was so good, Bonnington told me, that he just assumed that he would always be in the lead, much to the irritation of the other climbers on the team. By the time of his magnificent performance on the south-west face of Everest he was up there with the best in the world. The fact that he adequately survived a bivouac without a sleeping bag or oxygen at 28,000 feet and was able to come down next day unharmed in good order is a tribute to the man's ability and mental control. This is how Bonnington relates it, in Haston's words:

> I was locked in suffering silence except for the occasional quiet conversation . . . Hallucinations or dream? It seemed comforting and occasionally directed my mind away from the cold. That stopped and then it was a retreat so far into silence that I seemed to be going to sleep. Shaking awake, I decided to stay this way. We'd heard too many tales of people in survival situations falling asleep and not waking up . . . I don't know if anything we did or said that night was very rational or planned . . . but with a terrible will to get through the night all our survival instincts came right up front.

To which his companion, the mature and likeable Doug Scott, added after having arrived down at Camp VI: 'We had been so absorbed in surviving the night and the descent that at times it all seemed so much like a dream, just two of us and no one else in the world to share the cold swirling snow.' Mick Burke, who followed them up the face, never returned.

The driving force of Dougal Haston's life was his acceptance of the philosophy of Nietzsche; he believed that whatever he did, it was his right to do. An extract from his diary reads: 'I will do many things for people I respect, and for fools nothing. They deserve to be trampled on . . . thus spake DH.' Even the sympathetic biography by Jeff Connor reveals an ambitious, tough, introspective, ruthless individual, albeit a fantastic climbing companion. Doug Scott recalls how during the hellish, surreal night they spent in a snow hole at 28,700 feet, just below the summit of Everest, Dougal opened his down jacket to warm Scott's feet under his armpit.

Such qualities bring one to the top, but seldom make for warm friendships. Connor never met Haston. But Robin Campbell had climbed with him and knew him well:

> . . . his progress was lubricated by taking Nietzsche's philosophy seriously. God died about 1800; Morality and Authority died about 1964; so what should men live by? Haston evidently liked the Nietzschean idea of striving to move along a bridge from Mensch to Ubermensch by strengthening every virtue in him and who is to say he was wrong.

How could it be that someone of this calibre could die in a paltry powder snow avalanche on a slope of a mere 1,000 feet? It was on the north-east side of La Riondaz, a modest hill of some 6,330 feet above the village of Leysin in the Swiss Canton Vaud. Here is Campbell's agonised obituary: 'He's gone and, with him, a long loping stride, narrow hips, wide shoulders, a lipless grin and bright bivouacked eyes.'

It is said that on the morning of this death he had just put the finishing touches to his novel. This is an inexpert work of fiction, but the climbing sequences are gripping. The hero is Dougal by another name – a nice, honourable Dougal that one would love to meet. Was this the man he wished he had been, or as he had always seen himself misunderstood by the rest of the world? In all probability he was already evolving into a more normal human being. He lived with a lovely girlfriend. One would have thought that peace would now be settling on his soul, that he had everything to live for. One wonders whether his reckless descent of an avalanche-prone slope just after two feet of fresh powder had fallen was a deliberate tryst with death, letting God toss the dice. He was 34. Perhaps he felt that in terms of great exploits he was over the hill. Younger climbers were baying at his heels. Maybe the adrenalin rush that drove him was ebbing. But 30-odd is far from being too old, even for a high-standard climber. I recall my 30s as the most vigorous time of my life and my 40s as a close second. Another facet of his death was that, like Mozart, he died skint, with overdrafts at both his banks. He was living off his friends.

His old pal Moriarty is still around, genial, always ready to share a drink. One of the striking features of that group was their excessive addiction to booze. Haston was frequently totally and utterly stocious and yet within a few days, as he embarked upon a new adventure, would regain his astonishing physical fitness.

The better climbers of those days preferred their own tight groupings to the larger traditional clubs. Membership of the staid ancients like the Cairngorm Club (Scotland's oldest), The Fell and Rock Climbing Club of the Lake District (FRCC), the SMC and Grampian was not attractive. Small competitive groups arose which one could join only by invitation, and this on the basis of observed performance on crag and ice as well as geographical location. So we had the Alpine Climbing Group (AC), The Rock and Ice in Manchester, Carn Dearg in Dundee, the Etchachan in Aberdeen, the Creag Dhu in Glasgow, and the less regionally orientated Squirrrels who modelled themselves on the Scoiatoli in Italy. They erected an illicit hut above the gorge in Glencoe. It's still there.

In due course practically all these people joined the SMC, which for all the criticism of it as a male chauvinist cabal that takes itself too seriously, is in fact the financial bulwark that prevents English mountaineering from taking over Scotland. Up to 1958 there was some justification for this criticism. It was a gentlemanly club, some of whose members would have been more at home in the New Club in Edinburgh than in the sordid surroundings of Laggangarbh or enjoying the ambience of a doss in the Shelter Stone at the head of Loch Avon. This image was reflected in the rather boring *SMC Journal* of the times, edited by that worthy and remarkable mountain explorer Dr Jim Bell, whose pawky humour unfortunately failed to surface in the sober pages of his journal. Happily, in 1958 Geoff Dutton became editor and at once turned it into a literary publication where people, aesthetics and human interaction became more important than a plodding record of mountain achievement. Dutton is a man of great erudition, a poet and gardener of well-merited repute. His rapier wit keeps his friends entertained for hours. Once when sawing wood with him at his home, the blade jumped and almost nicked my finger. 'Ach!' he said, 'what's a finger or two to a piper like yourself.' He is also an actor. Sartorially impeccable, he will address an international conference on biochemistry, with the audience wondering when he will be up for a Nobel prize, and then at home in his garden resemble a down-and-out tramp, wearing a Burberry raincoat he bought as a student 55 years ago. A man of great spiritual and intellectual generosity, he is less so with his drams. Proffering a minuscule drop of the *craitur*, he enjoys the emotional response it creates in the recipient. No one who has read his first number of the *SMC Journal*, XXVII, in 1960, could continue to accuse the SMC membership of stuffiness. The droll writings of that issue continue to this day. McLennan's article, 'We Happy Few', brings tears of joy and was the harbinger of a literary style where you poked gentle fun at your companions.

The other mountaineering journals, of course, were important as records of mountain exploration. The Italian *Revista CAI* is a great record, likewise the *Alpine Journal,* but the best in English is probably the American *Alpine Journal,* which until recently was edited by the indefatigable (and now deceased) Ad Carter who, with contacts globally and an open house for climbers at his homes in Boston and New Hampshire, seemed to correspond with everyone in the mountaineering world.

For my part, as an identified SMC member, I was constantly subjected to teasing by climbers from other groups. In those days, with money scarce, if you came across a piton you took it out and added it to your equipment. If you were a member of the SMC you had scarcely time to bang one in before a scavenging Creag Dhu climber would be at your heels. Johnny Cunningham (alas drowned in an effort to save another climber), one of the best of the Creag Dhu climbers, was particularly expert at taking the mickey out of SMC members; but it was all in good part. The perception of the SMC as stuffy prevailed long after it was out of date. One aspect of this was that it was taken for granted that its members were rich. A reallocation of our gear and the illegal use of our huts were simply considered a legitimate step towards equality of opportunity.

At the period that Haston was at large there was one other *enfant terrible* on the Scottish scene: Robin Smith. His background was quite different. He came from a very correct middle-class background. He lived in a bungalow with a widowed mother and was educated at George Watson's College, a private Edinburgh boys' school. But he shared one thing with Dougal; he was always skint, doubtless due to his mother's meagre pension. Like Dougal he stole. Robin wore an innocent air that belied the real man. He had a puckish face and cheeky grin. While still a student Robin quickly became a rock-climbing star. He simply flowed up the rocks, barely stopping to take precautions. Like Haston, he didn't suffer fools gladly, but he was kinder. Whereas most climbers when recording their routes for posterity gave pitch by pitch directions so that others might know where to go, Robin's attitude was 'If you can't climb at my standard, why bother following?' He offered minimalist descriptions of his new routes, for example his superb 1,000-foot 'Thunder Rib' in Core a'Mhadaidh, Cuillins, which he described as follows: 'The rib is to the left of Deep Gash Gully. Follow the line of least resistance. Very Severe.' Another hard route he described as 'Follow the exiguous crack to the top. Hard Very Severe'. I remember looking up my dictionary to find out what exiguous meant. It was a good description. He wrote well, indeed he set a style of writing that many sought to copy. His description of his ascent of The Bat with Haston on Ben Nevis became a classic and was reprinted in *Games Climbers Play* by Ken Wilson. I appear obliquely in this story. Describing his arrival at the CIC hut, Smith wrote: 'We had to speak in whispers because old men were sleeping in other beds.' I was one of these *old* men. I was then 33!

He only once deigned to climb with me. My standard wasn't up to his, but what I did learn was that whether through poverty or inclination, he took very few safety precautions compared to a salvationist like myself. He put his faith in his skill. His gear was almost always tatty. But this was to change.

In 1962, as one of the architects of the joint SMC/Alpine Club expedition to the Pamirs, I negotiated that of the twelve British climbers, four would be Scots. Ken Bryan from Glasgow was to be one and Graham Nicol from Aberdeen another. Tom Patey was invited but had already arranged to go to the Karakorum. This left Haston and Smith as the obvious alternatives. Haston was rejected on account of his disagreeable reputation. Smith accepted. He was 23 and had just graduated with a first-class honours degree in philosophy at Edinburgh University. He made no secret of the fact that he considered his fellow Scots on the expedition incompetent degenerates. We took some consolation from the fact that when he met the English contingent he cast them in the same light, with the exception of Joe Brown and Ian McNaught-Davis.

The expedition was subsidised by the Mount Everest Foundation and, oddly, by a Texan oilman, but we were each expected to chip in a few hundred. This the poverty-stricken Robin could not do. We gave him time to pull together some cash. In preparation for the expedition various duties were devolved and headed notepaper distributed. Robin took full advantage of the fact that the letterhead bore the legend 'Leader, Sir John Hunt'. God knows what cock-and-bull stories he wrote, but he amassed a considerable amount of goods quite irrelevant to the expedition's needs which he flogged to friends and in pubs. Amongst these goodies were karabiners, virtual gold to the impecunious climbers of the day. Anyway, he paid his whack before we left for the Soviet Union.

Once we arrived in Soviet Asia his behaviour became quite bizarre. For example, while at Dushanbe swimming in the Lake of Komsomol Youth, Robin pushed my head under the water and kept it there. I expected this to be some playful gesture, but as time passed I ran out of breath and seriously thought I was going to drown. When he finally released me, he just grinned, offering no explanation. I practically needed a stomach pump. Later, at base camp, I was lying in my tent reading when the door flap opened. There was Robin with his penis hanging out. He then proceeded to pee into the tent. He certainly impressed the Russians with his fitness, doing round-trip load-carrying in half the time of the rest of us. Hunt organised us into three teams for a fortnight's high-altitude training. Happily Robin and I were in different teams. I never saw him again.

On the descent from Pik Garmo, Wilfred Noyce and Robin were roped together as they descended a shallow but steepening slope of sun-rotted snow on ice; not technically difficult. One of them slipped, dragging the other off his feet. They failed to brake and both slid 4,000 feet. It was impossible to survive such a fall. It was agreed by those who witnessed the fall never to reveal who slipped first. The context of this tale is given in Chapter 10. Robin was a truly free spirit who lived a shambolic existence of impoverished interdependence with his friends and associates. He came from nowhere, a shy boy who taught himself to climb and soon surpassed everyone. He lived by no rules or codes, but simply, as Jimmy Marshall put it:

> . . . by an unbounded enthusiasm at being born into an age of climbing where overhanging corners, bulging walls and seeping black cracks remained untouched. Couple this with a never-ending effort to improve his technical ability and a climbing history of inordinate experience and the result power-packed agreeable Smith . . . It is hard to avoid the pitfall of remorse and endless eulogies; but he himself would reject these, and we are best to remember him by his wild whoops, the tuneless ballads wailing from some fearful dank wall, the hair-raising climbs far into the night and his wanderings about moonlit snows of the Highland summits . . . he has left us with a legacy of great climbs.

Let me quote just a small excerpt from 'The Bat and the Wicked', describing a climb on the Carn Dearg Buttress of Ben Nevis that he finally achieved at a second try with Haston as his partner. At this point in the story he has fallen off twice from an attempt to overcome an overhang that blocked the exit of the route:

> By now night was creeping in. Peels were no longer upsetting,

but Dougal was fed up with sitting on a slab and wanted to go down for a brew. But that was all very well, he was going home in the morning, and then coming back for a whole week with a host of terrible tigers when I would be sitting exams. So I was very sly and said we had to get the gear and climbed past the roof to the sling at the pebbles leaving all the gear in place. There I was so exhausted that I put in a piton, only it was very low and I thought, so am I, *peccavi*, *peccabo*, and I put in another and rose indiscriminately until to my surprise I was past Dougal's ledge and still on the rock in a place to rest beside a solid chockstone. Sweat was pouring out of me, frosting my waist in the frozen mutterings flowing up the rope from Dougal. Overhead the right wall was swelling out like a bull-frog, but the crack grew to a tight shallow chimney in which it was even blacker than the rest of the night. I squeezed in and pulled on a real hold, and a vast block slid down and sat on my head. Dougal tried to hide on his slab, I wobbled my head and the block rolled down my back, and then there was a deathly hush until it thundered on to the screes and made for the hut like a fireball. I wriggled my last slings around chockstones and myself around the last bulges and I came out of the corner fighting into the light of a half moon rising over the north-east buttress. All around there were ledges and great good holds and bewildering easy angles and I lashed myself to about six belays.

What a man! What a loss to Scottish climbing!

How different was the third icon of that period, Tom Patey. He was one of that adventurous group from the Aberdeen University Larig Club that was active in the mid-1950s of the last century. They included Bill Brooker, Mike Taylor and Graham Nicol, all still at large. They were characterised by three things: they were tough, they set new standards in ice-climbing and they had a wonderful sense of humour. Tom played the accordion and invented hilarious parodies, such as 'Onward Christian Bonnington' to the tune of the famous hymn. The chorus ran:

> Onward Christian Bonnington, of the ACG,
> If you name the mountain, he will name the fee.

Tom did his national service in the Marines (as a doctor). He was notable for his lack of hygiene and on his departure was presented by the officers' mess with a box of black hankies. Once back in Scotland he settled as a general practitioner in Ullapool. His partner's recreation was fishing, so they split the weather between them. Patey attended to his patients when it was wet and climbed when it was dry. He unlocked the climbing potential of the north-west Highlands. His travels as a doctor gave him ample opportunity to identify new lines. Though he climbed to the highest standard, one of his finest new routes was the relatively easy but sensational 'Nose' on Sgurr a'Chaorachain in Applecross, which he climbed with Bonnington in 1961. Hamish MacInnes, with whom he often climbed, said 'he shifted the centre of gravity of British mountaineering several hundred miles northwards'. A politically attuned individual, he knew how to make the right gestures.

My first encounter with him was when he and some Aberdonians were illegally camping just below Zermatt. I was with a Glasgow group and we set up camp alongside. This desecration of the Swiss environment was not long tolerated. We were removed by the local officials and fined. That night, in revenge, somewhat drink-taken, we lifted up several signposts and rotated them by 90°. I often wondered how many hapless lederhosen-attired tourists intent on taking the Furi lift to the Schwarzsee found themselves at Findeln.

Tom and I met frequently at the barn attached to the farmhouse of Aberardair, the gateway to Creag Meagaidh, in the days when six people on the face was considered a crowd. In spite of it being 30 miles north, Saturday nights were spent at Karl Fuch's bar at Carrbridge where, after closing time, the door was locked and Tom got out his squeezebox, after which a riotous evening would ensue. As ever there was terrific competition between Glasgow and Aberdeen climbers. The Aberdonians had been extremely pipped when Norman Tennent and I snatched the first ascent of the South Post (a steep snow and ice couloir) before them.

On one particular occasion we got back late and by that stage Tom was very drunk. We slept in the barn, for this was before Creag Meagaidh had been bought by the Nature Conservancy and was still a sheep farm. On the Sunday morning Ken and I rose early, and silently made breakfast and hastened up the snowy track towards the cliffs of Coire Ardair. Just before the top of the old birch wood I looked back and could see Tom and party hastening after us. Rather than stress ourselves by trying to outpace them, we carefully reversed our steps using the existing foot prints in the snow, and then darted behind some bushes. In due course Patey and Nicol came past, with Tom saying, 'Hash on, Graeme. I can see their tracks. We've got to get ahead of them.' Once they were out of sight we enjoyed a leisurely ascent of the glen, and picked off another route, Eastern Corner.

Tom made many fine ascents on Creag Meagaidh. We had omitted the first pitch of the South Post. He straightened that out. We failed on the North Post, he succeeded. He made a girdle traverse (in winter) of the entire crag. Though he also made his name elsewhere in the Alps and Himalaya, he is remembered for his new routes in Scotland in winter. Yet for many of us there was an even more potent memory – his satirical wit. He was totally unmechanical and as is typical of such people, he made fun of those who were otherwise. It happened that during a boring period at my place of work I had set my mind to work out the dynamics of a belayed climber holding a falling leader. He lampooned this in the *SMC Journal* in 1958:

> Have you ever seen a rock climber with a climbing rope marked in inches, a pencil in one hand and a slide rule in the other? Have you noticed how he consults his slide rule and scribbles hurriedly on his anorak cuff before committing himself to a hard move? The climber was probably Dr Malcolm Slesser, the well-known Scottish Scientific Technologist, a man with an equal head for heights and figures. Slesser was the first to point out that:
>
> $$P2 /W - 2P = 20 \ T/EN$$
>
> How comforting to know that 'nylon mountaineering rope can absorb an impact kinetic energy of 0.235/foot length per lb. Tensile strength'!!! In a tight spot, a cool-headed leader will consult his Slesserian Tables to calculate the chances of the rope parting under the impact of a falling climber. Many leaders have probably fallen with their calculations incomplete. If that were the case, it would be doubly unfortunate, because the tables generally confirm what is already feared: the rope will break. It's impossible to argue with a mathematical equation.

Some of his ribald verses could hardly be published these politically correct days. He had a remarkable gift for seeing the comic, the absurd and the pretentious around him which he exposed in his satirical songs, as in:

> Two tiny climbers on a ghastly North Wall,
> And a huge hungry bergschrund just ripe for a fall

and

> Let the Valkyries howl in the pitiless sky,
> But the two tiny climbers must conquer or die.

He offered some strategies to ageing climbers in 'The Art of Climbing Down Gracefully':

> Mountaineering is becoming fiercely competitive. Every year marks the fall of another Last Great Problem, or yet another Last Great Problem Climber. Amid this seething anthill, one must not overlook the importance of staying alive. That is why I devote a few lines to the long dedicated decline to Dignified Decrepitude.

There are various ploys the ageing mountaineer can deploy to avoid risk to one's neck while retaining the respect of one's peers. The 'I'm afraid I'm a bit off form today' gambit is quite acceptable, but cannot be used too often or the rumour will circulate that 'poor old Slesser looks past it'. Another strategy is to cash in on one's great experience compared to that of the young tigers and denigrate the proposed route as being too trivial; try 'Well, after SC gully, which I did in the '40s, your proposed route looks a little boring', or 'I remember we did it direct in '44. I don't think I want to spoil my memory of that great occasion.' A more desperate ploy, only to be used as a last resort, and then only when there are no contemporaries present, is to lie. When invited to climb rocks you say 'Actually I'm a snow and ice man' or vice-versa if invited to climb ice. But the subtlest approach which no one can gainsay is to declare that you've reached the stage where you prefer your own company, that in this way you feel more in touch with nature and that anyway the rope is just a hindrance.

If, in spite of these ploys, you find yourself outmanoeuvred and obliged to tie onto somebody's rope and then put up a poor show, try Patey's suggestion: explain that nowadays you only really function well at over 20,000 feet.

It has to be said that Tom Patey was a terrible risk-taker. Unmechanical, disorganised, wild and careless, his early demise was probably inevitable. But a kinder, finer man you couldn't hope to meet.

To get a feel for the evolution of British mountaineering in the 1950s one should read his posthumous book *One Man's Mountains*. In one sense he wrote his own obituary in the satirical song 'The last of the grand old masters' (which particularly referred to Joe Brown):

> Live it up, drink it up
> Drown your sorrow,
> Sow your wild oats while you may,
> For the Grand Old Men of tomorrow,
> Were the Tigers of yesterday

Patey, like Haston and Smith, died needlessly through an error of judgement. He was roping down from a sea-stack in Sutherland known as The Maiden when the piton into which the rope was threaded came out.

All three were a huge loss to mountaineering, particularly to Scottish mountaineering. It's not quite true that only the good die young. So can the bad, the foolish, the proud and the famous.

NOTES
[1] This was finally achieved 40 years later through financing from the Scottish Mountaineering Trust.

route to Kommunizma

route to Garmo

route to Concord

route to Patriot

The author's impression of the Garmo Basin

Avodara

GARMO GLACIER

Pik Moskva

Pik Leningrad

Pik Abalakov

II

Ice Fall

BELAEV GLACIER

Pik Kirov

Smith's Peak

II

IIIb

IIIa

IV

IV

V

V

VAVILOVA GLACIER

IV

V

IV

V

Peak Concord

Pik Patriot

BELAEV GLACIER

Kuzmin Route

Pik Kuibyshev

Georgian Couloir

Former Molotov

SOUTH FACE

Pik Pravda

Ice Cave

III

Pik Kommunizma

VII

VI

V

Ice Fall

VI

Pik Garmo

CHAPTER 6

High Pique

Once a team of mountaineers are embarked upon an expedition their social world contracts to their own tiny community. To succeed in their endeavour they must forge a social unit. Each individual's capacity to tolerate another's foibles, suppress one's ego, adapt to changes of plan and work for the common good plays a huge role in bringing the venture to a successful conclusion. However accommodating the mountain and the weather might turn out to be, without social cohesion even a successful summit climb may leave a bitter taste in the mouths of the returning party. Norman Dyrenfurth's 1971 International Everest Expedition was a classic example. One climber, Pierre Mazeaud, said in exasperation, 'You expect me, Pierre Mazeaud, Member of the French Assembly, aged 42, to work as a Sherpa for Anglo-Saxons and Japanese. Never! This is not me, but France they have insulted.' Perhaps he had a point.

The problem is that you cannot say to friends and the public when you get back home, 'I made the first ascent of [say] the great tower of the Baltoro' when in fact you were merely part of the team that helped to get two of the expedition's climbers onto the summit. Your role was possibly indispensable to their success, to the expedition's success, but unless the public also see you as the expedition's leader, as with Sir John Hunt on Everest, your moment of fame will be a small paragraph in the expedition book. Thus climbers inevitably vie with each other for pole position, for the opportunity to be the best-placed person when the final push comes. Being identified as the person who got to the top brings real benefits. Firstly, if you are minded to go for some other mountain, raising finance is a lot easier. Then there is the matter of status. Doors seem to open that were hitherto shut. But for some, like those in the old Soviet Union, there was an even more tempting benefit; the freedom to climb free of supervision, when you wanted, where you wanted – a freedom Western mountaineers enjoyed as a matter of course.

My own experience of an international expedition was not one I sought. I had early on in my expeditioning recognised how difficult it was for mountaineers, whose very ability centres on their individualism, to pool their resources for a common aim, especially if the task is long-drawn-out and physically demanding. One of Chris Bonnington's undoubted claims to fame has been his ability to lead and channel highly individualistic climbers to a common purpose. On high mountains the stresses are amplified, stresses that may have nothing to do with your like or dislike of your tent companion's personal habits. Possibly food and one's stomach's reaction to it are amongst the greatest problems. Tummies do not readily adapt to high altitude and no food ration yet devised seems to quite fit the need for energy, low weight, digestibility and palatability. Stresses are doubly amplified when the climbers come from totally different cultural backgrounds. It takes great forbearance on everyone's part to bring such an enterprise to a successful social conclusion. And in the case of the British–Soviet Pamir Expedition of 1962 we failed. But let me start at the beginning of this remarkable story.

There are many factors that drive a climber to undertake the tedium associated with organising an expedition to a distant mountain range: a virgin peak of character is the usual and most compelling. For Ken Bryan and me, however, it was the curiosity to know what went on behind the Iron Curtain, as Churchill called it, that girdled the Soviet Union and to meet up with Soviet climbers. Not since the time of Lord Curzon had British travellers penetrated into the remote regions of what had become Soviet-controlled Asia and in particular into that knot of remote high mountains known as the Pamirs, whose highest summit was 24,595 feet.

The opportunity came as a result of the diplomacy of Sir John Hunt, the leader of the successful 1953 Mount Everest expedition. In 1958 he had visited the Caucasus with an Alpine Club party, the first such visit of British climbers since the origin of the Soviet Empire. In 1960 he arranged a return visit for some of their climbers and when in Scotland, Hunt politely brought in a few of the locals. The SMC threw a posh dinner party, where we met the Russian climbers (for they were all Russians, not from other parts of the USSR), in particular their charismatic spokesman, Eugene Gippenreiter, who spoke excellent English. Kenny Bryan and I left that meeting with the germ of an idea – to climb the highest mountain in the Soviet Union in the Pamirs, then rejoicing in the name Pik Stalina – what else in those days? With such an unusual objective it seemed to us we would have little difficulty in raising the media interest needed to meet the considerable expense likely to be incurred.

As it happened, we were not alone in this thinking. Hunt had been asked by a Climbers-cum-Alpine Club group to lead a party to the Pamirs. I approached him with a view to joining forces but he was not interested. He advised me to apply to the Soviets for permission in the name of the SMC. After months of waiting an identical telegram reached both of us, but in such a form as to throw us into confusion: it granted permission for a party of 12 climbers from the UK on condition that the SMC and the AC joined forces. What a dilemma! It was a bit like proposing that North and South Korea should cooperate on making a nuclear bomb. I often wonder if the Soviets chose deliberately to be mischievous. There was a perception in the Soviet Union that Scotland was a subjugated nation. Now where would that idea have come from? A female diplomat told me that while travelling in a taxi in Moscow the driver had asked where she came from. When she said 'Scotland', he said that was impossible as Scotland was a subject nation and therefore the people must be black.

The Soviet proposal was that we would be joined by 12 Soviet climbers. While Scots and English mountaineers mingled freely and easily on many high-altitude expeditions, such as the Tom Patey and Joe Brown team on the Mustagh Tower, there were also exceptions. Harold Raeburn had not gone down at all well with his English companions on the 1922 Everest expedition. Expeditions from Scotland tended to call themselves the 'Scottish something expedition' at the time and this was considered somewhat parochial by the English establishment.

I had been with Hunt on his 1960 expedition to Greenland with the lads from the Duke of Edinburgh Award scheme and formed a considerable respect for him. He was a gentleman to his fingertips. At that time he had already led the successful Everest expedition and been knighted: his name carried enormous weight. (He eventually became Lord Hunt and chairman of the Parole Board in England.) To Hunt it seemed obvious that the SMC's proportion of climbers should be according to the fraction of the Scots population, some 10 per cent of the UK whole. I viewed it differently; we had the right to equal representation, having made our own separate application. We settled for four Scots and eight English – you see how reasonable we both were! Thus we came together unintentionally, perhaps even unwillingly.

At this time, 1961, the cold war was almost at its peak and the Cuban missile crisis was about a year away. However, Stalin had died and his successor Kruschev brought a little kindness and relaxation into a society basically scared out of its wits. People began to talk and criticise more freely. Intellectual life became more vigorous and underground newspapers, the samizdats, circulated more freely. The satirical magazine *Krokodil* was seriously funny.

In November 1961, in response to a request from the USSR Federation of Mountaineering for someone to come to Moscow and work out details, Hunt asked me to go. As a single traveller I was obliged by Soviet visa regulations to travel on a businessman's ticket. This meant I was furnished with a full-time minder/interpreter, a car ever at my disposal, a berth in the ancient and gloomy Metropole Hotel, and a wad of meal vouchers that would have fed an entire Siberian *gulag* its Sunday treat. I mostly traded them with the corrupt waiters for Georgian wine No. 4, said to be Stalin's favourite. In that respect, anyway, the old villain had good taste.

From the very first meeting with representatives of the Federation of Mountaineering I sensed that the people around the table harboured a pathetic anxiety to speak their mind, but that they dared not. It was plainly up to me to make it as easy as possible for them. The negotiations were hard: there were questions of who paid for what, how we would get to the mountains, what Customs arrangements would be made, what we could and could not bring with us. Pik Stalina was in a prohibited area, but they would try to find a way round that. These discussions were carried out in an alcoholic haze, since the first act on sitting down was to plonk a 1-litre bottle of 55 per cent vodka on the table and pour out the equivalent of 3 drams into each glass. This was tossed down in a oner with cries of '*Nazdarovia*' and followed by a long gulp of lemonade.

'Why the soft drink?' I asked.

'Ha, ha. To hide the taste!'

The first encounter seemed to go well, but as I left, Gippenreiter whispered, 'I warn you not to hope for too much at the negotiations tomorrow.'

The next day saw the surfacing of many problems. The USSR Federation of Mountaineering had a clause to the effect that participants would at all times uphold and perpetuate Communist Party principles. I had no particular problem with this, since once on the mountain we would presumably share and share alike. However it was more than likely this condition would be publicised, the capitalist media back home would pillory us and we might lose potential sponsorship. I decided to upstage them by suggesting we consider this issue over a further bottle of vodka at my expense. They declined, citing the need to get back to their families and so forth. I chided them, pointing out that in my culture it was considered an insult to refuse the return drink. Mortified, they agreed to stay. I chose some Armenian brandy (very good) with ice cream. We were at that critical point of inebriation when tongues loosen. They talked intimately, explaining their own predicaments and insisting they would help us fight the forces of Soviet bureaucracy. As we tottered out to our respective limousines I felt I was in the company of friends. On the way to the hotel the Moscow lights were entertainingly fuzzy.

The next day my limousine was directed to the Federation of All Sports. Behind a massive desk was an immaculately dressed 50 year old whose smile sparkled with gold crowns. This was no mountaineer, but Comrade Antipinok, a high Communist Party official. After fulsome enquiries as to my health and comfort and those of practically everyone even remotely connected with our endeavour he eventually came to the point: 'Mr Slesser, you are here to make negotiations. But are you authorised to take decisions?'

There could be only one answer: 'Yes.'

'You will understand, Mr Slesser, our mountaineering is conducted on carefully planned lines. Since it was decided to grant you permission we are regretting that there has been a change in programme.'

I was aghast. Surely they hadn't allowed us to incur the expense of this Moscow trip simply to say 'niet'. He went on to explain that their committee had decided to put all their efforts in the coming season into the Caucasus and that they could not spare 12 Soviet climbers to join us. It seemed that in the Soviet Union you climbed where you were told to. He then explained that we could go, with 'a little Russian assistance', to wit six Russian climbers, one of whom, Anatole Ovchinnikov, was present. I was actually relieved at this news, since an expedition of 24 climbers is far too big for assimilation. All that remained was for me to make a fulsome speech as to how devastated we were at not having the privilege of climbing with 12 Soviet comrades, but that 6 was better than none and we accepted their terms and looked forward to closer cooperation between our climbers, and indeed our countries. At this everyone seemed overjoyed. The tension around the table palpably eased. Comrade Antipinok rose, his diplomatic role at an end.

The negotiations reopened and I was asked where we would like to climb. The question astonished me, for we had already stated this in our official request for an ascent of Pik Stalina by the Garmo Glacier. I asked for maps, for suggestions, for access data. None of my requests met with a reply that did not make the Garmo our only option. The form slowly emerged. I was pressed to say where we wanted to climb, while being denied the information to make a decision. It struck me that this was the procedure adopted in a Soviet show trial. Once the defendant confessed to what the State wanted, then things could be quickly wrapped up. I agreed to go to the Garmo.

One fact did make discussion tricky. De-Stalinisation was in process and the mountain had no name. I was later informed that the Supreme Soviet of the Autonomous Republic of Tajikistan had voted to call it Pik Kommunizma, 24,584 ft (7,495 m). I daresay they too had confessed to the appropriate name.

So now we knew we were going to the Pamirs in the summer of 1962. But who would be in the party? For the Soviets there was no problem. The climbers were selected by a top committee on the basis of their ability and worthiness. Of the six selected it turned out that three were already Masters of Sport. This is a coveted status, given to those climbers who summit five 5b-graded mountains (summits of 20,000 feet or over), since only such climbers were free to climb where they chose. The other three were within one summit of attaining this privilege. We did not make social contact until we finally reached base camp.

Back in the UK it was quite different. This was not Mt Everest. Hunt was not about to invite the cream of British mountaineering. After all it was not so much a mountaineering venture as a social exploration. Furthermore, though I was well enough known as a mountaineer, I was not in the top flight. He left me to sort out the Scottish end. Naturally one likes to choose compatible people: climbing ability and stamina were not the only qualities required. Ken Bryan was part of the initial plans, so he was in, and a superb climber anyway. He had been enormously helpful in the byzantine negotiations with Hunt. Tom Patey unfortunately couldn't get away, but Graham Nicol was from the same stable, a hardy Aberdonian with wonderful storytelling ability. He was also a doctor – always useful on an expedition. The remaining place I offered to Robin Smith, who at that time was one of the most talented young climbers around.

Hunt was also selecting on the basis of earlier promises and compatibility. I knew Ian McNaught-Davis from the 1960 Greenland trip, where we had done some great climbing together. George Lowe and Wilfred Noyce were old friends of Hunt, in what might be described as an older age group. Ted Wrangham was a landowner, a genial ex-Etonian. Later, when asked by the Russians what he did for a living, he teased them by saying he was a collective farmer. 'My peasants farm, I collect.' Joe Brown was perhaps the top English climber of the time (though Don Whillans would have disputed it). He came from a completely different social environment. Ralph Jones and Derek Bull were members of the Climbers Club and had been with Hunt in the Caucasus two years before.

In those days when you travelled in the Soviet Union, and perhaps even now in the new Russia, you were a prey to all sorts of hidden forces: we were shepherded around by representatives of the Federation of Mountaineering; arrangements that had been made after long discussion were suddenly changed and when explanations were sought none were given, but we could see that our hosts were embarrassed. One cancellation that really infuriated us was that we were not to be allowed to march into the mountains through the lush valleys of Gorno-Badakshan. Traditionally one gets physically fit for a high mountain expedition by the march in. We were instead to be transported by helicopter (at our considerable expense) and then dropped at a glade at an altitude of 9,000 feet above sea level, no less than 25 miles from our mountain and 15,000 feet below it. This was absurd, given that there would be no porters, such being considered, we were told, inappropriate in their egalitarian culture (though not in Communist China!). We suspected that the nearby valleys had been forcibly cleared of their population, as they were followers of the Aga Khan.

This created the first souring of international relations. It has to be remembered that as far as the West was concerned the Soviet Union was a totalitarian state, with a bad reputation for civil liberties. McNaught-Davis and Ralph Jones made sallies in rather bad taste about the Soviet system, which offended the Russian climbers, who after all were pawns in the great game. Our being dumped in this spot was not the work of the climbers but of some hidden higher authority. We were surrounded by hills best described as slag heaps, reminiscent of Spitsbergen in summer. Not an icy spire was to be seen. Distinctly depressing. We in the British party behaved rather like a bunch of kids who having been promised a birthday treat arrive to find there is no lemonade or cake. Criticism was in the air. I was reminded of the words of Ogden Nash:

> Such is the pride of prideful man
> from Austrians to Australians
> that wherever they go, they regard as theirs,
> and the others there as aliens.

We embarked upon a boring period of carrying loads up to the intended base camp at Avodara identified at my November negotiations, about 7 miles nearer the mountain and 2,000 feet higher. What further exacerbated the international divide was that the Soviet climbers were supremely fit while, apart from Robin Smith, we were not. My diary reads:

> We were out-of-puff individualists. The Russians had been training since January, going out on runs three mornings a week and taking cross-country ski trips at the weekends. They even went to the length of carrying each other on their backs in deep snow up the Lenin Hills by Moscow . . . I can only say that we were under no obligation to please anybody. A Russian climber is picked by a committee who see to it he is supplied with all his food and transportation (and salary). We, in some ways, picked ourselves and we ourselves paid for the pleasure of coming.

This was only partly true, however, with the expedition being subsidised by the generous Texan oil mogul.

Inevitably a sense of inferiority pervaded the British group, some of whom reacted in a petty manner, openly belittling things Soviet. McNaught-Davis's huge ego and outgoing nature were irrepressible. He taught the Russians that the polite way to greet John Hunt in the morning was to say, 'Balls to you'. Eventually they caught on to his mischievousness and Vladimir dubbed him MacHooligan, to which McNaught-Davis responded, sharp as a tack, 'And you are Bloodimir!'

The six Russian climbers made themselves as agreeable as they knew how. Tolya Ovchinnikov was the leader, a small, intense, powerful, considerate man, an engineer by profession. He spoke passable English. Three of us in the UK party had studied Russian and could make a stab at conversation. Hunt, in an effort to engender a sense of togetherness, arranged for one Russian to sleep in each three-man tent. I shared mine with a sort of human coiled spring named Nikolai (Kolya) Shalaev, who spoke no English. He had a lovely smile and I grew to be very fond of him. He was a carpenter by trade and a member of the Communist Party.

Avodara was at the snout of the Garmo Glacier. Here and for several miles along it was covered with debris. Grim, black, plunging hillsides added to the gloom. Up this horrible surface we would have to carry all of our supplies a further two days' march to reach the true foot of the mountains at 13,000 feet, the altitude at which a normal Himalyan expedition would start. It was soon apparent to Hunt that we would exhaust ourselves and have too little time for serious climbing, so he asked if it would be possible to helicopter food and materials to the junction of the Garmo and Vavilova Glaciers, which would be our Camp III. This is illustrated on Map 3. His request was granted. Why if it was now possible was it firmly rejected back in November? Our joy at this reduction in load carrying was muted by the fact that we had by now carried too much stuff to Avodara. More mutterings amongst the camp followers! We imagined that the helicopters would land at Camp III, but in fact things were tipped out from a height of 20 feet onto a moraine. The gear and tents survived all right, but the food boxes split open. On arrival we found that if you wanted to cook dried egg, you had to be content to have it mixed with tea leaves, sugar and lemonade crystals. It offered all the excitement of eating deep-fried Mars bars. Even so, the Russians admired the detailed manner in which the boxes were labelled to indicate each daily ration.

One incident on the way up the glacier illustrated the difficulty faced by our Russian colleagues. From my literature researches, I knew the names of most of the peaks and when the 22,559-foot (6,878-metre) Pik Molotov came into view, I remarked upon it to Vladimir Malachov. He winced and shook his head. 'Not Molotov.'

'What is it, then?' I asked. A discussion ensued amongst the Russians present. Then they turned to me, 'It is peak "Former Molotov".' The Pamirs had not caught up with the pace of de-Stalinisation. They were perfectly conscious of the irony.

Anyway, with the drudgery of the lower Garmo behind us, our spirits picked up as we settled into Camp III. We were now close to the mountains, and what a magnificent prospect it was, in particular the imposing 5,000-foot south face of Pik Kommunizma which was our planned route. Pik Garmo looked a veritable giant, hunched over the pristine tablecloth of the Vavilova Glacier. Across the way Pik Leningrad presented a monstrous bulk, like a stout maiden aunt whose modesty was protected by impenetrable hanging glaciers which were continually avalanching. I was spellbound by the 20,000-foot (6,000-metre) Pik Patriot directly opposite. So too were McNaught-Davis and Bryan. Joe Brown in his cautious way kept his opinion to himself.

Hunt and Ovchinnikov proposed that we split into three parties for an acclimatisation climb, each of four Brits and two Russians. Garmo would be tackled by Ovchinnikov's party, consisting of Wilfred Noyce, Robin Smith, Ted Wrangham, Derek Bull and Vladimir Sevastianov. My party would consist of Vladimir Malachov, Kolya Alchutov, Ken Bryan, Joe Brown and Ian McNaught-Davis (Mac). Hunt's party was composed of Eugene Gippenreiter, Ralph Jones, Graeme Nicol, Kolya Shalaev and George Lowe. They would head for a 19,000-foot virgin peak.

There now arose the delicate issue of who would be the leader of each of these parties. As far as the Brits were concerned no leader was needed, but this was not the Communist ethos. In an unbelievable piece of political correctness Hunt suggested the leadership should alternate each day. The rest of us thought he was losing his marbles. On Russian insistence, control times were set for a return to Camp III. No matter what, climbers had to be back on time; if not, a rescue party would set out.

Now that we were in groups of six and about to do something for which we were mentally and physically attuned, the prospects for international integration looked more promising. By common consent my party chose Pik Patriot. For the two Russians it had the added lure of being a 5b peak – if they climbed it, it would clinch their status as Masters of Sport. It had been ascended by the south ridge three years before. Five climbers had died, two being avalanched and three in attempting their rescue. We decided on a different route – the west ridge. As we humped heavy loads to set up Camp IV under Pik Patriot's west ridge, Mac teased Vladimir: 'Will you carry my load, Bloodimir? I will pay you many roubles.' To which Vladimir boomed, 'Oh, MacHooligan, you are decadent.' This was a Russian joke, but a little close to the bone for Mac. Later Vladimir told me how happy he was to be climbing with the conqueror of the Mustagh Tower, saying 'He is real mountaineer', as indeed he was and is. The Russians were well informed about mountaineering exploits around the world and names like Hunt, Noyce, McNaught-Davis and, of course, the legendary Joe Brown, were all familiar to them.

At last we had a group of individuals in touch with each other. With Vladimir's English improving rapidly we were able to have interesting camp conversation. He was a Communist Party member, a status held by one in seven of the population. We learnt that membership requires not just formal, but active participation, and a member must at all times demonstrate exemplary behaviour. He is the soul of respectability, upholder of moral tone and preserver of institutions. This image was completely at odds with that portrayed by the Western media. The dissolution of the Soviet Union by the tenets of the Harvard Business School has now destroyed all the old values. In 1961 the citizen put his or her four kopeks into a box on entry into a bus. No ticket was issued. It was a matter of honour to pay. Those few who did not and were identified were lampooned: their photos would be pinned up in the buses with rabbits' ears attached. Our Russian colleagues had seen the film *Room at the Top* which confirmed the Soviet propaganda that Britain's masses were downtrodden. Joe put them right.

This amity lasted a very short time. The issues that came to divide us were purpose and safety techniques. The Russians disagreed with the camping arrangements, wanting to reduce the number of tents and sleep three to a two-man tent. We disagreed. On the first day's serious climbing, while Ken and I went down from Camp IV to Camp III to bring up more supplies, Joe, Mac and the two Russians set off to forge a route to the ridge. Later that day, as Ken and I searched the face for signs of them, we could identify only three climbers. Shortly after, Joe Brown arrived back alone. He had just opted out. Joe later recorded that he told Mac it was madness to climb in the conditions which prevailed that day. Alchutov was determined to continue, however, and Mac agreed to go on with the Russians, 3 on a 300-foot rope. They came down at the end of the day having failed to find a route. Mac unburdened himself to us *sotto voce*: Kolya was a fine climber but his safety techniques left much to be desired; furthermore, the rock was appallingly loose and the snow rotten. Much of our enthusiasm for climbing was already petering out. This led to a discussion as to our purpose here. The British view was that we climbed for pleasure, and if it was not so, why climb? The Russian view was probably the same but coloured by their personal situation within a command economy. Once a 5b peak was under their belts the benefits for them were huge. I realised that if we were to climb this peak it would be for them, not for us. Nonetheless we did need to get acclimatised to altitude. Sadly, thereafter, the two Russians climbed only with each other.

Next day it was the turn of Ken and I to force the route, which we did, choosing a different line. But in all my days I had never climbed on such rubbish. It was rather like climbing bookshelves using the books as holds. If one drove a piton into the rock it split. The only possibility was to use horizontal cracks and depend on the weight of rock above to hold them in place. My recollection of that period is full of alarming little incidents. Mac understandably thought the whole enterprise pointless and too dangerous and, had it not been for Joe to jolly him out of his petulant moods, he would probably have walked off the mountain. Vladimir confided in me: 'Mac and Joe have no will for the mountain.' It was no less than the truth, but the Russians had so much to go for and provided the driving force. I watched with my heart in my mouth as Kolya climbed a pillar of rotten rock unroped. We did eventually reach the col, stocked it and set up Camp V. Scenically it was a superb position from which to watch the endless avalanches discharged from Pik Leningrad and examine more closely the ferocious south wall of Kommunizma. This was very relevant, because a route up this unclimbed face had been the expedition's objective. I knew at once that we would never do it. A route as steep as that could only be done if the rock was sound.

On 21 July Ken and I came up to Camp V for the third time with a view to remaining there until our turn came to try for the summit. It was 11 a.m. To our surprise the others were still there. The four of them had spent the previous evening in a vicious argument about whether to make an all-out assault on the last 3,000 feet of the peak. Mac and Joe had wearily given in and all were on the point of departure. Ken and I also came in for Russian criticism for not going with them. Frankly, we were exhausted. Vladimir brusquely asked me for my pen, the only writing implement, it seemed, amongst the six of us. 'Why?' I asked.

'So we can leave our names on the summit,' he replied. The pen bore the words British–Soviet Pamir Expedition. 'At least,' said Vladimir, 'your pen will reach the top.' Oh, how unkind!

They forged a route to the top of the next tower 1,000 feet above. Next morning we were alerted by a wolf whistle and in the thinning mist saw Mac shouting to us to the effect that they would make a summit attempt, and advising us not to come up as there was insufficient room for another tent. Ken and I dozed all day at Camp V. Having nothing to write with and nothing to read we spent the time fantasising. What would our ideal mountain be like? 'A bit like an ideal woman,' said Ken, the bachelor, 'shapely, seductive, mysterious.' Alpamayo in the Andes was put up for scrutiny: nice shape, but lousy tropical snow. It had to have good rock, something like Chamonix granite or Nevis porphyry. Well, we certainly would not find it here in the Pamirs. It would have a tiny summit, just enough for two people to stand on, like the Grépon. We decided that the quality of the snow was a key property. None of your sun-rotted snow on top of ice, but the crisp névé of Ben Nevis, with its toffee-textured ice – not the tropical or Pamirean overnight water-ice. As we roamed the world in search of our ideal mountain, we began to appreciate that it was quite pointless travelling far from home. Except for shape, the best was literally on our doorstep at home, while for shape, nothing could beat the Mont Blanc area – the Grandes Jorasses, the Dent du Geant, the Dru, and all the aiguilles, though I put in a plea for Greenland. We turned to make some tea, but there was none. The packet, broken in the helicopter drop, had emptied itself onto the floor of the tent.

The 24th was the last possible day for the group to make a summit attempt and be able to meet our control time. On the 22nd at 9 a.m. Ken and I reached Camp VI. Its platform was barely 6 x 6 feet levelled out of rock and banked with snow. We ransacked the tent for tea, but again there was none. By now the expedition's food provision had become a joke: not only had it been damaged by the airdrop, but it contained ridiculously heavy things like pickle in glass jars and barely cookable dried meats rich in sodium glutamate. Tummies were seriously upset. The Russians had a completely different diet, of which tea, caviar and kasha were the main ingredients. Kasha is a porridge made from wheat flour – our semolina. It is easily digested. I now include it in my own rations. Ken's feet were lifeless and we waited for the sun to warm the tent and him within it. At 11 a.m. we set off upwards. We were at about 18,400 feet and were working on a misapprehension that the peak was 20,000 feet high, whereas it turned out to be 20,800 feet. So while we thought we had but 1,300 feet to climb, in reality it was 2,500 feet. After a couple of pitches where we climbed like three-footed cows, we accepted the fact that the rope was more of a danger than a safeguard and unroped. There was nothing to belay to anyway. Ken was now ill but he struggled on to get a glimpse of the final ridge. There, below the final tower, were two figures. We heard a cheery yodel. Two pitches lower were Mac and Joe. We pressed on but at 19,000 feet Ken finally gave in. I was in little better shape. We had insufficient energy to continue. I think now that our lack of digestible food played a big part in our poor performance. This was seriously to affect us later.

To our consternation we saw Mac and Joe descending. Why? It was only two in the afternoon. Joe recorded the events in his book *The Hard Years*. I would like to have been able to quote the events up there as explained by Joe in his chapter on the Pamir expedition, but of all the people from whom I requested permission to quote from their writings, Joe Brown is the only one to have refused me. The gist of it was that he and Mac were appalled at the dreadfully dangerous snow conditions and decided to call it a day and descend. According to Vladimir, Mac sounded off his feelings with what would for him pass as a witty remark, but which for Vladimir was rather offensive: something like 'Bugger you, Bloodimir, and your lousy Soviet snow.'

Ken and I were unaware, of course, of this insensitive interchange. On arrival Mac said they had just lost interest, but it was not so simple. Joe had piles in a big way. I really felt for him – it is a disgusting ailment, usually brought on by climbing with a heavy pack. Joe and Mac descended to Camp IV, while Ken and I remained at Camp VI.

The Russians returned at 7 p.m., an hour before dark, having failed to reach the final tower leading to the summit. We had a meal ready for them. They were angry and didn't know how to express their feelings. A few remarks in defence of Joe and Mac brought out a furious reaction:

> Malcolm, I never wish to climb with famous climbers again. Two days we did nothing. We asked them many times to go up, but they would not. They laugh and say it is unpleasant.

I pointed out that Mac and Joe were two pretty good judges of what was safe. But the bottom line was that the Russians had a dream, that of becoming a Master of Sport. Joe understandably dreamt of a warm sleeping bag, a fag, lots of tea and no load carrying; Mac didn't give a bugger.

I offered Kolya and Vladimir two options: we would help them place a higher camp, in which case we would have to share the remaining four man-days of food at Camp VI, or Ken and I would descend at once, leaving them food enough for two days. They chose the latter option.

A day later Ken and I reached the squalid litter of Camp IV. Joe in his kindly way had prepared a drink made from throat pastilles – we had no tea left. It was like nectar. The two exhausted Russians reached us next day having reached the summit. Joe had a meal ready for them, but they declined, saying their first duty was to go to the memorial to those comrades who had died there three years ago. Visiting it later, I saw they had laid a bunch of wild flowers.

Amity was restored. The success of the Russians elated our group, though Vladimir could not understand it, since we had not also summited. Once again the dichotomy between the Western and the Communist ethos emerged. In their view they had succeeded; we had not. In our view the team as a whole had succeeded because we had worked together to put two men on the top.

CHAPTER 7

Peak of Communism

On the morning of 25 July I crossed the Vavilova Glacier to Camp III to report we were safe and sound. No one was there! Odd. That evening our meal at the Patriot camp was interrupted by the arrival of a haggard-looking John Hunt with a deeply sunburnt Graeme Nicol in tow. Hunt cut short our greetings: 'I had better tell you straightaway that Wilf and Robin fell 4,000 feet to their deaths on Garmo on 23 July.'

This news evoked a kaleidoscope of emotions, images and reactions. Given the appalling nature of the rock on Patriot, an accident had always been on the cards. Had Garmo been similar? Four thousand feet! What could such a fall have done to the bodies? But the sense of personal loss predominated. I had ice-climbed with Wilfred Noyce on Ben Nevis earlier in the year. I had admired his technique and caution, and enjoyed his company. He was a kindred spirit. Robin was a man I had not yet grown to love, but he was still in his formative stages, with a terrific future ahead of him both intellectually and as a mountaineer. Hunt, with tears in his eyes, gripped my arm: 'Wilf was one of my closest and oldest friends, Malcolm, one of the best.' Graeme pulled Ken and me to one side: 'How do you chaps feel about going on [with the expedition]?'

This was not an issue for me. In the past some of my friends had been killed on the mountains. We had lost Hans Jensen on the British North Greenland Expedition. It had never been mooted that we pack up and go home. On all the expeditionary trips I had run we had mutually agreed before leaving home that if anyone was killed the expedition should continue. So I wondered what lay behind Graeme's enquiry. He just said, 'I *am* glad. I told John I was sure the Scots would want to continue.'

The full story emerged over the next few days. It seems that Hunt's party had quickly and successfully put a team on the top of their virgin peak and named it Pik Sodroozhstvo, which roughly translates into Peak Concord. They then headed over to Noyce and Ovchinnikov's advanced base camp. All they found was an empty tent. It was now 24 July, the day that Vladimir and Kolya were making their summit bid on Patriot, one day to go before the control date. In search of the other group, John Hunt and Graeme Nicol climbed to an icefall from where they could see some figures descending slowly on exceptionally steep snow. 'Fantastically slowly,' added Hunt, as he described the events of that day. The figures turned out to be Derek Bull and Ted Wrangham, from whom they learnt of the accident. The snow conditions were awful and they decided to return to Bull's lower camp and look for the bodies the next day, it being assumed that no one who had fallen that far could still be living.

The tale was that Pik Garmo had been climbed by four of the party – Ovchinnikov, Noyce, Smith and Sevastianov. They had all safely come down from the summit rocks and were resting. The remainder of the route was on steep snow-covered glacier. Smith, who had been roped to Ovchinnikov, unroped. For reasons unknown, or unspoken – we were never sure which – he then attached himself to Noyce. The two of them then hastened off down the slope before the others, moving together. One man was seen to slip – he was not held by the other, who also fell. They slid and slid, out of control. Hearing this my mind flashed back to my time with Noyce on Ben Nevis. I had watched him crampon down the steep slope of hard névé that falls from the summit of Carn Mor Dearg to the CIC hut, pipe in mouth, one hand in the pocket, his ice axe cradled under his other arm, supremely confident. I was surprised. It would only have taken a tiny off-balance jerk to send him slithering down the slope helpless. He would never have been able to get at his axe to stop himself. Was it so on Garmo? Bull and Wrangham, who had not gone to the summit, had seen the entire episode. First one unidentified person slipped, then the other. Hypnotised by the spectacle they witnessed the entire fall, the bodies flashing past them only a few hundred feet away. No one would comment who fell first. I had the impresion from Hunt that the only person who knew was Ovchinnikov. Hunt swore him to secrecy. He was quite right to do so – though from a mountaineering point of view it is quite irrelevant who fell first, since they were roped and therefore mutually responsible. But in the lay world, and in particular in the media, the back-biting and accusations that would have flown if it became known who fell first would have caused endless and damaging debate that would percolate far beyond the small world of mountaineers to the press and the public. It would have been a reprise of the equally irrelevant issue of who had first stepped on the summit of Everest: Hillary or Tenzing?

It was only 30 years later when Ovchinnikov published his memoirs, *Alpinists of the Moscow School*, that more detail emerged. This is what he wrote:

> When we got down from the cliff [presumably the summit rocks] I saw Tolya [Sevastianov] doing up his crampons and Wilfred continuing down the snow slope. Robin was standing by Tolya. That moment Robin untied himself from my rope and unclipped Tolya from Wilfred's rope and put him onto mine. He then tied onto Wilfred's rope, telling us to follow. We were not in a hurry. I was doing up my crampons. Suddenly Tolya Sevastianov cried out 'They have fallen.' I raised my head but couldn't see anyone on the slope. Sevastianov explained that he too was doing up his crampons and had raised his head and saw a rucksack hurtling down [Wilfred had a rucksack] the slope which was quite gentle and we were not anxious until we got down to the brow of the slope and couldn't see anyone.

It seems that the sun-rotted snow that we had experienced on Patriot had been lying on top of ice. Joe Brown records climbing with Robin on Nevis in March 1961, commenting how quick and careful he was on difficult ground, yet so reckless on easier terrain. What is intriguing about Ovchinnikov's story is that Robin chose to detach himself from Ovchinnikov's rope and link himself to Wilfred's. Why? Did he dislike Ovchinnikov's style of climbing? Did he feel he should look after Wilfred? Apparently the slope was initially quite gentle. The whole point of being roped is that if one slips the other should be able to hold him. If it was considered that this might be impossible, they should either have been unroped, or taken to pitching the descent. It is really surprising that when the first fell the other failed to hold him. Were they just careless, or too confident?

The following morning the remainder of the two groups entered the icefall. After some hard climbing the bodies were found lying side by side, still roped. It was a dreadfully dangerous place to be. After discussion amongst the British members it was decided to bury the bodies there – like a burial at sea, they were pushed into a crevasse. Even as the group turned to go, the first of the day's falling stones came whirring by.

The fallouts from this sad incident were many and varied. On the Russian side they could not understand why the bodies were not recovered and given a proper burial. That would have been their code of conduct. There was also a little tut-tutting about climbing safety from the Russians. For those of us on Patriot who had viewed the Russian tactics at close quarters this was a bit rich. On the British side a thorough dislike of the rock had removed much of the intrinsic pleasure of climbing. Had we been on a climbing holiday, we would have decamped to a more salubrious area or sunned ourselves on the seacliffs of the Calanques. The snow conditions were also bad, but these could change and anyway were par for the course on high mountains at this latitude. Bull and Wrangham, close witnesses to the accident, decided to return home. Likewise George Lowe, who was an old friend of Noyce's.

While one could sympathise with their feelings, the fact was that we were not on some casual climbing holiday. The expedition had political overtones. It was an endeavour to cement British–Soviet relations. What we did or did not do would have ramifications far beyond our little group, far beyond the mountaineering world. The British party in a very real sense had to uphold the verities of the capitalist West and show that it was not the decadent beast portrayed by Soviet propaganda. It was therefore with astonishment that we learnt that John Hunt was also quitting. To Graeme, who has a strong martial streak (he was in the Territorial Army), it was like a general leaving his troops. Hunt felt he could no longer climb here after the loss of so dear a friend as Noyce. His duty, he said, was to return home and explain the situation to the world's media and to Noyce's wife and Robin's mother. He was certainly right, in that when the news broke the media were frantic for details. However, Hunt felt the expedition should continue in the interests of 'Anglo–Soviet [sic] relations'. His words. I let them pass.

There were three firm commitments to stay – the three Scots. Joe Brown, in his quiet cautious way, said, 'Oh, I'll stay, not that I particularly like climbing these mountains.' This, said Mac, put him in a fix as their two wives knew each other. Ralph said if Joe stayed, he'd stay. During the subsequent days, as we hirpled down the loathsome Garmo Glacier to base, numbers fluctuated between four and six. One thing was clear – the intended climb on the south face of Kommunizma was out of the count. The most we could do was save face by climbing the peak by the easiest route as a joint Soviet–British party. Tolya Ovchinnikov knew the way. It was called the Georgian Couloir. We would have to re-ascend the Garmo, pick up materials and food already lying at Camp III, move them to the junction of the Vavilova and Garmo Glaciers at 13,000 feet and then strike northwards up the Belaev Glacier, which was guarded by a ferocious icefall. Some relaying of food, fuel and materials would be required to the foot of the couloir at about 17,000 feet. It would take two camps to get there. This is illustrated on Map 3.

The tragedy brought us all a little closer together, Russians and British. On the other hand the impending departure of the four diminished the camaraderie of the British group. The base-camp glade was now filled with a huge Trades Union expedition called Spartak, led by the legendary Vitali Abalakov. He was extremely critical of Hunt's departure. He told me that there had been 420 applications by Soviet climbers to be on this expedition. This fact alone emphasised the importance of achieving some sort of successful joint venture. It was clear that we had, at the very least, to get to the summit of the highest peak, Pik Kommunizma, if only by the easiest route – and that we had to do so in good style alongside our Russian colleagues. It must be a truly joint ascent. Only Alchutov and Sevastianov would not be accompanying us, as they had already done this route.

Tolya joined our group of six who were staying on and nervously opened discussions. It was important, he emphasised, to be up and off early when the conditions were at their safest. No more British lying in their beds after dawn. He looked sternly at Joe and Mac. Vladimir must have been telling tales. Then he set the cat amongst the pigeons. Here are his actual words, recorded on tape:

> We must warn you Pik Kommunizma is a high mountain and it
> may not always be pleasure. Since the way will be hard, and
> sometimes dangerous, there is no place for weaklings, it will be
> better to have a medical examination.

I am sure he had no wish to hurt our feelings. He was too nice a man. It was indeed manifest how much fitter were his own climbers than we, but for all our apparent frailty, we were a pretty tough bunch who had an enormous amount of climbing experience. Joe and Mac had successful high-altitude climbs under their belts and we had all made ice climbs of a far higher grade than the Georgian Couloir route that was now envisaged. I was acutely aware of what each of us was thinking – 'No bloody Russian is going to decide whether I am fit to climb'. This affront was smoothed over. But that was not all. Tolya raised the issue of safety procedures. The British party had been far from impressed with the Russian safety procedures. I sensed exactly what was going through the minds of my colleagues who, in the interests of British–Soviet relations, kept their mouths shut. As Joe was to remark:

> No one is going to tell me, Joe Brown, one of the best climbers
> in England, how to get myself up this grotty pile of shit.

With these diplomatic cracks delicately papered over the party enjoyed a boisterous last evening before departure. This had not been an expedition with many laughs or much camaraderie, so we needed the amity it brought forth. We committed the unpardonable sin of bringing out the whisky bottle. If any of the climbers on the Spartak expedition had so much as sniffed it, he would have been sent home in disgrace. Indeed one man caught smoking was forbidden to go beyond base camp. Meanwhile Joe puffed at his fags. Our drinking confirmed, I later learnt, the Russian view that we were not serious high-altitude mountaineers.

However, we were now a more coherent group. We recognised that there was work to be done and that what faced us was duty rather than pleasure. Unfortunately, the British party was now to be divided by yet another trivial incident. Ken, Graeme and I had wrung out of the Russians the right to march down the valley for three or four days on our homeward journey. It would at least give us a flavour of that lovely region we had been denied visiting on the way here. It would, of course, delay the return home. Ralph and Mac were adamantly opposed. Their position was that they had agreed to stay on to climb the big peak only on the condition that they left for home immediately after. We could not afford two separate helicopter lifts, so once again we were polarised into north and south.

So heaving heavy sacks once again upon our backs, we left for the dreary plod up the Garmo. Facing us were 16,000 feet of climbing in 9 days – in fact more like 20,000 feet taking into account the relaying of loads. It was galling how fast the Russians moved compared to us.

They seemed almost intent on embarrassing us. On the first two days up the glacier there was no need for hurry. There were no dangers. We knew we would get there, but all the time Tolya was pushing us. Every one of the British party was perfectly capable of making his own decisions on the mountains. We were just not willing to be led by the nose. But then from the Russian side, it looked as if we were not willing to keep to our promise to climb all together. Two days later at the new Camp III, Tolya extracted a promise that from now on we'd be up early. Before us was the formidable Belaev Icefall. We had to carry loads up and be down again before the sun hit it at 9.30 a.m.

The icefall was not a pretty place and was exceedingly dangerous in the sun. In due course, having ferried loads through it twice, we established Camp IV on the flat upper glacier at 15,500 feet with enough food, tents and fuel for the remainder of the ascent. Not once did we manage to keep to Tolya's schedule. His irritation was plain to see. Ralph had wanted to turn back after the ferrying of loads to Camp IV, saying, 'I've done what I promised John I'd do,' but we chivvied him on, particularly Joe. So now we were all at Camp IV about 3,000 feet below the final ice slope – the Georgian Couloir – that led to the plateau above which the summit towered. Between here and there we would place a Camp V at about 17,000 feet. Joe and Mac were going well, but never moved with the Russians. At this time Ken, Graeme and I were plagued by food poisoning. It is very difficult to convey to another person, especially a super-fit Russian climber, what it is like to have a cement mixer churning away inside you, generating gas at a rate that could heat a small house. Ken became so ill that Graeme, as doctor, said he must descend, and Ralph kindly agreed to accompany him. Both Graeme and I had frightful bouts, and took purgatives and chloramphenicol antibiotic. Both of us made miraculous recoveries within 24 hours, but, nonetheless, this lost us a day and put another black mark against us as far as the Russians were concerned.

Tolya declined to wait. He was probably thinking how right he had been about a medical examination. Their team, he said, would place fixed ropes on the final stretch of the upper couloir (actually an ice slope of 60°) and then fill in the time ascending 'Former Molotov', 22,559 ft (6,878 m). This was a bit of lifemanship designed to rub home their superiority and it was with some pleasure we found out later that they too lost a day on the way between Camp V and the plateau. An absurd situation arose now: a shortage of climbing rope. The final

113

ascent to the plateau was with 4 of us on a 30-foot rope: not only dangerous, but clumsy. Joe and Mac unroped. As I cramponed up the final slopes, Joe threw me a line. I was as weak as a kitten. I crawled into my tent more a gasworks than a human being.

Next day we descended to a col at 19,000 feet, at the foot of the final 5,000 feet of the mountain. There stood a Russian tent. To our surprise it was empty. Then looking up we saw the specks of descending climbers. A party was helping down a sick member of the Spartak team. As doctor, Graeme was called in and pronounced a pulmonary oedema. The best cure is to get the person quickly to lower altitude, but the route required a prior ascent of 1,000 feet. The temporary answer was oxygen. We had carried an oxygen bottle for just such an event right up to Camp V, where it had been abandoned in the interest of lightening loads. Graeme pumped the invalid full of antibiotics. We reflected on the irony of the situation. We had arrived at base with 200 kg of medical stores. By Camp II it was down to 25 kg. By Camp V it was down to 4 kg. Now it was negligible.

Late that afternoon Tolya and Eugene came across for what he called a 'Trade Union meeting':

> So far we have not climbed this mountain as a joint party. We have been in three tents. English, Scottish, Russian. We do not mix. We do not see you. The way above is heavy, the snow is deep, for the wind has filled in the tracks of the Spartak party. We must share the burden of breaking the trail.

Some of this was true, some unfair. Surely they might have waited for us during the 24 hours of Graeme's illness. Joe was enthusiastic: 'Now we are here I really feel I want to climb this perishing mountain.' Graeme's medical opinion was that three of us were actually ill: our electrolytic balance was all to pot and food made Joe sick. Kolya kindly dropped in a tin of caviar – it was wonderfully digestible and palatable. Once again an early start was mooted.

So the new day dawned. Eugene passed by while we were still getting ready, telling us Spartak had dug an icecave at 22,500 feet, 3,300 feet above us. We would meet there. Given our weak condition I proposed to Mac and Joe that they go for it, while Graeme and I would carry some of their load to the icecave and then return. They would not hear of it. The proposal was defeated by kindness.

It was a dreadful inner battle for both Graeme and I to make that icecave. A couple of hundred feet below it I was all in and Joe took some of my load. Graeme's face had the pallor of anoxia, the blue colour of his Moncler down suit. At dusk we crawled into the cave, whose headroom was about four feet and a bit. The Russians were huddled together, leaving a space for us.

Eugene announced sternly, 'There will be no spoiling of the air or smoking.' Graeme and I had about as much control of our bodily functions as a parachutist has over gravity. The cave was sealed with snow, the stoves lit and the temperature rose to almost zero. It was comfortable. Looking back I am amazed at what we chose to eat that night: curried meat! We were woken at midnight by angry voices. Someone, probably me, had spoilt the air. The entrance seal was broken, and clean cold air swept into the cave, reducing the temperature to -25°C. In no time our sleeping bags were covered with an eiderdown of powder snow.

I emerged, dressed and ready for the summit attempt by 8 a.m. The Russians were champing at the bit. Graeme was not mentally functioning well, fumbling over simple things. We set off 20 minutes behind the Russians. Their steps were already filled in by the drifting snow – it would have been so much easier for us had they waited, but they seemed determined to demonstrate our frailty. Joe, too, was in poor condition. He had been sick that morning. I heard him confiding to Mac that he was all in, 'weak as a kitten', that he hadn't an ounce of strength in his limbs. He even urged Mac to go on without him – after all, English pride demanded that at least one of them should reach the top with the Russians. The possibility of Graeme and I, who he was later to describe as 'two dead-beat Scots', being the only ones of the British party to reach the top was probably more than he could bear. The very reputation of the Manchester Rock and Ice Group was at stake. However, he was a man of great fortitude and will. He shouldered his sack and stepped forth into the chill wind of the morning, and the British party set off in an effort to catch up with the Russians.

Today was the day. It was necessary to keep my mental faculties at the highest alert to be able to drink in all the many sensations open to a climber at high altitude. The view was of course fabulous, reaching to the distant Karakorum. Rhythm, that was the answer. Breathe once, twice, thrice, then step up. Pause, repeat, up again. Step after step. This gave reasonable speed. Pulse 140. For a while I could actually keep ahead of Joe and Mac.

To my delight we closed on the Russians, and for some reason, Tolya asked me to break the trail. It was a beautiful day. The wind was dropping. At 23,000 feet the slope narrowed to a ridge. Looking back, the Russian cordée made a colourful foreground to the distant Karakorum. I could not resist a photo. Until now all my pictures of them were of their backsides miles ahead.

Just 1,300 feet from the top both Graeme and I flagged badly. As the Russians passed I noted, with a touch of *schadenfreude*, that even Tolya and the steel-stranded Shalaev were affected by the altitude. The problem, of course, was that we were climbing this mountain too fast to properly acclimatise. However, Joe was looking better with every step. Mac never faltered. They would certainly make the top. I proposed something no climber would normally ever do – cut the climbing rope in half. Joe and Mac continued. Graeme and I sat down to contemplate defeat. We were both bitterly disappointed. Graeme reminded me of a remark made by Bob Scott, the well-known keeper at Luibeag on the Mar Estate near Braemar: 'Graeme, ye'll no let the glen doon, noo.' Graeme was looking frightful, his eyes unseeing. He had mild cyanosis. After a while the 'Bob Scott' factor was too much for Graeme and he rose to his feet: 'We must, man, we must.'

So we plodded on, stopping frequently. We made an excellent pair. He provided the determination, I the brains. Above us Mac and Joe had caught up with the Russians. All were resting. We closed on them, but when almost there they rose to go on. It seemed cruel at the time, but it was logical. What was brilliant, however, was that for the first time since Patriot, Russians and British were on the same rope. Tolya with Vladimir and Mac, Joe with Eugene and Kolya. According to what Eugene told me later, Tolya made a little speech about how all must go to the summit, the strong in front, the weak behind. Tolya then suggested that Joe took the lead. Mac, always ready to be witty, then turned to Joe saying: 'Better do what he says otherwise if we ever get back they will sentence us to the salt mines.' He then turned back to Eugene, teasing him, 'All right, you galloping Georgian revolutionary, we'll do your work for you.' Eugene Gippenreiter, whose mastery of English was almost colloquial, failed to find it humorous.

By 2 p.m. Graeme and I reached a slab of rock overlooking the great south face. The sun was warm. We were now at 24,100 feet. We suppressed the desire to quietly die there. But there was only 495 feet to go. We were higher than anything around. Former Molotov was way below us. In the distance we could see Kongur and Mustagh Attar in Sinkiang. Rising cloud then enclosed us.

We made that last 495 feet just 40 minutes behind the others. We were now off the snow onto shaley rock, so rotten that our crampon points bit through and attached themselves. To our amazement a Union Jack was flying alongside the Hammer and Sickle. It had been brought not by us but by Eugene, ever the politician. Joe and Mac were smoking – a wonderful piece of bravado. Vladimir enquired, 'How is it, Mac, that you can climb so well when you are so decadent?' No answer.

Once at rest I regained all my faculties. Even Graeme was coming round, a little Saltire peeping out of his anorak pocket. I was happy. Red pique had given way to red peak. At long last we were together: communists, capitalists, socialists, nationalists. The dedicated, the correctors, the castigators, the cynical, the devoted, the unsophisticated, the fastidious and the slummers – none of us was entirely one of these, but a mixture. I look upon the group photo on the summit with much affection. Ovchinnikov wrote in his memoirs:

> The joint expedition showed that friendship between ordinary people who have grown up in different ideological situations is entirely possible. I have retained friendly relations with John Hunt, Malcolm Slesser, Joe Brown and other British members of the expedition.

Mac's reply to those who felt his remarks were often insensitive was that what we lacked was a robust sense of humour.

The summit was not prepossessing: flakes of shale, a small cairn and a book to record names. Tolya Shalaev presented each of us with a little enamel badge. It was a nice gesture. That very day two Soviet Cosmonauts had been launched into space. The four Russians on Pik Kommunizma[1] were their nearest countrymen.

The end game has been described elsewhere, my own version of events in *Red Peak*, but one event calls for mention here. At base camp we found that the Spartak team had built a charming little memorial to Noyce and Smith. To Mac it was shaped like a fireplace. To Abalakov it represented Pik Garmo. On a stone slab below it Abalakov had carved 'Wilfred Noyce and Robin Smith, Pik Garmo, 24 July 1962' in roman not cyrillic letters. A white shroud wound around the memorial bore: 'To Robin Smith and Wilfred Noyce from all Soviet Alpinists'. To say we were slightly ashamed was an understatement. Why had we not done this? We had a small ceremony of dedication, attended by both our own expedition and the Spartak. We observed a minute's silence.

117

It was a perfect moment – the warm-coloured evening sun was streaming down; in its rays the summit of Pik Garmo was glinting like a pedestal of gold.

NOTES

[1] This, the highest mountain in the old Soviet Union hung onto its name until 2003, when it was renamed Pik Ismail Samani (or Ismoul Simoni depending on the source). Ismail Samani was the founder of the Samanid dynasty and state, which ruled large parts of Central Asia during the ninth and tenth centuries.

CHAPTER 8

Tropical Ice

To those mountaineers whose natural habitats are amongst the temperate regions of the world, ice is a wonderful medium for climbing. Routes impossible or even impassable in summer become feasible and usually much safer. The climber can treat ice as a sculptor works with stone: something to be carved and shaped. How different is tropical ice. There can be no better description of its perils than that given in Joe Simpson's *Touching the Void*. The tropics by definition lie between 23°N and 23°S: the tropics of Cancer and Capricorn. This convention is meaningful, for it is within this arc of the earth's north–south axis that the sun will at some time in the course of a year be vertically overhead; and it will never be less than 67°, an altitude attained in temperate regions only on midsummer's day at latitude 46°, such as that of Mont Blanc in the Alps. This high angle of the sun does peculiar things to snow and ice. For example, a speck of dirt, a leaf or a stone will absorb the sun's rays and so warmed will sink into the snow, creating a hole. In the temperate regions this also happens, but it soon sinks out of reach of the slanting rays. In the tropics, with the sun vertically above, these specks in the snow continue to absorb heat, sinking in ever deeper. Since dust is everywhere, the result is that the many snow surfaces resemble a giant egg carton.

Another feature of tropical mountains is that there is no clearly defined sunny and shaded side to the hill; in northern temperate regions the north slopes are always cooler and hold snow longer and, of course, vice-versa for southern temperate latitudes. But there is a

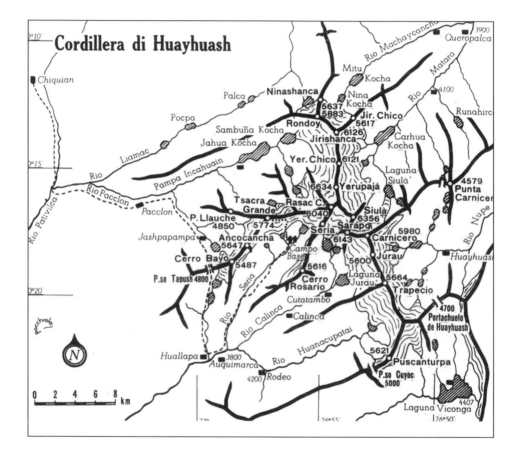

Cordillera di Huayhuash

third, more devastating effect of the near-vertical sun. Under its intense heat, which can be the equivalent of a one kilowatt electric heater on ten square feet, snow sublimes – it goes directly from solid to vapour, without the intermediate step of melting. This process results in a filigree of snow-ice so frail that the climber's axe can barely find anything solid, even deep down. Thus the security and opportunities offered by temperate-region ice are totally lacking in tropical ice. These factors are further exacerbated by the fact that to get ice at all, the altitude must be very high, high enough for there to be freezing conditions long enough for snow to accumulate. At these altitudes, which will be 15,000 feet and above, the transition at sunset from heat to cold is astonishingly swift.

The lowest altitude at which I have encountered tropical ice was on the 10,000-foot summit of the Indian Ocean island of Réunion, locally known as the 'Piton de Neige'. This little island, which is part of France, is one vast eroded volcano, bits of which still fling out lava. From the shore a dirt road winds its way upward around crumbling volcanic pinnacles and along shelves cut into cliffs of pumice. It could be the set from *The Lord of the Rings*. Once at the pastoral village of Cilaos (5,000 ft), however, you could believe you were in the Auvergne. Contented cows and sheep graze in the shade of familiar trees.

We stayed at the sole guesthouse. All ate around one big table. Two fellow guests were an English couple, ex school teachers, who had retired two years before. The day after their release (as they saw it) they went down to Southampton, bought a yacht, were shown the principles of sailing and promptly set off around the world. Here they were, having already crossed the Pacific, quite unfazed by the risks associated with their palpable ignorance of nautical matters. Luck can sometimes get you a long way. Their next port of call was to be Cape Town. I did not like to tell them about the terrors of the Alguhas Current. Ignorance is not bliss when the risks were as great as they were taking.

We rose before dawn and strode up a fine path to the summit at 10,130 feet in time to catch the night frost, which had squeezed moisture out of the damp soil, forming blades of ice. We were high above the serried ranks of cotton-wool cumuli that like an armada of galleons were sailing towards the African continent. This was what earth must look like to an angel in heaven.

There are certain advantages, of course, to climbing in the tropics – no cold fingers, for example. It was a picture of the famous sugar loaf mountain in Rio de Janeiro one winter's day that put me in mind of such benefits, so when offered a year's teaching in Brazil I leapt at it. They say you can smell the tropics from the sea before you can see the land, but the first proof of our arrival was one single brilliant beacon high in the sky when we were still 20 miles from land. This was the huge illuminated statue of Christ with outstretched arms that is perched on the summit of Corcovado (2,300 ft), one of the many mountains that rise out of the canyons of Rio. Little by little the breaking dawn revealed more and as the sun sprang out of the sea it delineated the features of its 1,500-foot-high sheer-granite east face. I naturally looked for a climbing line and found none. I later learnt that the face is virtually unassailable without bolts.

We slid into Guanabara Bay by the sugar loaf rock, the famous Pão de Azuçar. To my delight I found my office was but five minutes' walk away from the Praia Vermelha beach. The British Council invited me to give a lecture on the Pamir trip and there I met Brazilian climbers, in particular Luiz Minchietti. Built like an ox with southern Italian features and an equally friendly smile, Luiz was eminent amongst the small band of rock climbers in Rio. He took me under his wing. He led me deep into forests by barely detectable trails to show me granite precipices and towers dripping with vegetation but virtually devoid of holds. Nervous of snakes I asked him if any were poisonous. 'Not many,' he replied, 'the non-poisonous ones scuttle away, but watch out for poisonous toads.' He showed me where the routes on Rio's precipices began and where to get back down. He showed me which were safe from muggers and which to avoid, especially at night. He outlined the immense climbing potential of his country, in which a spine of mountains 2,000 miles long lay along the eastern seaboard. Their attributes as a *mise en scène* for climbing are determined by one singular fact: there is virtually never any frost, so there are few fractures and nearly all cracks are blind. This also means it is rare to find a rock spike belay or be able to use the normal means of protection. The local talent has solved this problem by drilling bolts, but at long intervals.

The Praia Vermelha is the first of the beaches that stretch southwards along Rio's Atlantic fringe. Luiz led me by a short walk through undergrowth to the foot of a chimney that cleaves the entire southern face of the Pão de Azuçar: the Cheminée Stopp, named after the German who first climbed it. Peering upwards all I could see were smooth granite walls and no stances. We were about to make 1,100 feet of back and knee ascent, dressed in shorts and vests. I went back to the office for some long trousers and a shirt!

The climbing, which was about Grade IV, proved arduous only because it went on for ever without a moment's let up. But unlike its loathsome counterpart in Skye, the Waterpipe Gully on Sgurr an Fhcadain, it was warm and welcoming. Rio was 37°C in the shade, but here in the belly of the mountain it was agreeably cool. Every now and then a small rugosity appeared on the otherwise glass-like surface of the rock. The tricky bits were when the chimney widened to the height of a person or narrowed to scarcely more than the depth of one's chest – then it seemed that there was every likelihood of my slipping down the crack and disappearing like a billiard ball into a pocket. Every 100 feet or so was a bolt. The evolving view was fabulous, revealing first the rugged hills to the south of the city, then Ipanema beach and finally, closer to hand, the surf-drenched Copacabana bordered by the magnificent Avenida Atlantica. That beach is never deserted. While lingering on my belay I could pleasurably observe a sample of the alleged 200,000 gorgeous, briefly clad, dark-haired females who cavort on the beach night and day.

Where else in the world, having emerged from a climb dirty and sweaty, will you find a toilet and washroom, a terrace restaurant providing excellent food and the finest beer in the world, together with a view to die for. On a clear day one can see Dedo De Deus (Finger of God), described in Chapter 12, poking out of the distant Serra dos Orgãos. At the descent *télépherique* they don't ask for tickets, it being assumed you must have paid to get up. A more detailed account of the joys of Brazilian granite is described in my article in *Mountain World 1966/7* or in *Brazil: Land Without Limit.*

One must go north to the state of Espiritu Santo to find the really hard stuff. Here also rises the country's highest summit, Pico de Bandiera 9,500 ft (2,896 m). My wife and I found we could drive up a considerable way to an altitude where the temperatures were very agreeable for walking. We stopped at a flat grassy spot to pitch our tent. When it was time to retire, my wife noted: 'The only trouble is that there is a snake occupying it [the tent].' We slept in the car, while fireflies circled ominously like attacking aircraft.

Perhaps the most remarkable summit is the pinnacle of Itabira in the state of Espiritu Santo, whose slim, holdless, granite walls may be seen from a great distance poking out of the foothills. Sylvio Mendes opened a face route here using untold numbers of bolts, and the route is now laced with steel ropes. On the Atlantic face is a Grade V chimney first climbed by Mauro Andrade and Patrick White in 1963. It is said that no second ascent has yet been made. The only trouble with these peaks is that there are so few holds and that almost all climbing requires artificial aids. These rock faces are inhabited by a species of deadly spider, making them dangerous in summer – it is too hot anyway – but come winter, when the sun can be as low as 67° at midday and temperatures fall to the low 20s, Brazil is simply a great place for climbing and walking: the food and drink is cheap; the people are great; the opportunities enormous.

Rio is a bit like Edinburgh. If you are wearied of your job, a short walk brings you to the crags. In Rio, right in of the midst of the canyons formed by the high-rise apartments of Copacabana, close to the favelas of the poor and destitute, soars the Agulhas da Inhanga, offering a variety of short, hard routes; and there are others nearby like Dois Irmãos in Ipanema, where on the summit is a Mucumba ritual site. Not a place to go at night – you might become the sacrifice!

Tropical Africa also offers ice. In fact Kirinyaga (known as Mt Kenya) 17,058 ft (5,199 m), is also exactly on the equator, so it has more vertical or near vertical sun than that other great tropical range, the Andes. It is a complex mountain, high enough to have permanent snow and ice and to attract heavy snowfall. My companions and I did what you should never do and made a dash for the peak over a long weekend in between commitments in Nairobi. I say this because the peak is so accessible that many who make these lightning forays are struck down with a pulmonary oedema through too fast an ascent to altitude. The start of the route is a mere 97 miles from Nairobi at Nyeri. There you have two choices. One is to go to the local hotel and hire porters to take your stuff up the hill to what is called McKinder's Camp, a permanent set of primitive tents nestling on an alp of the Teleki valley at 13,000 feet below the great east face. Better is to use a four-wheel-drive vehicle and drive up from Naru Moro police station to a roadhead at 10,000 feet, and walk from there – or there are other ways in from other sides of the massif.

We did not stay at McKinder's as we had keys to the Kenya Mountain Club's excellent hut nearby. To get there we had a 3,000-foot ascent, 1,000 feet of which was up what is aptly described as the 'vertical bog', outclassing anything that Skye or Connemara can offer. Beyond this, you walk through a strange and, to my mind, rather ugly landscape of giant Lobelias to the more familiar alpine environment of the rough pastures of Teleki. The setting is now truly magnificent. The two black summit-towers of Nelion and Batian are separated by the Diamond Couloir whose ribbon of ice descends fully 3,000 feet from the col between them. It is a popular, but demanding, ice climb. It usually requires two days and a bivouac. This is one problem with the tropics: long nights and darkness falls swiftly. Recent reports are that the couloir ice is in retreat.

On Kirinyaga, there are two rainy (and hence snowy) periods: long rains from mid-March to mid-June, and short rains from mid-October to late December. Being in Kenya on business we had no control over the season. It was 10 March 1984 as we tramped up the hideous black ooze of the vertical bog. We were all slightly breathless at the hut that night. Next day we plodded up the trail to Point Lenana at 16,355 feet leaving our rucksacks at the hut 700 feet below. This utterly squalid place cannot have been cleaned since it was built. We traversed the glacier and left climbing gear and food at the foot of the north wall of Batian in order hasten the proceedings on the morrow. From here the route is not more than a Grade III rock climb, somewhat akin in difficulty and length to the Tower Ridge on Ben Nevis. The traverse to Nelion is more demanding. We woke to ten inches of fresh snow! The climb was impossible and we could not wait as we were expected to be operational in Nairobi the day after the next. It was just as well. One of my companions was showing signs of oedema and was vomiting. We hastily descended to Nyeri at 6,000 ft. She quickly recovered, but there are many instances of people who do not.

No one should go to this mountain without first having read the penetrating and delightful book *No Picnic on Mount Kenya*, written by the Italian Felice Benuzzi who in 1943 escaped from a British prisoner of war camp located at the foot of the peak. Their object was simply to alleviate boredom, not to escape. They made a swift ascent of the peak before their captors could round them up. His widow is today the international secretary of the Mountain Wilderness Association, a body whose mission is to protect mountains everywhere from desecration.[1]

The ultimate tropical mountains, however, are the Andes of Ecuador, Peru and Bolivia. In spite of mountain exploration going back to the time of Humboldt, at the time of my first visit in 1966 there were still many, many virgin peaks. The invading Spaniards recorded in 1550 that Atacama and Quechua Indians had ascended some volcanoes, including the 20,000-foot Llullaiyco. These are technically easy hills. Equally easy by present-day standards were Humboldt's ascent of Chimborazo, 20,500 ft (6,250 m), and Reid's of Cotopaxi, 19,400 ft (5,896 m), in Ecuador in 1872, both virtually on the equator. In 1897, the Swiss guide Zurbriggen climbed Aconcagua, which at

22,900 ft (6,982 m) was found to be the highest peak in all the Americas. Much of the ascent can be made on a burro's back!

Two supreme mountain ranges from the climber's point of view are the well-named Cordillera Blanca, lying to the east of the valley of the Rio Santo near Lima, and in the stupendous walls of the Cordillera Huayhuash (Cordillera di Huayhuash) nearby. These are dream-like summits, pointed and steep in a way that few Himalayan peaks are. In the 1930s a stream of German and Austrian expeditions made many first ascents. Huascarán, the highest peak in Peru (which has an easy side), was climbed by an English lady and her guide. In the 1950s the Andes entered the golden era that the European Alps had enjoyed a century before. Literally hundreds of climbing expeditions took advantage of the simplicity of Andean organisation; easy access, cheap transport by burro and little bureaucracy. The New Zealanders climbed Cayesh, the French the exquisite pyramid of Alpamayo, the Austrians Jirishanca, the humming bird peak. In the Vilcabamba the French overcame the superbly defended Salcantay, and some young Englishmen, Clark and Gravina, climbed Pumasillo.

In this golden era of Andean mountain exploration one peak above all others resisted the blandishments of climbers: Yerupaja in the Cordillera Huayhuash. Hans Kinzl, a great authority on Peru, who had made a map of this great mountain range, regarded it as the most beautiful in South America. At 21,679 feet it is third in the pantheon of the American mountains, yielding only to Aconcagua in Argentina and Huascaran a little further north. The snowflake that falls upon the east side of Yerupaja is arguably the remotest source of the Amazon. The first ascent in 1950 ended with terrible consequences: two young American undergraduates, Dave Hurrah and Jim Maxwell, forced the south ridge to the summit, but were benighted on the descent and had to be rescued – Hurrah lost toes and fingers to frostbite.

Yerupaja is an Everest in its context. It is a mountaineering challenge that few can resist. Since Hurrah and Maxwell's ascent further assaults had been made from the north and west by the Austrians and Argentinians, but without success. Kinzl suggested to me that an eastern approach might offer a reasonable way up. In 1964 a bunch of us organised ourselves into the Scottish Andean Expedition. Yerupaja was to be the ultimate objective, but to limber up we would first explore new territory in eastern Peru. This idea came from the Swiss climber René Dittert. He had jabbed his finger at an area on the map north and east of Cuzco saying: 'The map is false, and here there are many virgin peaks.' It seemed like the place to go.

126

Serendipity was once again at work. We were befriended by a missionary from Ulster by the name of Alfie Bell, whose mission house at Calca, at 9,500 feet on the Rio Vilcanota, he put at the expedition's disposal. Alfie was a gentleman, always smiling, always helpful, never asking. It proved a great base. There was good news and bad. The good was that we had finagled our two cases of malt whisky and climbing gear through Customs without paying any dues. The bad news was that the mountains we had come to explore didn't exist! This emerged from the expedition's first ascent, a graceful virgin peak by the name of Sirijuani, 16,400 ft (5,000 m). Since the exploration of these mythical hills was the basis upon which we had sold the literary rights of the expedition, a key input to our finances, we were in a little trouble! All, however, was not lost, for Alfie told us of some unexplored peaks up a valley known as the Quebrada Huaccanhuayco, branching off the nearby Rio Cochac. With the help first of burros, then shouldering our own heavy packs, we entered a magic, remote, unpopulated pampa, nestling below a cirque of unclimbed glaciated peaks. It was the sort of camping place one dreams of: greensward for the tent, a stream, no biting insects, no wind and a staggering mountain prospect of peaks and icefalls. We even found fuel for a campfire to lighten the long Andean night. If we worried about anything, it was whether pumas were on the prowl out there in the darkness. It was a real pleasure to be in such a place with a bunch of true friends all in tune with one another. There was a temptation to do nothing and just be. What on earth is it that drives climbers to the effort and discomfort of climbing when they can lie back in their sleeping bags and pick out every step of a route by eye and imagine every nuance of the climb? However, such idleness was out of the question with someone like Evelyn McNicol in the party. This female dynamo was exactly my age and had been running on maximum power since about the age of 18. She wasn't about to slow down now. She was a consultant gynaecologist with three children and a long mountaineering record, including the first All Women's Himalayan Expedition. In addition we had three young tigers in the party: Ken Bryan, introduced in Chapter 4, and Rob Brooks, who had been introduced to the delights of snow and ice during Sir John Hunt's boys expedition to Greenland in 1960, and who had evolved into a very competent rock climber. Slim, witty, handy and skilful on the guitar, it was due to his prowess we were able to make a radio programme on our return called the 'Singing Mountaineers'. Finally, Jock Anderson, a student from Glasgow with a shock of red hair and the permanent air of one about to take flight. He was charged with looking after transport, but as he was addicted to his sleeping bag, he proved more useful as a climber than a transport wallah. Then we had some mature mountaineers. Donald Bennet, who was to become chairman of the Scottish Rights of Way Society, was an all-round climber with Alpine and virgin Himalayan peaks to his credit. He was a natural organiser, never happier than when doing or planning something, whether it was washing a mess tin or organising a team of burros. Robin Chalmers was our cameraman, a job he did for the BBC. His wry humour never failed to bring out our smiles. Small, wiry and handy with an ice axe, he was a great asset to the party. Then there was my old buddy, Norman Tennent, the fatalist introduced in Chapter 1. Norman and his wife ran a hotel in the Highlands. His jaundiced view of his customers led me to think this was not really his appropriate metier. He seemed happiest when cooking. All he sought was appreciation of his efforts. The oldest amongst us, he seemed destined to suffer an endless stream of vicissitudes that most of us manage to avoid. Last, but not least, we had Betty Stark, also of the All Women's Himalayan Expedition. Her very schoolmistress-like smile hid a talent for humour. She spoke creditable Spanish and I recall that once when I asked her to try to explain something to the donkey driver she replied, 'I don't think the subjunctive is quite my forte.'

Here, 14° south of the equator, at this season the sun was almost vertically overhead at midday. It was no surprise, therefore, that we encountered the egg-box snow surface. In fact it often resembled tightly packed wine glasses. There were places on steep snow where one could literally use these holes as handholds.

In the cirque above us were four virgin peaks whose access was guarded by an impressive icefall. Bryan forged a rock route up its edge to 17,000 feet to a point where with some ingenuity a platform was made for two small tents. If the icefall above could be ascended to an obvious col, it looked as if all four peaks would be accessible. The crowning summit of these peaks was Chainapuerto, 18,990 ft (5,790 m). It had that ineffable aura that mountaineers called 'character', which distinguishes a dull mountain from an interesting one – interesting in the same way as you instinctively judge a person, not merely by his or her looks, but by other qualities. The route to these four peaks was neither obvious nor, as it turned out, easy. We were each able to claim a virgin summit. Evelyn named hers after her daughter, Punta Erica.

The ascent of Chainapuerto by Donald Bennet and Ken Bryan was

Norman Tennent in 1960.

Anatole Ovchinnikov, leader of the Soviet team on the British–Soviet Pamir Expedition, 1962.

Robin Smith while in the Pamirs, 1962.

Joe Brown while in the Pamirs, 1962.

The team that attempted Yerupaja in 1966 at Camp II.
Left to right: Mike Kosterlitz, Rob Brooks, Dez Hadlum
(hooded against the sun) and Ian Howell.

On the shores of the Volquart Boons Coast, on the south shore of Scoresby Sund,
the morning after the crossing from the north side of the fjord:
Major Carlos Ziebell (*left*) and Allan Petit.

The Staunings Alps from the north, showing the three highest summits. *Left to right*: Hjørnspids, Danske Tinde, Norske Tinde.

On the lower Garmo Glacier in the Pamirs. The peak in the centre is Pik Kommunizma, showing its 5,000 ft south face, and to the right 'Former Molotov'. *Left to right*: Ian McNaught-Davis, Vladimir Malachov, Ken Bryan and Kolya Alchutov.

Members of the 1985 Peterman Peak Expedition on the summit of Ruth Island, looking west. *Left to right*: the author, Roland Zeyen and Iain Smart. The land to the left is Suess Land. Beyond lie Ymers Island and Antarctics Sund.

Luiz Minchietti below the
overhangs of Pedro de Gavea,
Rio de Janeiro, Brazil.

Chainapuerto in eastern Peru. The first ascent was made by Donald Bennet
and Ken Bryan during the 1964 Scottish Peruvian Expedition.

Charlie Orr sunbathing in the Roscoe Bjaerg in 1996. It is April and the temperature is -20°C. Dry air has very low conductivity, while the pollution-free atmosphere means that the sun's rays are scarcely attenuated. The result: it does not feel cold.

A kerosene-fuelled Primus stove is the lifeblood of an Arctic expedition. Here, young Calum Slesser, holidaying on the shores of Alpe Fjord, north-east Greenland, is the zealous keeper of the stove.

Geoff Dutton in 1953.

Donald Bennet in 1964.

Memorial erected by members of the Soviet Spartak Expedition in memory of Robin Smith and Wilfred Noyce.

Sir John (later Lord) Hunt, leader of the British–Soviet Pamir Expedition.

Bill Wallace forging a ski-trail in the Alps. Note the wind-slab avalanche debris ahead of him. This ground is now safe. Note also the considerable distance between the lead skier and the follower in the interests of safety.

The pristine, pollution-free environment of north-east Greenland in April 1999, looking north-east towards the Barents Sea from a summit in the Roscoe Bjaerg.

a brilliant piece of route finding and determined climbing. At the col they noticed that clouds were already forming over the steaming jungles of the Madre de Dios in the Amazon basin. It was time to hasten. Here are a few excerpts from Ken's own narration to give the flavour of this great climb:

> Above the terrace there was another giant crevasse. We found ourselves shill-shallying about on tottery ice blocks and balancing on thin blades of ice until a steep wall of snow and ice shot up in front of our noses. Donald, airily balanced on a narrow ledge, belayed the rope round an ice block, and I proceeded to cut steps up the wall. Half an hour later we climbed onto the snow dome above the central buttress . . . In front of us and seeming only a stone's throw away rose the broad summit pyramid, thrusting 600 feet to a corniced summit ridge.

Another feature of tropical snow is the existence of grotesque cornice formations, often 10 or even 20 feet high, that are as insubstantial as papier mâché and as brittle as polystyrene tiles. One cannot climb them. They simply have to be destroyed till more substantial rock or ice can be found underneath.

> To reach the base of the long ice-arête . . . we had to cross a shallow basin and climb a 400-foot face split by several large crevasses . . . It was now after 11.30 a.m. and the clouds which we had seen early in the morning above the jungles to the east had boiled over and were starting to break over the mountains in great steel-grey masses. The temperature began to drop very quickly, although at first we were kept too busy to really notice it.
>
> The snow face was not difficult, but the fight up the thigh-deep powder was extremely exhausting. By 12.30 p.m. we were standing at the base of the arête rising at an intimidating angle. We both felt duly impressed.
>
> The sky was by now almost completely covered in dark grey and streams of ice-cold mist whistled over the crest . . . The summit appeared in brief glimpses. Donald weighed up the situation. 'If we are not on our way down by 3 p.m. we will not have a hope of getting back to camp tonight.' I thought even 3 p.m. was pushing matters and the thought of spending the night at 18,000 feet in a blizzard made me shudder. Donald,

having got this far, was determined to reach the summit.

By the nature of things it was necessary to climb on the windward side . . . which was formed by a huge slab of ice which rose steadily at a very steep angle for 350 feet. Above this it swung to the right and became to all appearances vertical. One hundred and fifty feet beyond, the arête joined the final summit ridge whose cornices hung high above us.

I belayed Donald as he crossed the rimaye . . . he moved steadily cutting good steps mindful of the descent . . . As time was at a premium we took the risk of moving together. Owing to the very high angle, handholds often needed to be cut.

We crept up the great wall slowly, foot by foot . . . By now we were in a little world of our own, encircled in freezing mist and chilled by an icy wind . . . Seldom have I felt the 'fly on the wall' feeling quite so markedly . . . Donald anchored himself as best he could and I turned my attention to the wall. Not only did it steepen alarmingly, but gave way to snow held together by a skeleton framework of ice. For the next 50 feet I was frankly terrified. Most of the time I tried to indulge in some form of levitation hoping to avoid putting weight on anything . . . Feverishly I burrowed around for something solid to hang onto. I knew if I came off here there was little Donald could do about it . . . Worst of all was the cold. For a long time my hands and feet had been frozen into aching numbness. After years of climbing you gradually accept this as perfectly normal . . . but now the numbness was spreading over my arms and legs. It was becoming increasingly difficult to keep control over my movements . . . I eventually found a narrow icy crack into which I was able to jam my ice axe and bring Donald up . . . It was already past 3 p.m., but now with only a few rope lengths to go, no one mentioned the time. Donald led out along the heavily corniced ridge . . . I joined and took over the lead for another 50 feet. Peering through the mist I saw what appeared to be a huge mushroom of ice blocking the ridge. It overhung its base and was stratified like a layer cake. We both stared at the obstacle realising it was the summit.

It was dark by the time they reached the tent. At these sort of altitudes one could be forgiven for thinking one was no longer in the tropics. Nonetheless the poor quality of the snow and ice was the precise consequence of the near-vertical sun.

We may have been drawn to Peru for its mountains, but it has one tourist attraction we had no intention of missing: the ruins of the Inca city of Machu Picchu. If I could visit only one marvel of the ancient world, I would choose this over the Taj Mahal, the astronomic observatory at Jaipur, the sculptures at Mahabarpuram in Madras, the amphitheatre at Verona, the Victoria Falls, Petra in Jordan or the Great Wall of China. It is stunning! The city was rediscovered by the American archaeologist Hiram Bingham in 1911. The tourist in the clutches of a travel agency may well pay thousands of dollars to get there. It cost us 8 Peruvian soles each, about a tenth of £1.

From Arequipa on the coast an incredible railway rises all the way to Lake Titicaca, then on to Cuzco and down to the Amazon Basin. From Cuzco this quaint little railway follows the Urubamba River past Ollantaytambo, a picturesque town with well-preserved Inca ruins, and terminates in the Amazon Basin at Quillabamba. Alfie Bell drove us down to the Urubamba valley to pick up the train. We each secured first-class tickets at 20p for a 20-mile journey that took the wood-burning locomotive all of 2 hours. I doubt if we ever exceeded 15 mph. I wrote in my diary:

> The valley grew lusher, and at one place widened out to present a positively English park-like appearance. In the midst stood a noble white house, the first we'd seen not built of adobe . . . To the right, deep valleys led up to fancy mountains the Cancha Cancha Towers reminiscent of the Canadian Rockies at Assiniboine; gentle ice fields of the Yucay, like some Arctic ice sheet; the steel blue pinnacles of Saguasiray.

We alighted. The altitude was 7,000 feet. The air felt humid after the aridity of altiplano. We woke the driver of a battered pick-up and asked him to take us to the ruins. He demanded 20 soles each (then about 33p). We negotiated 80 for the lot of us. Taking all 18 blind hairpin bends at full speed, he safely brought us to the tourist hotel. I wrote:

> We stood our rucksacks against the fence and congregated in the shelter of the garage. It was raining. What a spectacle we were! Battered boots, worn climbing breeches and heavy all-enveloping anoraks. Donald Bennet wore the sort of straw hat the master gives to the servant and the servant to the tramp. Betty wore a khaki parka whose fur hood dripped beads of water. Even Norman had lost his country-gentleman look. It

131

would have taken a perceptive person to see what magnificent men and women lay beneath these rugged exteriors. Fortunately the receptionist at the desk had the necessary percipience. 'We would be delighted to serve you lunch. Will you wait in the lounge, sir?'

The little Peruvian spoke perfect English (and French and German) and had manners to match. 'May I enquire whether you are staying the night?'

I said we were mountaineers and had hoped to bivouac in the ruins. 'No need for that, sir. One of the Inca dwellings has been roofed with thatch. If it suits you, you may use that.'

The Inca dwelling had one side completely unwalled – a picture window on the world, offering a bird's eye view of Huayna Picchu. This peak, a bastion rising sheer from the valley, forces the Urubamba River to make a right-angled turn. The river's deep roar was occasionally swept away by the light wind. Once we heard the tooting of the old train. We simply had to climb Huayna Picchu. Though it was one of the easiest mountaineering ascents of my life, I am not sure if it was not the finest. This little peak stands about 1,200 feet above the ruins, which themselves stand 1,500 feet above the river on a saddle between the peak and the main mountain behind. Seen from the ruins it rises like some Fitzroy, Tower of Paine or Chamonix aiguille. Its southern flank falls 2,000 feet in a sheer granite wall. That there might even be a mountaineer's route up the 'easy' side seemed unlikely. Yet, in fact, one can walk to its summit. The Incas had made a set of steps that wind to and fro across the north-western edge of the peak:

> . . . the path is steep without hand rails . . . Two hundred feet from the top one comes upon the remains of impressive stone terraces, then a little ruined house, so small that it is reminiscent of St Columba's beehive cell on Eilean na Clerich on the Garbhalach Islands in Argyll . . . It was so redolent of an abandoned Highland croft. There were small trees like oak, ferns, familiar flowers and blueberries . . . We scrambled to the pure white summit to see one of the world's finest views.

The expedition continued to make many explorations and ascents, none of them as hard and demanding as Chainapuerto. The next step was to travel back to Lima, then north to the Cordillera Huayhuash and tackle Yerupaja. This mountain is the topic of Chapter 9. But first we had to get there and our finances were seriously depleted. Alfie put the word out that we needed a truck to take us to Lima. We made our choice out of poverty, not safety. The truck on offer looked as if it had been left abandoned after a military campaign: its springs were enhanced by strips of inner tubes and the tyres had a vestigial thread, but bald patches could be seen. As the nominal leader I was shoved into the cab, while the gang enjoyed the safer position on top of the gear, from whence they could jump clear if the truck went off the road. Betty Stark, our interpreter, wrote down for me a few key Spanish phrases like 'Are your brakes OK?', 'Go slowly please', and 'Stop here'.

Belching unburned diesel the truck drew away and was soon on dirt roads grunting its way at 10 mph up a long incline. My companions were singing at the top of their voices to the accompaniment of Rob Brooks' guitar, callously indifferent to the danger faced by those of us imprisoned in the cab below. The driver, a Quechua Indian with a time-worn face, placidly chewed coca. The Madonna stuck on the windscreen, together with a pendulous cross that swayed to and fro provided, in his view, sufficient protection from harm.

We came upon an Army checkpoint in the middle of nowhere; just an adobe hut sprouting telephone wires. The barren brown earth was relieved by some agave cactus, and in the distance could be seen the serrated outline of some impressive mountains. A cool wind tempered the heat from a cloudless sky. Out popped two squat fellows in bottle-green uniforms with brass buttons and epaulettes. Their American GI-type helmets coupled to their swarthy features and unshaven chins gave them an absurd appearance. Their uniforms were too large for their small Quechua Indian bodies, all of which imparted a somewhat yokelish look, inclining one not to take them too seriously. This vanished as they approached with carbines at the ready. I reminded myself that they were there because the country was being subjected to an armed insurrection. I had no wish to take sides.

'Where are you going, *gringos* [white foreigners]?' they asked in Spanish. They were grinning broadly, intent on enjoying the prospect of humiliating the hated gringos. I could hardly blame them. We were a ragged bunch, looking just like the revolutionary cadres that the military were seeking to suppress.

Betty replied in very adequate Spanish that we were mountaineers in search of virgin peaks. This caused great mirth; maybe it was the word 'virgin'.

'OK,' they said disbelievingly. 'Let's see your passes.'

Passes? Passes! Betty slowly got off the truck. '*Jefe*,' she said, pointing at me. Any expedition organiser will recognise this manoeuvre. When things are going well, no one wants to hear a sound from the leader/organiser/heid bummer. As soon as things start going wrong, all eyes swivel in one direction! We had no inkling that passes might be needed. Betty engaged the soldiers in banter while we considered our options. Here we were on the altiplano, at least 400 miles from officialdom, which I suspected would be indifferent to our fate. The idea of getting a telephone contact from here with someone important enough to resolve the situation seemed beyond reasonable hope. We couldn't bribe the soldiers since we had very little money. Norman had a Diner's Club card: not useful for bribes. The only recourse was bluff. With the air of one searching one's pockets for a mislaid document I stumbled upon a Glasgow city tram ticket. In those far-off days a tram ticket was a stiff piece of coloured cardboard with a serial number on it, and a hole punched at an appropriate point.

I made a show of bringing it out of my wallet and gave it to Betty, who cleverly caught on and presented it with due gravity to the soldiers. The first soldier studiously examined it and then shared his puzzlement with his mate. It was fairly obvious that both were barely literate. They were probably used to some standard document – and this was not it. Betty explained that as we were gringos, this was a special sort of *laissez-passer* designed for mountaineering expeditions. We brandished our ice axes by way of proof.

'Ah, si, ah si,' they responded gravely. Like most people in the lowest ranks, they didn't want to get into trouble with their superiors, especially with gringos, who tended to have friends in high places. It was difficult to keep a straight face as they laboriously wrote down the number of the tram ticket and handed it back with a distinct air of respect. I did have a slight twinge of conscience.

With the ticket again in our possession we proceeded, but not far. Five miles further on yet another manned checkpoint loomed up. On a demand for our passes, Betty confidently presented the tram ticket. Consternation! What was this? This was no proper document. 'All you have to do,' said Betty sweetly, 'is telephone the checkpoint down the road and you will get confirmation.' This they did, turning the handle of some primitive communication device. It was indeed confirmed and we were on our way once more.

This is an old trick which must have been played hundreds of times by adventurers all over the world. That ticket never failed us. I hate to think what would happen nowadays. Our expedition party would probably be a cipher on some intolerant computer. Bribery might still be the only immediate solution, but it would have happened again and again at each checkpoint. Modern life gets ever more and more expensive for the libertarian and the explorer.

NOTES

[1] The address for this organisation is Mountain Wilderness Italia, Piazza Europa, 6/P, 25030, Coccagio (BS), Italy.

CHAPTER 9

Yerupaja – Queen of the Andes

We had every reason to be optimistic. After our campaign in eastern Peru we were fit and ready to tackle a peak of the reputation of Yerupaja. We had three weeks at our disposal. After dropping off Donald Bennet at Lima our hired truck took us north along the Pan-American Highway, our headlights stabbing the perpetual fog that hangs there for several months of the year like a North Sea haar. The road climbed steadily until we were above the fog sea which still obliterated the view of the Pacific Ocean, just a few miles away. The protesting vehicle ground its way up towards an arid mountain pass of 15,000 feet where there was not so much as a blade of grass to relieve the dun hillsides. At a refreshment stop I asked a wizened old fellow in a poncho if it ever rained. 'Not in my lifetime,' he responded.

As the road dipped to the east side of the coast range we entered a great green plain, then onto verdant hillsides populated by tiny crofts. The harvest was in and the natives could be seen winnowing the seed by tossing it into the air, where a light wind took away the dross. This road terminates at Chiquian, a charming roadhead town perched on a belvedere overlooking the Patavilca valley with an unobstructed view of the Cordillera Huayhuash. I wondered how anybody could go about their business with such a stupendous view always before them.

The story of our residence in the gaol at Chiquian (the convicts were evicted temporarily) and of haggling with an *arriero* (donkey driver) for the conveyance of our gear to the mountain (for a fee which was less than the previous Italian expedition had given as a tip) is told in my book *The Andes Are Prickly*. It took some days to get the mule transport organised. Meanwhile our expedition, for all its poverty, became highly popular by virtue of Rob Brooks' skill on the guitar – in the evenings small boys would knock on the gaol compound beseeching 'Robeeee' to entertain the village yet again. In the plaza one poncho-clad fellow with an intelligent face asked me where we were heading. I replied, 'Yerupaja, by the east face. It has already been climbed from the south.'

'Aaiihh!!! So it is said, señor, but nobody believes it.'

'Why?'

'It is said, señor.'

No one could ever know. Unlike mountains in polar or temperate regions, these summits are so braided with fluted cornices, standing 10 or even 20 feet high, that it is impossible to build a cairn or leave any record such as the proverbial sardine tin.

Our 3-day mule trip took us down to the well-watered Patavilca valley at 8,000 feet through many villages of adobe huts and back up to the grassy altiplano populated by sheep and cattle. Our arriero, Bedon, having accepted our penny-pinching deal, exhibited no hard feelings. As we plodded up the dusty track to his home village of Pocllon, he kept asking me of Norman 'Why is señor so *triste*?'

'If he says that once more, he'll be triste,' gritted Norman, who was perfectly happy.

At Pocllon they had just completed a village brew of *chicha*. The entire population appeared to be drunk. A band of young women dressed in multiple skirts and broad-rimmed hats took a fancy to Ken Bryan. He was last seen sprinting out of the village with the girls hot on his heels – it was hours before we saw him again. He refused to discuss how he had spent the intervening time. Next day, as we climbed up towards a pass, Bedon asked me how many children I had. 'One,' I replied.

'One!' He looked at me in astonishment and then in pity, as if I must be suffering from some grave masculine defect. 'Why, I have seven children, many of whom live in my own house.'

When forming our plans we did not realise one grave disadvantage of climbing from the Amazon side, one that had showed up dramatically in the ascent of Chainapuerto, as described earlier: namely that the moisture-laden air of the Amazon forests would daily rise, then flow west, depositing a filigree of hoar frost and snow on the wafer-thin summit arêtes. These deposits would grow and grow and grow to become double-sided cornices which of necessity must from time to time collapse. Of this we were still ignorant as we crossed the continental divide at the Cacanan pass that leads down to the lake of Caruacocha at the foot of our mountain.

Our base camp at 13,600 feet, at the foot of the east face of Yerupaja, must count as one of the most beautiful on the planet. We pitched camp on an alp of springy turf, so alive with flowers that it bore comparison with a Uist *machair* in May. A stone shelter with a thatched roof housed a shepherd, his young wife and two children. They greeted us warmly. We bought a sheep and they swiftly cooked it on stones first heated by a fire of dried grass. Below us spread the waters of Caruacocha, whose deep blue-green was a sapphire jewel at the altar of Yerupaja. We experienced the spectacle of a tantalising striptease as veils of mist drifted by, revealing now a buttress, then an icefall, then the summit ridge. We were titillated and tremendously excited. How we longed for the denoucment. And when she did stand naked next morning we were pretty speechless. Of the 8,000 feet to the summit 6,000 of them were going to be very serious climbing.

The setting was magnificent: to the left rose the needle of Siula Grande, which would be the scene of Joe Simpson's purgatory 20 years later, described in his *Touching the Void* – avalanches tumbled down it hour after hour; to the right stood the north margin of the east face, which rose at a very reasonable angle for climbing. It looked as if Kinzl's advice was sound. All we had to do was get on to it. But first we had to negotiate an icefall, an intimidating barrier of seracs and climb a near-vertical rock face.

There is no saying what the prospects are until one rubs noses with the mountain. As we hauled loads up to our first high camp only 17 days remained at our disposal. We badly needed the cooperation of the weather. It took several days to find a safe route through the barrier above Camp I, onto a glacier basin below the wall that was the key to the ridge. It became immediately apparent that no route lay this way. There was a barrier of seracs, the passage through which, though feasible, as all icefalls are if one takes time and risks, was unjustifiable, for it would have to be a trade route as loads were carried to and fro to build up higher camps. My diary records that the basin terminated in:

> . . . a 2,000-foot leap of splintered ice masonry: the demolition of a half-frozen city of water . . . Every half hour a thunderous avalanche would sweep part of the face, and it was worth waiting for. It would start as the crack of a door catch. Then a mass of ice the size of a house would peel away, fall and

> pulverise, rolling down 1,000 feet coming to a stop in a great fan
> of ice rubble . . . I thought in speechless wonder of Toni Egger
> and Siegfried Jungmeir who, having climbed Yerupaja Chico
> [Little Yerupaja], had risked descending this way.

As Ken Bryan observed, 'I suppose anybody can climb anything if they don't mind being killed.' Egger died in the mountains shortly afterwards.

We turned our attention to the only alternative: the ridge bounding the north (left) side of the east face. These two edges, the north and the south, met at the apex of the triangular east face at about 20,000 feet and then ran upwards in a catenary of cornices to the summit. Our optimism had received a nasty setback. Nonetheless we resolved to try this north approach. It required us to gain a col at about 17,700 feet between Yerupaja Chico, 18,600 ft (5,660 m), and the start of the south ridge.

First we needed a safe intermediate camp, which was located at 17,000 feet, on a dome of snow overlooking the valley below. The summit now stood the height of Ben Nevis above us. Our efforts were hampered by frequent rain squalls, snow, hail and thunderstorms. We never had a full day of clear weather. Though the party rallied magnificently, building up supplies at this Camp II, as the days passed and our remaining time diminished, it became increasingly plain that we would never get high enough to launch a bid for the summit. Still the urge to explore, to push into the unknown, is very strong. Mountain exploration is almost as satisfying as reaching the top. This was neither war nor a campaign, but we felt that what we could learn of the route on this expedition might help us on the next one. So we continued to probe the mountain's defences. The real problem was that the snow and ice was rotted and rotten. The weather was simply too warm and humid. We were too late in the season. Added to this we had lost the support of the two women who were obliged to return home. We were down to six climbers. On top of this two of the party fell prey to various bugs. Ken Bryan, however, one of our two strongest climbers, together with the tough and resilient Norman Tennent, reached the col after dealing with truly treacherous conditions, virtually climbing Yerupaja Chico in the process.

With time running out we made one last thrust. From the col the way to the putative summit ridge, the north edge of the east face, was barred by an overhang. Tennent tried it. I tried it. We both failed. Next day Rob Brooks took the lead. I wrote:

> He climbed the overhang beautifully, using seven pegs. It was a
> faultless series of manoeuvres . . . One could see his body in
> profile against the tremendous sweep of Suila's upper ice slopes.

As we watched him, a vortex of wind whinnied up, enveloping us in
tendrils of powder snow. It seemed hostile. I felt it was sending us a
message. By the time Norman and I joined Rob it was already 3 p.m.
Darkness arrives abruptly this close to the equator. I wanted to settle,
once and for all, whether there was a feasible route here. I led quickly
up a sebaceous groove of compact dolomite. There were few positive
holds and no pitonable cracks. It was about my limit and I enjoyed it
to the full. I found a belay where Rob joined me. I set off again on
brittle ice, which provided no placement for ice pitons. Steps had to be
cut. I hacked with all my energy, hellbent on getting somewhere before
the onset of darkness forced us down. With the rope entirely run out I
had still not found a place for a piton and so rammed in my ice axe to
create some sort of belay. It broke in two! One often utters the
hyperbole 'I could have wept'. In this instance I did. A climber without
an ice axe is like a cripple without a crutch. Fate had defeated us. It was
time to go home.

Though all of us declared our desire to come back and have another
crack at the route, only two of us managed to free ourselves to do so.
Two years later, in 1966, Rob Brooks and I joined forces with three
others: Ian Howell, a very able English climber who wore the
meditative air of a poet – he lived in Kenya; Mike Kosterlitz of the
Alpine Club had recently graduated and oozed bonhomie and energy;
and Dez Hadlum from Manchester, a powerful rock climber and friend
of Ian's. Apart from the fact that he was not belligerent, he had a
remarkable likeness to Don Whillans, resembling a houseplant that
had outgrown its pot. We were a disparate group, unknown to each
other, who got on remarkably well. This time we arrived at the
mountain in early July, the supposed best season. Looking up at the
summit ridge, the cornices certainly looked less formidable.

Rob Brooks and I went back to the col. We bivouacked in a crevasse
and I had just found deep sleep when Rob shook me awake to say
someone was shining a torch. It was the moon rising over the Amazon
plain! I cursed him and never slept another wink. Next morning we
probed again the 1964 route but it was soon apparent that this was no
route to the summit. Happily the glacier had changed. The 1964
barrier of seracs had slipped downhill and a reasonably safe way was
open to the foot of the wall leading to the north side of the east face.

The only problem was that from its top edge rained down a ceaseless fusillade of stones, indelibly recorded in the heavily pock-marked glacier surface below. You could hear the zinging sound as they plummeted at speeds of hundreds of feet per second. As they hit the surface they sprayed out snow like some meteor landing in Siberia.

We were not to be deterred and the consensus was that once we reached the wall it would be pretty safe with the stones passing clear of us. So with our rucksacks on top of our heads for protection, we took a deep breath and dashed the last 300 feet to the safety of the wall. No one was hit or hurt. Things were looking good: nice weather and the wall proved to be a simple, unexacting rock climb until the top where we had to put in some bolts and a fixed rope. Kosterlitz wrote:

> We soon reached the crest to be greeted by a breathtaking sight.
> The ridge above seemed to stretch upwards into the dim
> distance in a never-ending sweep of grey and yellow slab.

Adjacent to the ridge, so close that one could almost stretch out and touch them, were the seracs of the south face. As I stood transfixed by their sheer size, one of them in slow, slow motion simply eased itself off its perch, tilted and then plunged down the face, instigating a violent avalanche. We were in no danger, simply voyeurs of the awesome power of ice and gravity.

This was to be our Camp II at 17,500 feet. The problem was where to put it. A sort of ledge was found. Some excavation and a bit of dry-stone dyking resulted in a passable platform. It was never popular. As it slowly subsided, spikes of rock poked through the groundsheet. We had to sling ropes around it in case the tent made an involuntary descent of the east face. Unknown to us two climbers were at that very moment placing their tent at the same height at the foot of the west face on the other side of the mountain. Lief-Norman Patterson, an American, had joined forces with Jorge Peterek, a Polish climber, to make an Alpine-style ascent of the west face.

What was intended by them to be a quick scamper up the face turned out to be a 12-day, foot-by-foot, hack at the ice. They had 1,500 feet of line for fixed ropes. Each day they cut steps up a few rope lengths (on some occasions as little as two!), then descended to their tent. When they had ascended 1,500 feet they reached a short ice wall and crevasse, within which they relocated their camp. Patterson wrote:

> This platform, partly covered by a dripping ice cliff, sheltered us

> beautifully . . . Not a breath of wind nor a sound other than our
> own hearts disturbed the dying day . . . No jokes about surplus
> food. This was the fourth day and progress was decreasing
> exponentially . . . we had really hit hard ice. Today I had even
> given up getting in the ice-screws a couple of times. The face
> was steepening . . . as day after day faded away, the weather
> became even better . . . we were two insects scratching tiny
> marks on a great white wall . . . at the end of the sixth day we
> made our home over the airy void in a little cave dug in a big
> crevasse.

They had now climbed 3,000 of the 4,600 feet to the summit. They
rested. They explored. On the ninth day they attempted to climb rock
bands below the summit, but they were too steep and smooth.
Descending, they looked for an escape route:

> This easy 'escape', starting with a simple walk along the
> crevasse . . . consumed the next two days! . . . we were exposed
> to all the finest cornices on the mountain . . . The relief of setting
> foot on the ridge felt like pardon for a 'lifer' . . . Right in front
> towered the dark triangle of the summit. We knew Hurrah and
> Maxwell had beaten it once; yet things had changed: more rock,
> less snow. And we were weakening. Our food was finished.

They were incredibly lucky. Twelve days on the face without a break
in the superb weather is luck enough, yet it still held. They bivvied in
an icecave on the summit ridge, melted snow with the last of their fuel,
and traversed the ridge to the summit next day:

> Eventually we, the snails, stood on the partly corniced little
> summit ridge; at each end was a small tower and in the middle
> a man-sized block leaned precariously over the wild flutings . . .
> To starboard the south-east ridge thrust out and down. It would
> give the Scots a handful.

The 'Scots' were our expedition on the east face of whom I was the
only Scot. They bivvied one more night on the ridge, now without
food or water:

> Pete declared that he could not climb up any more and that his
> feet were freezing. Clouds ominously created themselves out of

143

nothing. My own limbs felt strangely jelly-like. The sneaking fear that paralyses a trapped animal raised its blind head . . . What should we do? Starve, and wait for the black rider?

Fortunately their expedition companions, who were attempting the south-west ridge, seemed not far away. They shouted for help. It was agreed, though by what means of communication is not clear – perhaps they had radios as we had – that they would use their remaining strength to gain the south summit where the others would try to reach them. All ended well, but just in the nick of time for the weather then turned sour.

While this saga was being enacted on the western slopes we were building up supplies at our precarious Camp II on the ridge. As the bad weather that almost trapped the Patterson–Strepek team arrived, we descended to base to pamper our tired bodies and satisfy our appetites with something better to eat than dehydrated meat and chicken noodle soup. The storm dragged on for a week, making us all very edgy. I had to leave as I only had a month's vacation, so I never got back to Camp II. My consolation prize was a donkey ride out to a new roadhead through the most exquisitely beautiful countryside. But I was rather sad. I had nurtured this route for many years, and would not be there to witness its successful execution.

Rob Brooks and Dez Hadlum took on the task of forging the next part of the route. Brooks wrote:

> The superb nature of the rock and the hot Peruvian sun made climbing a real pleasure. Our aim was to reach a pinnacle of rock we had spied from Camp I, the height of which we estimated as 19,000 feet . . . We reached the rock, dubbed the pulpit, to find that the ledge we had hoped for was a slab of rock sweeping away down the mountain. We found a ledge above the pulpit just wide enough to hold a two-man tent; Camp III. This was the most spectacular of sites. Hanging as it was at the top of the first great wall one could drop, say, a tea bag over the side and it would not stop until it hit the ice 3,000 feet below . . . one could see into the basin of the Amazon.

The four climbers put a huge effort into overcoming the difficulties of the ridge above. Kosterlitz wrote:

> The first section above Camp III was simple enough . . . Then

came a hair-raising traverse beneath a large and apparently detached cornice on steep, crumbly snow to a commodious ledge below the first of the great ice-roofs which was about 20 feet across . . .

The non-climbing reader should be aware that ice-roofs like these overhang and are bound sooner or later to break off. Moving beneath one is definitely a form of Russian roulette, but they were well aware of the danger, and accepted it:

> Then came a sensational traverse six feet from the lip, and short vertical wall of ice, to gain an easier angled ice field above. Exhaustion set in from continuous step cutting at 19,500 feet, so we retreated to camp.

Brooks and Hadlum were meanwhile at Camp II. Brooks wrote:

> Each evening we tuned in our radio to learn how Howell and Kosterlitz had progressed . . . For five nights we listened to terrifying stories of near-vertical and perpendicular snow and ice rotten with heat from the sun, frost-shattered rock pitches down which great boulders hurtled at irregular intervals . . . Ice-roofs of such magnitude that icicles 100 feet long or more dangled from their rims.

The weather closed in again and the party once again retreated to base. Three days later they embarked on a final all-out attempt on the summit. Brooks writes:

> After a rather cramped night at Camp III we started up the route which Howell and Kosterlitz had already prepared. Following the ridge for a while we passed under two very large snow bulges, then broke diagonally right and onto the first of the great ice-roofs. From there, with ever-increasing difficulty, the route progressed for 2,000 feet following the diagonal line of the fixed ropes . . . Because of the anticipated bivouacs involved in this attempt to reach the top from so far down [they were 1,500 vertical feet below the summit still] we were carrying fairly heavy sacks. At 5.30 p.m., with still a few hundred feet to go to the highest point reached by Howell and Kosterlitz, we bivouacked . . . sharing two minute ledges with our legs

145

> dangling over a drop of 6,000 feet . . . we waited for dawn and
> gratefully watched the sun rise out of the valleys of the
> Amazon. By 11 a.m. we reached the top of the fixed ropes.
> Above us stretched a steep snow face which was rapidly
> deteriorating in the increasing heat of the sun . . . The route
> disappeared under a giant snow mushroom . . . beyond, the
> snow turned into green water-ice and moved into the
> perpendicular for 500 feet.

Continuing would have been fruitless. Their supplies were insufficient
to sustain them beyond three days. The nature of the ground was
terribly dangerous and the going would be painfully slow. Very wisely,
they retreated. Yerupaja had once again rebuffed climbers. It is
interesting how different were the conditions between the east and west
faces. The west face was a coherent, steep smooth slope of mainly very
hard, but high-quality ice. The east face was utterly different. Kinzl had
not well advised us.

It is not easy to make the decision to retreat – even though it is
dangerous to go on – when one has put in such a huge effort in time
and money to get to the mountain, and when so much mental resource
and physical output has been expended. High up there at almost
20,000 feet they were truly out on a limb. Bivouacking meant suffering
night temperatures as low as -20C. It was dark for ten hours. They
were utterly at the mercy of the weather. The best outcome might have
been frostbite, the worst extinction. Brooks described their retreat:

> The descent was the most strenuous and exacting any of us had
> ever made. Because of the late hour the snow was at its foulest
> state: the trip could be likened to swimming down vertical slush
> for 2,000 feet and it was well after dark when we finally made
> Camp III, utterly spent. The weather was changing to its worst.
> Again bitter gusts brought heavy snow clouds hurtling from the
> north-east. We were grateful for the tent and content in the
> knowledge that had we ventured to climb the 500 feet to the
> ridge we would never have returned.

It may be difficult for the non-climber to appreciate the intense mental
effort such a descent calls for. This was no chess game where the board
could be reset. No one could afford a false move or allow the rope to
snag. There could be no lapses in concentration. There were no second
chances. Each man was dependent on the other three and they on him.

146

Safety was indeed a matter of acute awareness. It is to their enormous credit that their exit from the mountain was done in such exemplary fashion.

It is interesting, too, to reflect that both these climbs were done using techniques now regarded as out of date. It is rare now to cut steps. A route like the west face would be climbed by front-pointing on crampons with a tool in each hand. What Patterson took six days to do would surely be done in one today. This would be less so for the eastern party where the quality of snow and ice was quite different. To put modern climbing techniques and attitudes into perspective, in 1984 Gerard Van Sprang, a Dutch climber, climbed Yerupaja by the west face up and down solo in 12 hours! You might think that this makes a mockery of earlier efforts, but I believe not. I have known a few solo climbers, and not one of them is now alive. You have only to make one tiny mistake and it's curtains. Nobody can be perfect 100 per cent of the time. You cannot help but admire the virtuosity and technical competence, the self-assurance, and the physical fitness of someone who can climb the 4,500-foot west face of Yerupaja at an average angle of 55° solo, let alone do it in 12 hours. It is a wonder that challenges can still exist for such a person.

Rob Brooks was not to be cheated of his summit. Two years later, in 1968, he returned with a New Zealand team led by Graham Dingle. They came early in the season and on 21 June the north summit was gained via the north west spur. The south summit was reached on 27 June. Rob Brooks was in the team that reached the top on 30 June.

CHAPTER 10

Safety is Awareness

Now I wonder if a survivalist as you are has written about the time you and I ended up in Point Five Gully (Ben Nevis) in a hail/ice storm with one ice axe between us, and you in canvas boots in May. I do remember hanging upside down determined to get a piton out – not ours – with you muttering away above me. And the only other time I have seriously climbed with you, me a relative novice glad to be in safe hands, after apologising to me for underestimating me, you suddenly announced that you'd led me into quite the wrong gully, and your advice to me was – run!

Leslie Hills
Climber and TV Producer

What is safety? That one will come to no harm? Is it the flip side of risk? To what extent should we be responsible for our own welfare? Today the populace increasingly expects to be safe and when harm comes their way, believe someone is by definition to blame. Wrists must be slapped, a suit for damages pursued or someone hounded by the law and sent to jail. We are destroying ourselves and our society if we persist in thinking this way. Risk is endemic in the act of living. Freud observed:

Life is impoverished, it loses its interest, when the highest stakes in the game of living, life itself, may not be risked.

149

However, as Louis Pasteur, the microbiologist, observed, 'Chance favours the prepared mind.' This is the essence of safety. The trick is how to reap the benefits of risk without paying its price.

So to what extent should we expect to be bailed out if we overplay our hand in pursuit of excitement or adventure? It seems these days we expect as a matter of course to be rescued. There have been some incredibly chancy escapes. That of Tony Bullimore, a Vendée Globe competitor, from his upturned yacht in the Southern Ocean must rank among the most remarkable. Not only was his determination to survive phenomenal but it was the longest-range rescue ever carried out, at the very limit of the scope of the Australian Navy.

Helicopter crews take tremendous risks lifting mountaineers off cliff faces and seamen off the decks of heaving ships in stormy waters. Some German sailors whose trawler sank far off the west coast of the Hebrides in 2002 were rescued by RAF choppers at the limit of their range. They made Benbecula with literally a few seconds of fuel remaining. A similar rescue off the US coast, characterised in the book and film *The Perfect Storm*, resulted in the loss of a helicopter and its crew when it ran out of fuel on its homeward leg. But in every case, however risky, however remote, however much the fault may lie with some foolish act on the part of the victims, every effort, regardless of cost, is made to save human life. That's the good part of today's society.

Unfortunately there are people who put themselves at risk for the publicity they gain; some even have to pretend they are at risk, knowing full well they will be rescued if plans don't work out, people like Pen Hadow, Hemplewell-Adams or Evel Knievel. Imagine, then, deliberately putting yourself in a position where no rescue was possible for at least three months. This was the situation facing three members of the British North Greenland Expedition. They were to spend the winter of 1952–3 in the middle of the Greenland ice cap, 8,000 feet above sea level: for two months it would be totally dark; for four months there would be no sight of the sun: the temperature would fall to -60°C; winter gales would bury their hut in drifted snow; they would be entirely on their own. Theirs would be an environment where even a trivial mistake could have serious consequences. Every action had to be prudent, well thought out: no trusting to luck. To behave always like this, day after day, is very demanding and, as we all know, quite minor injuries can sometimes grow into major problems. But we can always trot off to the doctor to be mended.

The story of their journey to the centre of the north Greenland ice cap from Queen Louise Land, of the RAF Hastings bomber which crashed as it was dropping their supplies and the rescue of its crew is well told in Simpson's *North Ice*. They arrived at the chosen spot on 15 September when at that latitude (78°04'N) daylight was already dwindling fast. Stores, fuel and a hut were airdropped, 87 tons in all. The hut was assembled close to the crashed plane, which was to become their store. The airdrop was not complete until 9 October. On 18 October, one week before the sun set permanently for the winter, the support party of Commander Simpson, Angus Erskine and Richard Hamilton left to fight their way through the autumn gales back to base at Queen Louise Land. The courageous three remaining were Graham Rollit, a lieutenant commander in the Navy, Buck Taylor, an Army telegraphist, and Peter Taylor, a glaciologist. They were now beyond rescue, no matter what happened. No plane could land, no sledge team could make the 250 miles from base in the dead of winter with the prospect of gales and temperatures reaching -60°C. How could an injured or sick man have survived such a journey anyway? Their safety lay entirely in their own hands, in their awareness of their situation. It's a lesson all we mountaineers should take to heart.

Happily they survived unscathed and made their observations in the name of science. This is an enormous tribute to the care and caution with which they conducted themselves in a potentially dangerous situation. Probably their greatest risk was that of carbon monoxide poisoning, for their electrical power came from a petrol generator. Admiral Byrd, who wintered alone near the South Pole in 1933, was poisoned by carbon monoxide from just such a generator and was able to rouse himself just in time. This simple molecule of carbon and oxygen can chemically link to the haemoglobin in the blood preventing the uptake of oxygen. It took an entire winter for Byrd to recover. His is a remarkable story of the triumph of willpower over physical disability. Incidentally, it is quite possible to unintentionally expire in a well-sealed bivvy tent from as innocent and harmless a gas as carbon dioxide – the ingredient in fizzy drinks. You can use up enough of the oxygen, which is replaced by carbon dioxide in the course of breathing, to induce a coma. You just quietly fade away.

How different are matters today as far as rescue is concerned. Climbers in difficulties can open up their mobile phones and call for help, in some cases simply for advice. Yachtsmen trigger their EPIRB (distress beacon) and the world's maritime rescue services swing into action. The knowledge that however foolish you are, however much your situation is due to your hubris or rashness, you can be sure of being plucked from danger, must diminish the sense of adventure

151

offered by these activities. If that be so, what is the point of engaging in them? Are we to reduce climbing a mountain to mere technical competence, the great outdoors to an extension of the indoor climbing wall? Calculated risk is an essential ingredient in mountaineering, indeed in all adventure. Assessing and managing that risk is what distinguishes the competent from the foolhardy. Should you embark on the Eiger Nordwand, a face notorious for objective dangers, assuming that someone will risk their life to rescue you if things turn out badly? Surely not. In the UK there now exists the Adventure Activities Licensing Authority. Is this the right way to go? Are we not in danger of destroying the very quality of the experience we seek to enhance? One cannot have adventure without risk.

I am not immune to appealing to the rescue services. On one occasion in 2001 I was making a ski traverse on the Cairngorms with two friends. We were coming off the upper slopes at the end of the day onto steep snow-covered heather. While making a kick turn a woman in the party tripped and fell down sideways about a dozen feet, dislocating her shoulder. This is very painful, but she was adamant she could hirple down through the forest to the private road below. What was needed was an ambulance to await her and this required the authority to open locked gates. Out came the mobile phone. The following conversation ensued with the Sergeant at Aviemore Police Station, who had a delightful West Highland accent.

> 'And what age would be the injured party?' he enquired in solicitous tones.
> '65.'
> 'And what age would be the other gentleman?'
> '70.'
> 'And what age are you yourself, sir?'
> '75.'
> 'I think I'd better send a helicopter!'

The following day *The Times* reported that three elderly ladies had been airlifted from the Cairngorms.

In this game of risk, what can we learn from the experiences of others? Where should we draw the balance between safety and risk? And who should make the decision? It has to be the climbers themselves. When Dougal Haston embarked on the direct route on the Eiger he was in no doubt about the risks he ran. When a storm hit, he sat it out. I feel sure that even if mobile phones had existed then, he would not have used one. One of Dougal's companions, Harland, had fallen on this route when a fixed rope broke. He completed the route in memory of his fallen friend.

When George Mallory made his third attempt on Mt Everest in 1924 he already knew he would not be offered another chance. Is this what drove him to push on beyond 27,000 feet on the north ridge? He would be aware that if anything happened to them, they were beyond rescue. Was he rash or was he just plain unlucky? Lack of oxygen at high altitude can easily confuse the mind. Could it be that he had to assist his companion Irvine, whose technical competence did not quite match his own? Irvine's body has never been found. Mallory's was discovered 67 years later on the western flank, his hands outstretched, his fingers clawing at the rock as if endeavouring to stop his fall. The answers to these questions are unknowable. What can be said is that they embarked on the climb of their own free will into an environment that no human being had hitherto penetrated. They were free to turn back. There was no third party dictating their movements. Who today can judge whether their decision to go on was 'constructive boldness or destructive folly'? High-altitude statistics show that one in seven climbers on the two highest mountains in the world, K2 in the Karakorum and Mt Everest in the Himalayas, have died on the descent from the summit. Some will have died through lack of stamina in the face of bad weather, or occasionally in heroic efforts to help another person. Others will be alive because they were sufficiently aware of their condition or judged the circumstances inappropriate for an attempt and turned back. At this outer limit of human survival very little in the way of rescue can be mounted. Dead bodies litter the South Col of Everest. No climber on his or her way up believes that they have but a one in seven chance of getting off the hill. The salient point is that we should not depend on luck for our survival; that's Russian roulette. You have to be aware to stay alive. Crossing a crevassed glacier calls for considerable concentration to identify just where the crevasses lie. One doesn't step on a snow bridge without probing its strength. This happened unintentionally to Bill Wallace, an experienced Scottish climber and one-time President of the SMC, as he stylishly skied down to his waiting friends on the Findelen Glacier after having traversed the Adler Joch. In an elegant sweeping turn he came to halt beside them. Unfortunately that spot was a snow bridge. He jammed 20 feet down and lost his skis!

What is held to be bad luck may be bad judgement. There will never be any shortage of critics after an accident, but this was not deserved in the case of Jamie Andrew and his friend James Fisher. These were two hyper-fit, experienced, tough young climbers who went to the Mont Blanc range in January 1999 to make the winter ascent of the north-east ridge of the Aiguille Droites, a 13,000-foot peak near Mont Blanc. This is a serious undertaking even in summer, but in winter with short days and long nights, rocks so cold one must climb with gloves on and cracks filled with ice and snow on the ledges, it is many times more challenging. But that's why they were drawn to it. They knew they were up to the technical difficulties and they were accustomed to cold and ice from their experiences in Scotland in winter. They assessed the risks and planned accordingly. They would have to spend at least one night out, perhaps two, so their rucksacks were weighed down with food, a sleeping bag, a small stove and a few litres of that most vital commodity, even with snow all around – water. This extra weight must have slowed them down. It is one of the intractable equations to be solved in big-route climbing. If you carry enough to survive a night out you risk moving too slowly and will probably have to bivouac. If you carry nothing, you will go faster, but risk disaster if you're caught out. Balancing risk is part of the intellectual entertainment of climbing to a high standard.

They waited for a good three-day weather forecast before setting off. The first day went well. They bivouacked, expecting to gain the summit the next day and rope down onto easy ground to be cosseted in a warm hut by nightfall. But the forecast, as so often, proved wrong. On that second day the wind got up and clouds drifted in. It started snowing heavily, slowing them down. The last six rope lengths to the Brêche des Droites were done in the dark. In principle the descent route was easy enough. It lay down steep snow slopes to the Talêfre Glacier, but that night nothing was visible in the spindrift generated by the gale. One has to have experienced the impact of a change in climate from the still cold of their first day to the damp airstream of the second to appreciate the physical and psychological stress they were suddenly subjected to. In cold, still, dry air, even at -20°C, one can be quite comfortable in shirtsleeves. Once the clouds come in, the humidity of the air increases and its conductivity rises enormously. Heat leaks out of the body like water through a sieve. The wind exacerbates the rate of the loss. You become a wet-bulb thermometer. For them, that night, weary from the climb, there was nothing for it but to remain where they were until daylight. They cut a platform in the snow and crawled into their sleeping bags, pulled on their bivvy bags, drew the hoods over their heads and waited for the storm to blow over. No stove could be lit, no food heated. It was a grim case of hanging on and waiting.

Next day the storm was, if anything, worse. They decided to remain, believing it must pass over soon. But the next day, and the next, and the next, the blizzard persisted. Four days elapsed. By now they were beyond fighting their own way down. Their future lay in other hands. Jamie's girlfriend, Anne, was in the valley. They were confident that she would raise the alarm. Sure enough as the sky cleared on the fourth day they heard the welcome sound of a helicopter of the French rescue services. But such was the wind that it could not reach them. The clouds closed in and the sound of the helicopter faded. By now they had lost all feeling in their hands and feet. Some time in the following three days James Fisher died. On the seventh day, the sixth without food or heat, the weather cleared and the rescue team were able to reach the peak. Jamie Andrew was alive but unable to move, his hands and feet literally blocks of ice. The French doctors did everything they could but he lost them all.

No two people are the same in such circumstances. Amazingly Judith Leslie, 30, who collapsed from hypothermia in 1994, was found to have a core temperature of only 22°C when brought to hospital, yet she made a complete recovery.

Obviously, had Fisher and Andrews visualised such an outcome, they would never have embarked upon the climb. This was not war, or the need for some outrageous performance to attract the attention of the media. Being bold means taking risks, but they were indeed unlucky.

Should luck be factored into the decision analysis, weather forecasting being the uncertain art it is? Was the knowledge that the Chamonix guides provided a first-class rescue service thought of as their back-stop? Is it really good mountaineering to proceed on the assumption that if worse comes to worst, someone will rescue you? Coping with bad luck is part of the game. As Geoff Tabin so aptly observed:

> To have a great adventure and survive, requires good judgement. Good judgement comes from experience. Experience, of course, is the result of poor judgement.

Getting off the mountain oneself unaided is part of the ethos of climbing. In 1937 Vorg and Rebitsch were in line to be the first to ascend the Eiger Nordwand. They had reached 11,000 feet when poor weather closed in. It took them two days and one night to descend; a brilliant accomplishment in the face of stone-fall, rain, cold and with sodden clothing. Such continual uncertainty stretches both mind and body to the ultimate. Another example is the descent from Yerupaja by Brooks and party described in Chapter 9. If they had yielded to tiredness it would have meant a night in the open and no living dawn. Many other climbers have taken equivalent risks, been lucky with the conditions and have lived to tell the tale. Lived, indeed, to dine off the tale. Even lived to write a best-selling book about it. Perhaps one of the most compelling is that written by Maurice Herzog of his ascent of Annapurna in 1950, the first 8,000-metre summit ever to be climbed. It is an epic tale of heroism, horror, *schadenfreude*, and tragedy. Herzog too lost his hands and feet.

It is remarkable what fortitude and courage people will manifest when placed *in extremis*. I particularly admire Martin Boysen's mental struggle on the Trango Tower in the Karakorum in 1975. This peak is a monstrously steep rock pinnacle of 20,470 ft (6,240 m), whose barely fissured face offered climbing so hard that the team were only overcoming 3 pitches of 100 feet each day. They had almost run out of food, but only one last overhang stood between them and what looked like easier climbing to the top. Boysen led; a brilliant effort. As he reached the lip of the overhang he had only one safety device remaining, a large metal wedge known as a bong, with a sling threaded through it. Thankfully he placed it in the crack above his head and clipped in his rope. He now knew he would come to little harm if he fell off. He relates the subsequent events:

> I eased my knee gently into the crack, flexed it and moved up. But then when I tried to repeat the move, I found my knee was stuck. I was merely irritated at first. I hadn't enough energy to waste wriggling my knee about. I slumped down on it and felt the grip tighten, and the first wave of panic began to lap inside my skull. I was very much alone . . . I struggled furiously, trying to tear the material of my breeches, but to no effect.

It is hard to imagine a more grotesque situation. You are the fox in the Inuit's trap; unhurt but captive. All around is the most magnificent scenery, the very environment you sought as balm to your soul. You are well and strong. This should not happen. Worst of all, you are able to think through the consequences. Like the fox you will simply die through starvation or hypothermia. Boysen continues:

I was rapidly tiring, becoming more fearful as time sped by . . .
I collapsed, limp and defeated, and slowly sank into a trance-
like, painless oblivion. My mind wandered aimlessly, picking
out memories, seizing trivia, until the anguish inside me welled
up uncontrollably and forced itself into my unwilling
conscienceness. I choked out a single sob, the distillation of my
despair. I would never see my daughter Katie, my wife
Margaret, never smell the warmth of love and life. I would miss
everything, utterly. How futile my wasted life seemed: how
precarious the balance between my passion for climbing and my
passion for life.

Three hours slipped by and, as the sun moved lower, I was
certain of my coming death . . . Then I remembered I had a
knife blade in my pocket. I found it and started trying to cut my
breeches. But the blade wouldn't bite, so I pounded it with my
hammer and produced a wicked saw edge. With this I cut and
gouged the thick material within the crack with my last
strength. Blood began to ooze thickly from my thigh, my fingers
and knuckles were skinned, but I continued cutting without
regard. At last I felt the material give. All my hopes were pinned
on my next few moves – I hardly dared to start easing at my
knee. I tried, gently at first, then harder. But it would not budge,
and all hope drained away. My body sagged, and then – I could
hardly believe it, my knee slipped out, and I half slid, half fell,
onto the bong [which held].

The will to survive is innate, yet in many situations in bad weather it
is terribly easy to slide into a numb, virtually painless apathy, and so
into coma, then death. Such was the case of one of two hillwalkers
caught in a southerly blizzard on the Cairngorm plateau. Here the
weather can be as bad as anywhere in the world. The two of them
forced their tired bodies through the blinding spindrift towards the
northern edge of the plateau below whose lip they could expect some
shelter from the chilling power of the northerly gale. The only problem
was to know in that white-out where, for sure, they were. This was
vitally important, for many cliffs abound in this region. It is painfully
easy in a white-out to walk off the top of a cliff. One moment your foot
is on firm ground; the next moment in space. Tragically the woman,
declaring herself beyond further effort, lay down and passed away
during the night.

Fighting just such a temptation engaged all the willpower of two

New Zealand climbers, the brothers Doole and Mark Inglis. It was early summer as they set off to climb the country's highest peak, Mt Cook, or Aorangi – the cloud piercer. This 12,349-foot peak sits on the spine of the South Island, a bulwark against the warm wet winds whistling over the Tasman Sea. The rising air cools and deposits huge amounts of snow and frequently encases the mountain in cloud, often with blizzard conditions. The pair knew a front was coming in but banked on getting up and down before it hit. They were unprepared for the icy blast that hit them as they gained the summit ridge. On the lee side was a *schrund* or crevasse and gratefully they climbed into its windless interior and prepared to wait out the storm. Usually these pass within 12 hours. They had some food and were well enough equipped to bivouac one night. Unfortunately the storm lasted 14 days! Their feet went numb in spite of continual massaging. By the fifth day they believed they no longer had the strength to descend even if the wind abated. Their only hope lay with others.

Down in the valley there was deep concern, but the conditions precluded a rescue effort. On the eighth day a bold helicopter pilot hovered over them to drop food, sleeping bags and a radio. They were like 'kids at Christmas' as they opened the supplies, they later told reporters. The weather again closed in. As the days passed, the cold penetrated deeper and deeper. Their feet no longer felt pain. There was an overwhelming desire to just drift away into oblivion, which they managed to resist. The 14th day was calm. The rescuers arrived by helicopter.

Those who have the strength of will to reject the drug of climbing may find it hard to understand why any of the climbers in these three tales chose to put themselves at such risk. Was it hubris? Was it the need to prove oneself? Was it driven by the spur of competition? Or was it just bad judgement? Herzog on Annapurna was so obsessed with getting to the top that he knowingly threw caution to the winds. Jamie Andrew and James Fisher appreciated the risks they were running, resting their faith in their equipment and skills, while the Inglis brothers were simply out for a good day's climbing on an admittedly dangerous mountain: 850 people before them had climbed Mt Cook, though 40 have died doing so.

Mountaineers are very conscious of the distinction between subjective and objective dangers. We like to think we are in control of the former, and assess the latter clinically. The ascent of Mt Cook even by its easiest route invokes objective danger. The day I went to climb it the weather had prohibited flying to the plateau hut and we were forced to make the tedious tramp up the moraines of the Tasman Glacier, followed by a relentless steep scrub-covered ridge, an ascent of some 5,000 feet. Dawn next day saw us outside the hut watching Aorangi's icy cone turn first rose then the yellow of an old candle. Then the eye was drawn down and down past buttresses of chocolate brown rock and steep gullies to the icefall. And there it stopped. In the growing light we focused on this well-known objective danger on the way to the summit of Mt Cook. This is how one Kiwi climber, Peter Radcliffe, describes it in *Land of Mountains*:

> Tumbled piles of broken seracs lie at the bottom of long, splayed out chutes where avalanches have lost their momentum. Crevasses carve blue-black lines of menace in our path. Huge green blocks poised ready to drop stare down from the hanging glaciers high on Teichelmann, frozen in mid-flight like figures on a Grecian urn.

The *easy* route to Mt Cook takes one below this icefall. Speed is your only ally. We didn't need any knowledge of accident statistics to tell us that we were looking at a prime example of objective danger. This was Russian roulette, though the odds were better than 6:1. In fact, looking at the accident statistics, they were 21:1. No amount of skill can reduce the risk, only speed.

That day I chose not to risk it. I was 60 and, though fit for my age, I was tired from the heave up from the valley the day before. I could not see myself going fast enough and I felt that my tiredness would slow down my reactions if any of the seracs did crumble. Instead we climbed the Anzac Peak and sat on its summit in awe of the great east face with its intimidating corniced summit ridge, every bit as impressive as any Himalayan giant.

What may astonish non-climbers even more is that in every case, fitted with artificial limbs to feet and hands, all these injured climbers returned to climbing. The Inglis brothers even managed to ascend Mt Cook, aided by many helpers. Jamie Andrew has climbed Ben Nevis to raise funds for people reduced to artificial limbs. He plans to ascend Kilimanjaro to raise money for charity. He even skis. Herzog became a hero in his native France.

For people of this calibre the issue is, where do you go once you've already done the hardest there is? It is said that Dougal Haston had this feeling in the weeks before his death. Unlike many physical sports, mountain climbing has such a strong aesthetic aspect that many climbers become monomaniacs, addicted to the hills for all of their lives. However, only those that learn that safety is awareness will die in their beds. Too many brilliant mountaineers have died needlessly from just a moment's inattention. Fritz Kasparek, who shared the first ascent of the Eiger Nordwand with Heinrich Harrer, fell through a cornice on Salcantay in Peru. Herman Buhl also fell through a cornice. Tom Patey, Dougal Haston and Robin Smith all died as a result of their own inattention to danger. There is a saying that goes 'There are bold mountaineers, and old mountaineers, but very few bold, old mountaineers'. Not everyone will agree with Kurt Diemberger's comment on Herman Buhl's demise: 'For people who love mountains, to die there is to die where your heart is.' OK, but surely in a great endeavour, not through inattention.

The technology of climbing has reached such an advanced stage today that falling off is the least of a top-class modern climber's worries, for if the cliff is steep enough, he or she will simply bound into space, to be held by an intermediate belay (called a runner) with the shock absorbed by the phenomenal elasticity and strength of a modern climbing rope.

So does this mean there is no risk left in climbing steep cliff faces? No, it does not, because human nature being what it is, the advance of technology, in this case of the equipment available, simply means that climbers embark on harder, chancier, or more remote climbs, expecting the same odds in their favour as that of earlier generations. Moreover, with modern outdoor clothing people can now survive nights out on the mountain wall with no shelter, though how one still longs for the dawn. This means that one can embark on routes of such severity that failing to complete them in one day would not necessarily commit one to a slow death by hypothermia, or the calling out of rescue parties. Of course, this expectation of survival is based on the idea that all hazards spring from external origins which through superior technology can be outwitted, just in the way a driver of a BMW 3 Series erroneously believes he is safer at 100 mph than in a Fiat Punto at 50 mph.

Of many incidents my most bizarre escape from death was not even on a mountain, but when camping in Utah. Our tent was pitched in the shade of a venerable cottonwood tree. In the dry climate of Utah such trees, as they die, wither into brittle spiky branches as tough as steel and as pointed as a rapier. In the middle of the night a limb of this tree, perhaps ten feet long, chose its moment of rest. We awoke to the sound of a cracking branch, and suddenly three sharp spikes penetrated the tent, pinning me down between the two outer, while the third penetrated my sleeping bag, passed between my legs, brushing against my testicles. I do consider that a lucky escape and not one I could have anticipated. It just demonstrates the extent of awareness called for to stay alive in this highly diverse world. The previous evening we had been discussing God. In retrospect we wondered whether this was a warning shot. Safety indeed lies in awareness, but just how aware must we be? John Simpson, the widely respected BBC foreign correspondent, whom one sees popping up everywhere there is trouble, had this to say of the risks he took in pursuit of a good story:

> Perhaps my upbringing has given me a rather Victorian view of life and death. I find it hard to accept the contemporary view that life of any kind, no matter how restricted and feeble, is better than no life at all. The thing doesn't seem to me to be worth clinging onto at all costs, regardless of quality. Like an ancient Roman, I would prefer to get out while ahead; if that involves taking my chances in an air war of extraordinary proportions, so be it.

Let me give the last word to one salvationist who died in his bed, Harry Spilsbury of the Fell and Rock Climbing Club of the Lake District, (FRCC). Here are the words of one of his witty songs:

> We are mountaineers ingenuous,
> and of ourselves we take great care.
> We never tackle anything strenuous
> and when danger looms we're never there.
> But if we see some moderate mountain,
> not too near nor yet too far,
> We do it in, we do it in,
> To show what mountaineers we are (repeat).

> With apologies to Gilbert and Sullivan

CHAPTER 11

Pushing the Boat Out

Imagine yourself gliding along in a small boat on a glass-like surface of transparent blue-green sea, surrounded by snow-capped peaks, with little auks and eiders bobbing and diving ahead of you, the nearby land glowing russet after the summer's heat. Irresistible? Well, certainly to any Arctic enthusiast or naturalist. Sounds like a bit of travel-agent hype, but it's not. Just such conditions are to be found in the Arctic Riviera, that region of east Greenland around Kong Oscars Fjord at latitude 72°N. The magic of the Arctic stillness, the subtle variation of the frost-tinted tundra coupled to the oblique shadows cast by a low sun that never quite sets, is utterly compelling.[1]

I had just such an image in my mind when I proposed to Iain Smart a small boat voyage down the east Greenland coast to climb the highest unclimbed mountain in Greenland, the 10,800-foot-high Borg Tinde, situated in a remote and inaccessible range known as the Ejnar Mikkelsen's Fjaeld. Iain is endowed with a vivid imagination. He is not so much a lateral thinker as a traveller of the mind. Such is his breadth of experience and power of imagination that he can imagine a visit to Petra and the scented whiff of the desert's dawn wind or the ascent of an icy mountain in all its fine detail without stirring from his armchair. He is also a master at intellectualising adversity. I could think of no better companion if I could just persuade him that what he would experience was beyond even his vivid imagination. I pointed out that the interior of this coast was Terra Incognito. I argued that a small boat journey was a uniquely intimate way of seeing the land and the fauna.

An opportunity like this was like offering a wine lover the keys to the Rothschild caves. He gave in. I needed two other people, yet to be recruited.

Once committed, we warmed our prospects by imagining our boat bobbing at anchor in little coves, backed by lush tundra, the still, crisp evening air rent only by the keening of a red-throated diver. There would be driftwood fires, a good dram in the hand, some excellent conversation. Forays into the interior would reveal unexpected discoveries. Such is the stuff that dreams are made of and without them America would never have been discovered.

The reality turned out to be that south of the giant fjord of Scoresby Sund and its settlement of the same name at 70°30' N, Greenland puts on a sourer face and maintains it for the next 5° of latitude – 300 nautical miles of ice fronts, high mountains and rough capes, all guarded by the pack ice that irresistibly flows down from the polar basin. This barrier played an important part in the historical north–south Inuit migrations in these parts.

In 1833 Lieutenant Jules de Blosseville, commanding the *Lilloise*, reached the vicinity of a bay now called de Reste Bugt, sighted a remarkable high peak, sailed to Iceland with the news and then returned and was never heard of again. No trace of the ship or its crew has ever been found and we hoped that we might make a sighting. It is in his memory that this shore is now named the Blosseville Kyst. The first published report resulted from a small boat voyage by Lieutentant (later Admiral) Amdrup in 1900. Funded by the Carlsberg Foundation (of beer fame), this was Amdrup's second attempt, the previous 1899 effort being thwarted by dense pack ice. Dropped off from the mother ship in a 16-foot dory, he left Kap Dalton 69°25' N on 22 July, and took until 2 September to reach the then most northerly Inuit settlement at Tasiilaq. He produced a very creditable outline map of the coastline. He found Inuit ruins and hot springs in a region he named Henry Land, but made no penetration into the interior. When in 1923 the colony of Scoresbysund (renamed Ittoqqortoormiit when Greenland declared its autonomy) was established to open new hunting grounds for the Tasiilaq Inuit, those hunters often sledged as far south as Kap Dalton in the spring, using the refuge hut built by Amdrup. The hunters always found open water south of Kap Dalton, even in winter. This is a measure of the strength of the east Greenland current.

In 1933, Knud Rasmussen made a coastal journey in a large vessel, meeting very little resistance from the polar pack ice. The year 1934 saw the Italian Bonzi making a try, but he was held up by the pack ice at 69°50' N. Similarly in the same year the French explorer Charcot was also forced back. So, how did we imagine we might succeed where these heavyweights with large and well-funded expeditions had failed? I had a theory.

It had been my experience that a small boat can often make progress whatever the state of the pack ice by using a narrow strip of clear water, perhaps just a few feet wide, that is usually to be found between the pack, which would be grounded on the sea floor, and the shore. This, however, would only be the case if the shore was shallow. It would not hold if the shoreline plunged quickly into deep water. My proposal was to take a similar boat to Amdrup's. There were three criteria to be satisfied. It had to have a shallow draught. It had to be able to stand up to compression if wedged between ice floes. It had to be light enough that four men could haul it out of the water. Iain and I had once circumnavigated the Isle of Mull in an open 16-foot Norwegian clinker-built dinghy constructed of slow-grown Arctic larch. We had been impressed with its seagoing qualities, so why not this craft? We knew that even heavily laden it could be propelled by a 5 horsepower (hp) outboard at about 6 mph at a fuel consumption of 8 miles to the gallon (almost 2 nautical miles per litre). The wisdom of such a choice was borne out the following year when Andrew Ross attempted to reach the Mikkelsen area using a 45 hp boat that did only 2 miles to the gallon. He was unable to carry enough fuel and ran out. A further aspect of our combination was that in event of engine failure we could propel it with oars. Belt and braces principle.

Our ideas were encouraged by aerial photos of the Blosseville Kyst, which had been surveyed by the Danish Geodetic Survey. They were taken in August which was when we planned our voyage. They showed a widely dispersed pack. So, with our image of windless days on a mirror-like sea surface, open pack and a boat that could do 5–6 miles an hour, a shoreline voyage down 200 sea miles of the coast seemed no more challenging than an outing to Ailsa Craig from Dunoon. Of course, there would be two crucial stages. Ittoqqortoormiit on the north coast was the only possible bridgehead, so the first crux would be the 20-mile crossing of the great fjord. The second was getting to the mountain from the coast. As for the mountain itself, we knew nothing of its quality. A blow-up of an aerial picture revealed a steep summit cone of snow or ice atop steep buttresses. Perched on this was a final rock pinnacle – in other words a quality mountain. While it was unlikely to be a hard climb in a modern context, getting to it would be a challenge.

I presented these plans to the Ministry for Greenland in Copenhagen for approval. I had some difficulty in persuading them that we would not finish up a liability and have to be rescued. To this end I undertook to leave food and fuel depots along the coast as we went south, so that if the boat were lost, we could at least walk back to the Inuit summer settlement near Kap Brewster (now Kangikajik) on the south shore of Scoresby Sund and shelter there until the winter freeze would allow us to cross to Ittoqqortoormiit on foot or sledge. I even planned to cache a typewriter and a ream of A4 paper so that I could spend the time writing my memoirs. The man at the Ministry, Eske Brun, urged me to recruit an experienced Greenland trapper and suggested a certain Major Carlos Ziebell.

We met at the railway station. He was a small man in his 60s whose wrinkled features told you he had comfortably faced hardship in his time. He had the loose dynamic body of a man who kept himself fit. I took an instant liking to him. He called me Sleazer and continued to do so throughout our acquaintance in spite of my protestations. I outlined our plans over coffee and pastry in the buffet. He was intrigued. He had for two decades made a living as a trapper on the east Greenland coast and had been marooned there by the Second World War. Like the other Danish and Norwegian trappers in that situation he had been recruited to form the East Greenland Sledge Patrol. That was how he became 'Major'. This tiny group of about 20 men were supplied by airdrops from the UK. Their primary task was to round up German groups that had been landed by submarine to set up weather stations. Carlos loved Greenland and hadn't been there for a decade. Our trip tempted him. However, he made only a scanty living as a smallholder in Denmark and had no money. We would have to pay his travel. We set a rendezvous at Ittoqqortoormiit on 28 July 1969.

Back home I ordered the clinker-built boat to be sent from Trondheim to Copenhagen for shipment to Ittoqqortoormiit together with an inflatable Avon dinghy, which would serve as tender and liferaft. We planned on enough fuel for a round trip of up to 500 miles, with food for 56 days, but intending only 35. The time schedule was tight. Until late July Scoresby Sund is choked with the remains of winter ice. By early September the frosts would return and the sea begin to freeze. Our craft was no icebreaker. We had at the most 35 days at our disposal. The boats would be powered by low-consumption outboard engines – a twin Evinrude and a single-cylinder Swedish Cresta.

Our fourth member had to be a top-class climber in case we met real difficulties on the mountain. Allan Petit was recommended by Iain with whom he had shared an expedition to Greenland when he was an undergraduate. A dentist by profession he used hypnotism in place of painkillers – though not on me. I was not susceptible! He was a totally laid-back character whose lean and saturnine features hinted at a lurking intelligence.

The actual march from the coast to the mountain we could not plan with any precision. As far as we could judge from the photos, if we could reach Grivel Bugt we would find an accommodating glacier-free shore where the boat could be hauled out and be safe while we were on the hill. It looked as if a reasonably low col would lead through to the snout of the Vedel Brae, where at some distance beyond soared our objective. There was no reason to think it would be fiercely crevassed. Some glaciers in Greenland are like highways, such as the Roslin and lower Bersaerker Brae in the Staunings Alps. But it was always possible they could be swift moving, highly crevassed and time-consuming like the Rinks Glacier mentioned in Chapter 2.

All that remained now was to finance the venture. The Mt Everest Foundation provided some funds and we contracted with the *Scotsman* newspaper to send regular radio telegrams from the field. We left for Reykjavik on 28 July. Ziebell had been unable to secure a berth on the annual ship to Ittoqqortoormiit, but, using his not inconsiderable wits, got himself by air to Mesters Vig for nothing, then by helicopter to Gurraholm deep inside Scoresby Sund on its north shore, some 120 miles from our rendezvous. He set off to walk towards Ittoqqortoormiit along the south shore of Jameson Land, content once again to be in his beloved Greenland. He underestimated what he was about. There were big meltwater streams that required him to make major diversions inland to find crossing places. Finally, on the ninth day, just as his food ran out, he arrived at the Kap Stewart hut where Hurry Fjord joins Scoresby Sund. Between him and the settlement of Kap Hope lay ten miles of ice-strewn water! Using a mirror he attracted the attention of the Inuit there. He was spotted and rescued. He was extremely fortunate. There was much sea-level fog at that time in the area. The concatenation of sun and randomly catching a passing eye is pretty low. He stayed with his old Inuit *keefak* (housekeeper), Sophia, who comforted him until we arrived.

Meanwhile, the rest of us kicked our heels in frustration at Reykjavik as gales and fog precluded flying. It was not until 2 August that we took off in a chartered twin-engined Cessna from Isafjordur on the north coast of Iceland. Soon the icy bastions of the Blosseville Kyst

167

were glinting in the sun. To our dismay the pack lay like a lace trimming hard against the coast. With high pressure to the north and a low to the south, a strong easterly airflow was pushing the ice firmly against the land. We could only hope that my theory of an inshore passage for small boats would turn out to be valid. But winds change, do they not?

In those days small planes landed on a tundra strip two miles from the settlement. Today, as a result of oil exploration in neighbouring Jameson Land, there is a proper airstrip with radar, control tower, refuelling facilities and so forth on the shores of Hurry Fjord at Constable Point, 30 miles distant. Connection is by helicopter, which is maintained the year round. In relation to their remoteness and small population, Ittoqqortoormiit residents today must be amongst the most pampered in the world. All is paid for by the Danish State. If someone needs the dentist he or she is flown to Constable Point and on to Iceland for treatment – free. If the inhabitants of the Western Isles of Scotland or the Peleponese got to know, they would be green with envy.

In 1969 Ittoqqortoormiit was still very much an Inuit village. Every house had its dog team chained outside. There was a government store. Liquor was rationed. The way of life was hunting and skins were their export. The women wore traditional *kamiks*, ornate thigh-high boots made of sealskin and beautifully embroidered. Today there are few dog teams. Every house has a skidoo outside. The women wear rather fashionable Western clothes and look good in them. The children's clothing is indistinguishable from that of any American schoolchild. There is a supermarket, where Aberdeen Angus steaks mingle with musk-ox joints. Pornographic videos are available for purchase or hire. Most houses have satellite TV. Hunting is in decline. Hardly anyone still uses a kayak to hunt. One really asks oneself what is the point of supporting their living here. It is just another suburbia. Today the main money-earner is tourism.

Back then, on 2 August 1969, we had no time to waste. With minimal courtesies to the Danish administrator at Ittoqqortoormiit, we loaded the two boats and pushed off. The natives thought we were mad to cross the fjord in such a small boat. In a reversal of the usual tourist scene, Inuits with Polaroid cameras photographed our departure! We arranged a radio schedule with Kap Tobin. The frequency we had been issued with happened also to be that of helicopters serving a major geological expedition in inner Northwest Fjord. An enormous amount of confusion resulted. I said to the operator, 'If you don't hear from us, do nothing until the end of September.' He laughed. 'If anyone rescues you it will be from Scotland.'

Calling in at the sordid but genuine hunting settlement of Kap Hope we were deluged with advice. A gale was in the offing. The next few days would be calm. Go straight to Kangikajik. Go first further into the fjord to Kap Stewart. From a small eminence behind the village we scanned the great fjord. Bands of pack ice lay in our path but didn't seem serious obstacles.

Carlos indulged in an agonising farewell to Sophia. We politely averted our gaze. It was raining but calm as we left that evening; time of day has no meaning at this latitude. Five miles out we were on the edge of the first band of pack floating on mirror-like water, making our first radio call. '*Kap Tobin her er Ejnar Mikkelsens expedijon – skifter.*' No reply.

Suddenly the wind rose and we became acutely conscious that our tonne of pay load left little freeboard. We nosed into the pack for shelter, where lumps of winter sea ice tossed about us threatening to grind the *Scotto Dan* (as Carlos had named our vessel) to pieces. The inflatable boat couldn't keep up. We then linked the two boats with a rope. We ended up in a cul-de-sac of heaving pack ice. By common consent we retreated to Kap Stewart, cold, dispirited and having used far too much fuel to no good end.

By next morning the Arctic had resumed its riviera image. We dried out in the sun, all in good spirits. From a high vantage point we scanned the fjord. Binoculars revealed in detail the grim façade of the south coast – the Volquart Boons Kyst – where almost every cranny is filled with glaciers cascading from brooding black mountains into the sea. What, one wonders, had Volquart Boon ever done to deserve to be linked to such an evil place? But the wind had fallen and it was time to be off. At 6 p.m. we sallied forth on placid water. Only at one set of floes did we have to get out and push the pack aside manually. Usually nosing the prow in between two floes and putting the engine on full throttle was enough to prise open a passage provided there was no wind acting on the pack. We were relaxed even though the setting was awesome. Iain shot eight little auks. By midnight using a compass fix we were pleased to find we were only four miles from the dreaded south coast, which now looked fearsomely inhospitable. The wind came up, bringing squalls of rain. There was only one word to describe the scene: the good Scots word *dreich*. Grey waves of glacier-silted water dashed against the boat, spilling in. There was just too little freeboard.

169

The risk of being swamped deterred us from making a dash for the shore. Seeking safety we held along the edge of the pack, moving eastwards with the current. Every inch of the coastline was scanned through our binoculars. Simply no havens were to be seen.

We passed a large floe, so big that it had its own topography: hills, valleys and a harbour. It was raining hard. A wet sleeting January day in Glencoe could not have been more miserable. We tied up alongside, unloaded the boats, and pulled them onto the ice. We pitched a tent and lit the stove. Blessed heat. Carlos handed round the cigars, we cracked open the Dalmore. Life was transformed. Was this, I wondered, fiction becoming reality? Not a week earlier, when interviewed on TV this was exactly the picture I had presented to viewers when asked what we would do if we got stuck in the pack ice. My diary reads:

> The crucial decision was when to move on. Allan [Petit] now exhibits an unsuspected skill: to fall asleep when danger looms. We have made a big mistake. The sea is angrier. We should have gone for it [the shore] when we had the chance. At 3 a.m. we face facts and relaunch ourselves and edge towards the shore in the lee of whatever ice floes we can find until we are surrounded by pack half a mile from the shore, with no way through. We moor ourselves to a large mass of polar pack and reflect on what to do. Kap Brewster settlement is clearly visible. Carlos looses off a salvo of shots, but there is nothing anyone on shore can do to help us. We become conscious that the scenery is passing quickly. In no time we shall be around Kap Brewster and swept into Denmark Strait. Panic. Action stations.

In every adventurous undertaking there is always the option of the daring action versus the cautious. The bold stroke here would have been to stay camped on ice floe, and be whisked out into the open sea of the Denmark Strait, and taken south on the current. Provided the floe didn't break up we could have floated southwards until opposite our objective and then force the boat through the pack to shore. However, two things stayed our hand. Firstly, once out in the sea proper with all that ice around, if we were forced to launch our boats and then the wind got up, our little wooden boat would be ground to wood chips like the proverbial frog in the food processor. Secondly, there was little guarantee we could make it to the shore even if our floe remained intact. Finally we had promised the Greenland Ministry to lay depots along the coastline in case of losing the boat. I was very conscious of the need never to have to be rescued. It was a point of honour. My diary continues:

> In our haste the boat is not well loaded with too much weight high up. We make for an open shore lead. It closes as we reach it. Back to the polar floe. Another lead opens out, we race for it. The bow is inserted. All hands heave at the ice with oars on each side. We prise the floes apart, and squeeze through, dragging the inflatable behind. The screech of ragged ice on the butyl rubber makes us wince, but it doesn't puncture. We are surrounded by masses of brash ice, some lumps weighing half a ton, swirling and moving like the parts of a gigantic mixer. We back off. A gap appears and we rush for it, and make it through. Kap Brewster is near, too near. With open water now we head west away from it. We desperately need a landing. We're back in open rough water, taking on the waves. Iain leaps into the Rubba Dan [the inflatable] and gets the Cresta engine going. We are now beyond being afraid . . . We are committed. It's like a pitch where the holds peter out with no hope of climbing back down. Its either up or falling off. Three miles back up the fjord, and only one file of ice floes remaining to penetrate now. A lead opens up. We dash for it. It closes, and we turn around. We have just passed a vast iceberg, which is now bearing down upon us. We just skip past it as it crashes into a mass of large floes and splinters them like so much matchwood. Even Carlos looks anxious. That was too close for comfort. The shear pin goes on the Cresta engine, and it screams at top revs. Iain searches madly for a spare. Finds it. It won't start. Has to replace the plug. I look around. Allan is asleep! Carlos is crooning a tuneless Jutish song. But luck is with us. A lead appears, we dash through and there on shore just where we need it a rib of moraine runs out into the sea, creating a breakwater.

The journey had taken 23 hours and 3 of us had not slept for over 30 hours. That night the weather alternated between drizzle and pelting rain. Both Iain and I had anxiety dreams about polar bears. This trip so far was definitely not according to the envisaged scenario. Yet next day our faith was restored as the clouds parted and we dried out in the sun. Ours was a humorous party. Carlos was much older than the rest of us and with his less than perfect English missed much of our wit. I happened to crunch on a prune stone and broke a tooth. I appealed to the resident dentist for help. 'I'm on holiday,' was Allan's callous reply. After a bit of nagging I persuaded him to look into my mouth. 'Aye, that'll give you a lot of trouble' he opined and continued eating his breakfast. He was eventually goaded into action. Having no equipment he took a pebble and ground down the sharp edges of the tooth.

With the boat reloaded, we followed the shore leads to the Kangikajik settlement where we received a warm welcome. Here three families with two pretty young wives and five adorable children dressed in cast-offs were spending the summer hunting seals, walrus and narwhal. The squalor was unimaginable. Waste, human and kitchen, was just thrown out of the door. What was edible, including faeces, was scoffed by the dogs. Everything else would be picked over by foxes in the winter and by spring, we were assured, all would again be pristine – except for the tins. Yes, except for the tins.

We moved towards the next crux: the mighty Kangikajik where the Scoresby current joined the east Greenland in tumult. With binoculars we could see spindrift torn from the wave tops. Not for us today. Just short of the cape we found a windless zone and a passable campsite. Here we adopted a technique to ease our efforts, one that we used time and time again. Instead of beaching the boat and then unloading it each time we camped, we threw out a stern anchor with a long line from the stern to the shore. If the two lines were set right, the boat would lie head to the waves.

Above us soared 1,000-foot sorrel-draped cliffs. They were alive with kittiwakes, fulmars and Brünnich's guillemots. Wherever vegetation got a grip there was saxifrage, cerestium, white flower draba, scurvy-grass, sedum, rununculus, bistort, horsetail, even gentians. Climbing a gully to the top we looked south to our projected route. The wind was Force 7; a huge swell beat on a cheerless shore. Mist was pouring over the cliffs. It was a grim sight for small boaters. It was now 7 August. We were a week behind schedule. We needed to make all haste.

As with most impending cruxes where you pluck up your courage for the plunge it ended with an anticlimax. We engaged the great cape with anxious minds at the bottom of the tide. Yesterday's wave top spray had given way to a huge swell. As is often the case, for example with Cape Wrath, the inner passage just a few metres from cliffs is the calmest. Once on the outer coast our anxieties were displaced by the sight of a school of narwhal, those incredible beasts with single dagger-like tusks, highly valued by the Inuit both for food and ivory. The shore was boulder strewn, pitiless and barren, quite impossible to consider making a landing. Fifteen miles of this brought us to Kap Russell and a hoped-for relief, only to be hit by the full force of a katabatic wind howling down the Sfinx Brae from the ice cap. There was neither a way ahead nor back and no place to beach the boats. We were incredibly lucky to find a tiny cove about 30 feet in diameter, with almost vertical walls of the same dimension. Tying the *Scotto Dan* fore and aft in such a way that she could swing in the swell without touching the sides, we rock-climbed out of the cove to find ourselves on an almost vegetation-free, wind-scoured boulder field: bleakness personified.

The gale blew for four days. The sea was 2°C and the air 5°C. Iain, who couldn't tolerate my anxious state, withdrew into the caverns of his imagination or hunted for botanical specimens. Alan appeared to sleep 22 hours a day, waking only when food was offered. Carlos stalked the hills for game. He cooked the little auks and shot two hares. He reported no evidence of musk ox, but saw polar bear droppings that he reckoned to be about three weeks old. I worried about the exposed position of the boat and the fact that we had a contract with a newspaper to pay the expedition expenses and nothing much to report. In the course of sending a radio telegram, the Kap Tobin operator asked me to spell the word 'fit' in phonetic alphabet. As I was searching my mind for the official word for 'F' (which is 'foxtrot') Iain muttered in my ear 'phallus' and before I could stop myself I was dictating 'Phallus India Tango'. Since the entire east Greenland radio system was listening, it occasioned enormous amusement. Once when a tin outside the tent rattled for hours, Iain's brilliant imagination likened it to 'hearing two skeletons fornicating on a tin roof'. It may have been lousy weather, but we had a highly sociable time of it. We still had ten bottles left of our case of Dalmore. They had been gifted by the distillery.

We ate well. Several times the tents were blown down as the guys chaffed against the boulders. It was now likely that our mountain was beyond reach in the time at our disposal. We had 40 gallons of fuel left. Kap Dalton in a straight line was 50 miles off and Grival Bugt 50 miles beyond that. But already, to achieve 32 direct miles we had covered 80. The only way to make the best of our situation was to investigate the hinterland. Iain concentrated on plants and kept an excellent botanical record that was later published. He augmented our diet with a discovery of blueberries. We found reindeer horns, which was

173

interesting as it was thought they had never penetrated here. Carlos found a fox trap of the sort used by palaeo-Eskimos. Most intriguingly we found fossilised trees.

Every now and then we would peer down anxiously at the boat tossing in the cove. Little by little we extracted more and more gear, food and fuel just to be on the safe side. At one stage, after a particularly stormy night, we found the boat awash with three inches of water. Then an ice floe drifted in and started to bump against it. At last the wind slackened enough and we were able to get into the boat to bail it.

Then with a clearing of the mist we strode up on to the hills above the Sfinx Brae and bagged an unclimbed peak of no great merit that we called Edzell Tinde. The three mountaineers in the party were worried about Carlos who, for all his great experience, was clearly not at home on rock and ice, and had never worn crampons. Understandably he liked to go off on his own, but we were always anxious until he returned.

On 15 August, the day we should theoretically have been loading our rucksacks for the march to Borg Tinde, the wind dropped. The inflatable, *Rubba Dan*, was left at Kap Russell together with a depot of food and fuel. The pack had withdrawn and we had a fast journey in a heavy swell to the peninsula of Manby Halvö. This was more like it! We lunched at some delightful little islands and watched a Gyr falcon do its routine search for food. Rounding the peninsula on clear water, we crossed Deichmann's Fjord, and entered the channel between Turner Island and the mainland, only to be stopped by dense pack. By now my theory of a passage between the shore and ice had been shot to pieces. Withdrawing, we scouted the seaward side, but again were brought to a halt by impenetrable ice. Retreating again we anchored in a superb lush bay. For the moment Greenland was as we liked to imagine it. Next day we tried again. The wind was in the east and ice was more pressed in than ever. We waited to see if the tide cycle would loosen things up, but no luck. We retreated to Turner Island channel where we encountered a walrus. This event starkly revealed our differing attitudes and experience. Carlos was all for approaching the beast, camera in hand. The rest of us, imagining it rearing up and popping its tusks over the gunwale, were all for heading in the opposite direction as fast as possible. After all, it weighed as much as the loaded boat. Carlos grabbed the tiller. Iain grabbed it back. A row ensued and I took the opportunity to head the boat away as fast as the engine would take us. Allan snapped a shaky photo. Shortly after we found a superb little bay, free of ice, backed by the sort of tundra a good Greenland valley should have. Beyond, through a gap, was a fine mountain. It was time to be mountaineers again so, carrying some bivvy gear, we crossed Stenos Brae and bagged a modest virgin peak of 4,933 feet, which we named MacDhui in recognition of its pudding shape.

Back at camp we found that Carlos had not wasted his time. In the course of a five-and-a-half-mile scour of the coast he had come upon some large boat timbers with eight-inch wrought-iron nails attached and a stern post six feet high. Was this from the *Lilloise*? If so, should there not be other signs, like human skeletons and primitive shelters. Though we searched we found none. The wood was later shown to be pine. Though enquiries were made at British, Danish and French nautical museums, no data with regard to the *Lilloise* came to light. In the absence of a more thorough examination of the coast by a properly equipped scientific expedition nothing more can be said. These timbers might, after all, be from some eighteenth-century whaler which, like many, never returned to home.

On 19 August the ice cleared from the Turner channel letting us enter Römer Fjord. Stopping to get a perspective on the pack ice beyond we stumbled on an Inuit village, long abandoned, with hot springs gushing water at 58°C supporting a flora never usually seen this far north. These were new finds. To me, as the person responsible for the expedition financing, this discovery was a godsend. At least we had something to report that was newsworthy.

Later analyses of the hot springs revealed significant amounts of iron, titanium, manganese, magnesium and aluminium and, of course, silicon. The sites of several winter houses were discernible, of which two were clearly visible. These were built into the ground just where flat ground sloped into the hillside. Although much overgrown, the entrance tunnels could be clearly seen and in one house a niche was identifiable on an inside wall. The houses were squarish, about 6 x 6 feet, not much larger than a three-man tent. Carlos found a tiny flint. It was extremely sharp and was later identified in Copenhagen as being associated with the Inuit migration southward from Independence Fjord 4,000 years ago.

Naturally, we could not rake around. This must be left to professional archaeologists. But it does add something to solving the history of the various Inuit migrations. It was already known that a northward migration had been traced as far as latitude 77°N. This new find might help to determine how far south had come the eastward migration originating from Qaanaaq that rounded the top of Greenland. Until our discovery, the most southerly site of the southward migration had been at Zachenberg, 3° further north. At this point Allan Petit saved the expedition's mountaineering pretensions by a solo climb of a fine virgin peak which he named Guthrie Tinde.

It was now 21 August. Flakes of new ice already lay on the surface of the sea each morning. It was time to head home. Carlos Ziebell was booked on the ship leaving Ittoqqortoormiit on 2 September, while the rest of us had a passage reserved on a flight out of Mesters Vig, 200 miles further to the north on 7 September. Another cogent reason to get out of the pack was the state of the *Scotto Dan*'s prow. It had been so far shaved by the ice as to have lost one of its two inches! Another half inch and the copper nails would start popping out.

The way north, which had been ice-free a few days before, was now blocked. With difficulty we forced a passage through the ice-choked Deichmann's Fjord and camped on the Manby Peninsula. Next morning I ascended a nearby hill to scan the fjord for a way through. I could see a promising lead and hastened down. We swiftly decamped. Looking back we saw a polar bear sauntering to the very hilltop I had just vacated! With four people and one rifle our policy was that it should remain where it could protect the greatest number, hence the rifle on this occasion had remained in camp. A polar bear can move at 30 mph, so fleeing is fruitless. But like other sorts of bears it does not necessarily want to pounce on you. It may depend on how hungry it is, or your attitude. There is the case of the person on an expedition led by Geoffrey Halliday, the botanist, who had left the party to relieve his bowels. Squatting on the tundra he looked up to see a polar bear scrutinising him. The bear twitched its nose, clearly disliking the smell emanating from the human, turned around and ambled off.

Three days later we rounded Kangikajik in a rising wind that turned into a three-day blizzard. The Inuit at Kangikajik took us in and we spent much of the time exchanging language. However, they kept their huts so hot we had difficulty sleeping. The storm abated on the 27th. The grim, black basalt of Volquart Boons Kyst was now covered by a brilliant mantle of snow down to the fjord edge. As we sped back across the Sund, now almost free of pack ice, we had our last contretemps. The *Rubba Dan* was attached to the *Scotto Dan* by a towrope and had its engine running. We were all in the wooden boat, myself at the bow. We were in mid-fjord when Iain called out 'Fire!'. The engine on *Rubba Dan* was in flames. I realised we had seconds only to save the boat. As if propelled by a rocket I ran the length of the *Scotto Dan* and using that momentum leapt the eight or so feet to the inflatable. A moment's rational thought and I would never have tried such a jump. With my hands I scooped up water onto the burning engine. Meanwhile Iain was offering the good advice that water merely spreads a petrol fire. He was right, but what else was to be done? I managed to douse the flames and we duly rigged a new petrol pipe.

At Ittoqqortoormitt we were entertained like conquering heroes, which we were not. After warm farewells Carlos took ship for home, the rest of us took off again on the *Scotto Dan*. Our plan was to walk up the Schuichart strath that Iain and I had walked in 1958. In two days we reached Gurraholm, having covered 120 miles. Oh, that the outer coast had been like this. Another year, another try? Alan was keen to do so. There now remained a 100-mile walk to Mesters Vig over country that Iain and I knew well. The Arctic Riviera was restored. The colours were magnificent, the going easy. Out of nowhere a helicopter from the Danish Geological Expedition swooped down upon us and offered a free lift 25 miles up the valley: taken with gratitude. As I stepped out the Swiss pilot gave me his card.

And so we retreated in good order. As Iain remarked, it is a great mistake to tell the world about your objective until you get home. The International Mt Mikkelsen Expedition was a failure. However, had we waited until we got home, we could have called it the Römer Fjord Archeological Expedition and basked in its success. Looking back, as all four of us have, the risks we took were rather great. There's no trap like the one you set yourself. Several times we were lucky. I have never been happy with an adventure whose outcome depends too much on luck. Iain Smart got it off his chest with a brilliant article in the *Scottish Mountaineering Club Journal* entitled 'Pushing the boat out', in which he posed the question of whether what we did was 'constructive boldness or destructive folly'.

The following year Andrew Ross with three companions left Ittoqqortoormitt in a 17-foot twin-hulled fibre-glass speedboat powered by a 45 hp engine. Having excellent open pack and calm weather it took them only four days to make the 280 miles to Wiedemann's Fjord. Ascending by the Kroneberg Brae they made a swift dash for the peak, climbed it, but failed to ascend its final rock tower. Technically speaking, therefore, Borg Tinde is still virgin. But the east Greenland current and the pack is no place for plastic speedboats. On the return they ran out of fuel. They were overtaken by a storm. One of the hulls was breached. They reached shore by the skin of their teeth and had to be rescued at considerable cost. What was worst, from my point of

177

view, was that without my permission Ross had my name printed on his expedition notepaper as patron. I had firmly refused this honour, not having approved of his plans. I was not pleased when the Ministry for Greenland presented me with a bill for £70,000!

NOTES

[1] If anyone thinks this is an exaggeration, see Ernst Hofer's photobook *The Arctic Riviera* (Kummerly & Fry, Berne, 1957).

CHAPTER 12

Two Sides to a Coin

How is it that two people listening to the same weather forecast extract different information from it? It is not therefore too surprising that when two people share an experience their stories differ, sometimes wildly. This is not a case of history being written by the victors. Facts may be 'chiels that winna ding', as Robert Burns put it, but there are many ways of interpreting them. We are victims of our perceptions, moulded no doubt by our characters. Here are three tales in which three friends, with whom I shared high places, saw things differently from me.

THE FINGER OF GOD

My first story concerns an American professor: Ernest Henley. A genial and eminent man in his field, author of many textbooks, he occupied the office next to me in Rio de Janeiro where we were both teaching in a school of engineering. Ernie was middle-aged and balding, but a ferocious tennis player, endowed with a strong competitive spirit. He was a sportsman but not a climber. He viewed the world through cynical eyes. He probably voted Republican. Learning that I was a climber he introduced me to a young Brazilian rock climber, Carlos Costa Ribeiro. He in turn proposed an ascent of a spire of granite they call Dedo de Deus (Finger of God). Ernie decided to come along to watch. It was such a hilarious occasion that I wrote it up for the *SMC Journal*. The editor, Geoff Dutton, smelling discord, invited Henley to send in his version, which was published in the same issue. Both were later published in the 25th anniversary edition of *Ascent*, the journal published by the US Sierra Club. His opening stanza tells the reader at once what his game is:

> Professor Slesser's version of our ascent of the Dedo de Deus
> and how he transformed an old, frayed nylon rope into a case
> of Chivas Regal is badly in need of elaboration.

There is a hint here of duplicity on my part that cannot go unchallenged. The rope was brand new and far from being a case of Chivas Regal, it was a well-known cooking whisky: Dewar's White Label, if I recall. His version continued:

> His overly modest account of what must surely be acclaimed as
> the 'rope trick of the year' hardly makes him out to be the rogue
> and blackguard he really is. Indeed, the true saga of how a
> feeble, middle-aged, New York cliff dweller whose previous
> highest ascent had been to the top of the Empire State Building
> (in an elevator) found himself nearly strangled . . . may serve as
> a deterrent to other novice climbers.

However, I was not to know that one day these calumnies were to be heaped upon me as, ensconced in Ernie's luxurious Chrysler, I watched him skilfully negotiate the hairpin bends on the road that gives access to the 6,000-foot-high Serra dos Orgãos that form such a magnificent backdrop to Rio, one of the most dramatic cities in the world. As dawn was breaking we parked by a shrine, aware of the sounds of birds and animals in the slowly awakening forest. The granite finger could be seen poking through the forest canopy 3,000 feet above. It was my first foray into jungle, and my fears were not of the climb but of Cor de Rosa snakes, anacondas and poisonous toads. Shamelessly I let the others scramble through the undergrowth ahead of me to frighten off these venomous beasties. An hour or more of climbing through vegetation at a 45° angle brought us to the first rocks; a sebaceous groove set amongst festering vegetation with 100-foot-high trees still towering above us. 'We leave sacks here,' commanded Carlos, whose black hair and burning eyes gave him the air of a youthful Che Guevara. For all he was a student with two professors in tow, Carlos was very much in command.

Ernie wore his hunting boots, no doubt Abercrombie & Fitch's best – the professor was not short of a penny or two. Carlos did not consider a rope necessary yet, and we overcame the groove by grabbing the roots of a once noble Ipé tree that had fallen asleep and never wakened. Thereafter, thanks to tufts of vegetation lodged in the intercises of a series of granite slabs, we made height. I thought Ernie was pretty game for a New York cliff dweller. When I caught up with the others they were sitting on a plinth of rock gazing at the majestic final 1,000 feet of the east face of this formidable obelisk. It appeared to be composed of four vast detached pieces of rock, which, like some child's puzzle, had been reassembled in the shape of a spire, no doubt by God. Ernie had now ascended close on 2,000 vertical feet, mostly on his fingers and was knackered. He had probably never exerted himself so much. What neither he nor I knew was that Carlos was leading us towards a rarely climbed Grade IV route whose crux was an artificial pitch, rejoicing in the name Maria Cebolla. The origin of this curious name, for *cebolla* means onion in Spanish, was never explained. At this point Carlos produced for the professor's use a pair of *alpogados*, rope-soled shoes once common in the Pyrénées, but definitely out of fashion. According to Ernie's later account in the *SMC Journal* he had planned to rest here, read *Red Peak* (excellent choice, if I may say so), and consume a picnic of Beaujolais and roast chicken. Curiously none of this he mentioned to us at the time, though we observed his rucksack seemed uncommonly bulky considering he had no climbing equipment nor need for warm clothing. We roped up and, led by Carlos, ascended rock so smooth that it was like solidified syrup. There were no belay points. Our security lay entirely in tree roots that over the centuries had somehow gained a foothold in the granite's blind cracks. On one occasion I found Carlos belayed to an agave cactus, so tenuously adhering to the rock that I was able to lift it free with one hand! I cannot better Ernie's own account of the subsequent proceedings:

> The procedure was roughly as follows. Ribeiro would shimmy gracefully up a crevice or tree, and then fix a rope so I could pull myself up. My legs never touched the side of the mountain. I was, however, making good use of my knees and elbows, which were a bloody mess. I do not know how Slesser negotiated the climb because whenever I reached Ribeiro, I collapsed in a soggy heap. No one was paying any attention to me at all. Slesser was alternately complimenting Ribeiro on his artistry as a climber and then berating him for his complete disregard for safety precautions.

Continuing the climb with my version:

> We reached a cave and thankfully crawled into the shade. Out right under an overhang I saw the first of several bolts . . . The rock being holdless. This was the famous Maria Cebolla.

At this point Ernie's eye for detail was superior to mine. He wrote:

> The *jeito* [trick] for reaching the open face was to crawl along the branch of a small tree. If done properly, the tree bends and drops you against the side of the cliff, whereon is fastened an iron spike. As you clutch the spike and pull yourself out onto a barely perceptible ledge, the tree moves away from you; it is literally a point of no return unless one is wearing a parachute. It was an ideal place to settle down with my remaining bottle of wine and book. Why didn't I? . . . When I proposed that I stay and wait for the two protagonists . . . I was vetoed. I became an unwilling participant in an Olympic event.

I tried to explain to the professor that one does not abandon one's companion in the middle of a cliff. Meanwhile, Carlos had executed the tricky traverse and was out of sight and high above. The wind distorted communication. The rope tightened on Ernie. I urged him onto the smooth slab. He then announced he had neither the strength nor inclination to continue and would go down. Informed of this Carlos slackened the rope whereupon the hapless Ernie slid wildly to the right (outwards). 'What do I do?' he shouted to me. 'Impossible to get back,' I replied encouragingly. With a tight rope and a great deal of immoderate grunting, to his eternal credit, Ernie got up the pitch.

And so to the summit by easier ground, via a final ladder, where we wolfed down Ernie's picnic. It was one hour to dusk: haste was called for. The *voie normale* is a series of easy chimneys with ledges between, but as a tyro, Ernie found climbing down impossibly difficult, so we arranged rappels, a manoeuvre unknown to him. The third rappel was above a void with a sense of exposure exacerbated by the gathering dusk. Ernie, after peering into the gloom, demanded a safety line and my rope was now put in play. I went down first. Carlos offered to belay the professor and come down last. As I wrote:

> I had descended and was enjoying a quiet contemplation of cavorting mists and mysterious walls, when the rasping sound

of Ernie's skin on the rope stopped and he started gurgling badly. The safety line had jammed in a karabiner. I shouted to him to haul himself up on his arms while Carlos freed it, but his arms were done.

'Cut the rope,' he demanded in a high-pitched voice that was not like him at all. Cut the rope! Whoever heard of such a thing! Ernie clearly had no notion of mountain ethics. All encouragement to raise himself momentarily on the abseil rope so that Carlos could free the safety line fell upon unwilling ears. Panic had destroyed rational analysis, something that in the comfort of his study he was particularly good at. How do you put a wounded animal out of its misery? My problem was that I had but one rope with me in Brazil. There were no climbing shops where I might buy a new one, so I demurred.

'Cut the rope. I'll buy you a new one.' They say that people undergoing torture will say anything to even momentarily alleviate the pain. It was not that I didn't believe his goodwill, I just couldn't think where he could buy a new rope. A repetition of this promise uttered in the tearful tones of someone breathing his last left me with no choice, sceptical though I was of his being able to implement it. Carlos cut the safety rope – my rope!

Now the professor's account may only differ marginally in one sense, but in a crudely inappropriate manner in another, for it suggested that my objection to cutting the rope was based on a meanness internationally associated with all those of Scottish (and particularly Aberdonian) origin. It was like suggesting that all Americans are like George W. Bush. He wrote:

> 'Don't you dare,' bellowed Slesser, 'that's my rope. It cost £7'
> . . . I am convinced to this day that had I not offered Slesser a case of Scotch I would still be hanging battered and bruised above the foot of the Dedo de Deus. If Malcolm Slesser saw, as he wrote, that the Finger of God was wagging at him as we left the scene, it was because Deus was saying 'For shame, for shame.'

My article concludes:

> Next day Ernie, a good colleague if there was one, offered to send to New York for a new rope. 'Forget it. Just one of those things.'

183

His cigar smoke penetrated my booth. 'Malcolm, you get whisky?'

'No.' I had no diplomatic privileges, unlike Ernie.

'A case any good to you?'

If the Finger of God wagged at me, I never saw it.

We continue to exchange Christmas cards and insults.

WE TWO OUGHT NOT TO CLIMB TOGETHER

Most climbers have their mates with whom they do all their routes. For a long time, my winter companion was Norman Tennent, who first surfaced in Chapter 1. It was never clear to me whether he climbed with me because he couldn't find anyone else, or whether I was the only person with whom he could exercise his mordant wit without causing offence. He was a small, compact red-head who affected an exaggerated country-gentleman drawl which we learnt to imitate when recounting some of his episodes. There were several reasons why we should not have climbed together. I was warmly attached to life (having made in my time a few mathematical calculations about the forces at work when someone falls off and the problems of holding a falling leader, I was well aware of the procedures required). Tennent, on the other hand, regarded belaying as a ritual: a formal requirement, but as pointless as lighting a candle in the expectation of better weather. He held to what one might describe as the Foreign Guide School of Mountaineering approach: follow me and you'll be all right. Another reason was that he was tough, barely affected by wind, rain or cold. I was a softie. But the third reason was perhaps the most significant. He liked to shift responsibility for decisions onto others. So when we met, whether by design or chance, I was left to believe I was making the decisions for both of us. On one occasion he wrote:

> Slesser was in good organising form. 'Have you put some more water in the tea?' he cried, munching my wholemeal bread and Oxford marmalade, and tramping his tricounis up and down over my fankled rope. Ten years in the catering trade has taught me never to argue with a difficult customer. Without mentioning that I wanted coffee, I fell to musing about this Man of Destiny with whom I was associated, and this place to which we were drawn irresistibly every winter.

Our first winter ascent of the South Post of Creag Meagaidh was very much in this vein. We had camped up the glen just beyond the last trees, in sight of both Loch Laggan and the Post face of Coire Ardair. It was February, but mild. The face was dripping. We had food, a stove and a tent. We lacked a watch, a guidebook and any specific idea of what to climb. As I wrote later in an article for the *SMC Journal*:

> Tennent, his deep-seated whimsicality ripened by good wine, adroitly parried my suggestions. Finally, ordering whisky and gazing fondly into its amber depths, he muttered 'You're the boss' and refused to discuss the matter further.

This was no more than a cunning ruse. I am now quite sure he had decided exactly where and what we were going to climb. As he went on to write:

> I had not seen many birthdays when I bought my first *Journal* [*SMC Journal*]. It contained a long account of Dr Bell's Coire Ardair explorations. I doubt if Chapman's Homer opened up more to Keats. Soon afterwards I discovered that wonderful men in Norfolk jackets with long ice axes really existed. Their reserve and obviously assumed reticence about Coire Ardair drove me nearly frantic . . . And now Slesser. I don't care if we are old fashioned; we climb for the pleasure we seem to find in each other's company despite everything, and whether we succeed or fail.

You see what I mean! It was to some extent the old problem of the two cultures, so well told in C.P. Snow's novels. I was scientifically trained, with the inevitable tendency to analyse and enumerate. Tennent, though he had been a submariner during the Second World War and was presumably pretty clued up in handling complicated technology, was innumerate, deliberately, obstinately so, and indifferent to money, which he spent so generously that eventually he had none left. He read literature and was forever dropping nuggets of Shakespeare and quotations from the works of other literary giants into his everyday speech. It was a bit like climbing with a *Guardian* literary critic. I felt quite out of my depth being uneducated in the classical sense.

We camped for two nights, waiting out the thaw. We played chess, at which we were evenly matched, using matchsticks as pieces on a roughly scored sheet of paper. Typical of the man, just when it looked as if I might at last checkmate his king, he sneezed. The lightweight pieces flew into the air. I was familiar with this insouciant approach to defeat. The third day dawned crisp and frosty, and first light saw us at the foot of the cliffs. I knew nothing of what had been climbed beyond the Centre Post. Our equipment, by the standards of today, was laughable: no crampons; one steel ice piton (if one can ascribe such a grand description to a piece of iron with a few notches at one end and a welded ring at the other); an ice axe each; and one slater's hammer with a sling attached. I was skilfully manoeuvred by my companion towards the foot of the South Post. The brief overnight frost had not been enough to harden the initial icefall, but by moving a short height up Easy Gully Tennent reckoned there was a way to traverse in above the icefall. He led across frozen turf to the frost-hardened névé of the steep couloir itself. Four hundred feet of step-cutting ensued to the next ice pitch. He wrote:

> Its [the climb's] dream-like quality was not diminished later by reading his [Slesser's] account in the *Journal*. It seemed a pity that I had not been able to publish my version alongside; and then – surprise! – to divulge that both described the same climb. I remember Slesser's magnificent long lead up vertical and overhanging snow, of the sort supposedly only found on the south side of the Andes . . . He recalls nothing but hard crisp conditions. Only when water squirted up his sleeve at a blow from his axe did he consider the wisdom of proceeding, long after I knew we had burned our boats. He saw an eagle circling above; but I think we were being eyed speculatively by common carrion eaters. We were in agreement, however, at that moment we took to be our last, in thinking that bomber which suddenly roared overhead was an avalanche.

Our ignorance of Creag Meagaidh's history also led to our climbing Staghorn Gully, believing it to be a first ascent. That it was not changed nothing, for we enjoyed all the excitement that goes with exploring unknown territory. A rising shelf brings you onto the north face, from which a gully gives access to the summit plateau – it is guarded by two short ice pitches. Tennent led the first and I embarked on the second. I was 30 feet up my pitch when, looking round, I saw that he had put aside the rope and was photographing me. I felt distinctly exposed. Remember, we were climbing without crampons, cutting steps, so one's adhesion to ice was tenuous and one tired quickly. I was most irritated. This is how Tennent reported the incident:

I was smiling happily and, I thought encouragingly, up at Slesser, who laid into the ice with mighty blows. He seemed to grow out from the side of the gully like a tree above a river. For a time all went well. Then he happened to stop and look down. 'Put that camera away!' he roared. Then, 'Which arm is the rope belayed around?'

'Both,' I replied.

Next moment his axe flashed down past my nose like a thunderbolt from Jove, to stick in the névé below. [It is unlikely I would part with my only security!] When Slesser himself descended, terrible in his wrath, the rope was round both my arms and my neck as well. I was made to ascend the pitch; not too difficult a task as the step cutting was nearly done.

'I happen to take these things seriously,' he said.

On a later occasion we thought to climb the Centre Post. We were now equipped with crampons. The conditions were foul, up top a howling gale. Tennent again:

I cut one or two steps, gingerly tried them, and then returned to where Slesser was ensconced.

'What's the matter?' he asked.

I thought the question unnecessary. He only had to look at me. In descending a few feet I had turned my head to see the steps below. Ice had instantly sealed my right eye, and my cheek felt like mutton from a deep freeze. 'Windy,' I said.

He was not satisfied, and set out to try the right traverse. It took a prolonged session of brainwashing in the cascade of powder snow and spindrift to weaken his determination. But even then he had been anchored on the face for some time before I launched my appeal. I told him about a Catalonian recipe for which I had the ingredients and then he said: 'What about lots of coffee, our sleeping bags and a game or two of chess?' Then, lowering himself down, he added, 'We ought not to climb together. We are both sybarites.'

Sadly my friend Norman is dead. I enormously miss the cut and thrust we shared.

ONE OF US IS NOT ONE OF US

Iain Smart, whom I have known for half a century, is the sort of friend who gives you the excoriating criticism that your enemies would hesitate about. On one occasion we sat side by side watching the slides of someone relating their recent experiences in Greenland, during the annual bun-fight at the Scottish Arctic Club. 'Remember Ruth Island?' he whispered. I could not. 'What,' he said, a trifle impatiently, as if yet again having to deal with my incipient senility, 'is the point of doing these things if you don't remember them?' What could I say? He was right.

My excuse, which I kept to myself, was that this had been a trip that had been less than perfect in terms of human relationships. I must have subconsciously wiped from my memory all but the salient points. It had been a boat trip to reach and then climb Peterman Peak (73°05'N), a 10,000-foot-high summit, cradled deep within the vast fjords of north-east Greenland. The peak had already been climbed twice.

It was only ten years later when I read Smart's retrospective account of that trip that I fully understood how it was that five perfectly likeable people alone in a wilderness, each of which respected the others, found the thickness of two tent walls enough to separate them into two distant groups. His account is pure poetry. It deserves to be widely read, if only as good writing. He starts:

> Madeira wine improves in flavour when carried around the world in the hold of a ship. So is the memory of a good expedition if allowed to rock around for a few years in the bottom of your mind . . . The immediate account . . . is the new wine drunk fresh from the bottle, sparkling and youthful . . . As expeditions go it was a good vintage and what follows is a flagon drawn from a cask ten years later.

He, however, drew from a different cask than me. Had ten years dulled his memory or had he been oblivious to the undercurrents? The answer, I now realised, lay in the fact that one of us had not been quite one of us, as Margaret Thatcher would have put it, and that that particular person enjoyed special favours. Qualifications for membership of the Peterman trip were rudimentary. You had to have enough money to pay your whack, a modest record of competence and be compatible with Iain Smart. This did not, of course, mean that each one of us was compatible with the others. We were far too mature a bunch to let this visibly surface, but the fact was that within hours of departure this schism emerged.

Here is Iain's description of our group:

> Pat was a man of many talents: an internationally acclaimed birdsong recordist . . . possessor of vast stores of arcane lore. Roland was superbly fit and utterly competent . . . without him and Phil we geriatrics would never have made it.

Phil was a software creator, a consultant to Sony and other big corporations who sent their staff to learn at his feet.

Our two accounts do not differ in material respects. The opening stanza of my own version, the new wine drunk fresh from the bottle, is an interpretation constructed immediately after the trip:

> Like all endeavours it started with an urge. For us [Iain and myself], there was the passage of time, and who knew, as Dr Smart so picturesquely put it, when the Grim Reaper might bear down upon us. Smart, whose brilliant exploration career had been enhanced by the skilful avoidance of any organisational chores on the specious grounds that he was incompetent, had, as a result of a rare misplaced move in the chess game that precedes all expeditions, found himself in the role of leader and organiser. Always a devolutionist, he practised what he preached, and from his eyrie in Glen Shee maintained contact with his lieutenants. Once after a happy day on the hill and his generous offer of a pint and a large malt, he had elicited from me an unintentional off-the-cuff offer to 'do' the food and be the treasurer. I had forgotten about it by the second dram. Not Smart. I had written down some figures on a beer mat, and Smart, pocketing it, later used it as evidence of my acceptance of both roles. One has to be up very early to get the better of Dr Smart.

The game plan was to make use of a sizeable inflatable boat powered by two 40 hp outboard engines left at Mesters Vig (72°13'N) by the polar explorer Wally Herbert at the conclusion of his attempt to circumnavigate Greenland. We flew to the airstrip, inflated the boats and set forth for the 140 miles to the head of Kejser Franz Josephs Fjord, from which point the peak was accessible by foot. By day three of our voyage we had made exactly three miles, for the winter pack ice was still pretty firm. We took refuge on tiny Ran Island near the south shore of Kong Oscars Fjord. Smart describes it eloquently:

> The pack drifted to and fro with the tide but didn't loosen. The island, meanwhile, started to make itself felt. It was a colourful, intricate place . . . It was like living on the palette of an artist confident with primary colours and bold forms. From the centre of the magic island the outside world was invisible except for the bright, blue sky . . . A peace began to descend on the mind . . . A month here would be an interesting educational experience. This led to questions. Was all this desire for movement merely an excuse to avoid thinking? Were we missing the point? We had maps of everything ahead of us, aerial photographs too; others had been this way before. Were we passing the time playing a hands-on computer game in real time in a sort of actual reality instead of trying to do something original? This island suggested there were unexplored territories on offer to a mind not preoccupied with movement. Intellectual vistas on the other side of the backdrop of the apparent scenery kept opening up for attention. This would never do; people [the rest of the crew!] were fidgeting and pacing restlessly. We were getting nowhere fast . . . As we loaded the boat I had a wild urge to throw out a few food boxes and say: 'Pick me up on your way back.' If I had, I might have done some original journey into wild and wonderful new territory. It was very tempting to snatch such an opportunity for original exploration but, alas, I had not the strength of character to bring off so bold an action . . . I had to go. I was supposed to be the leader.

I knew Smart well enough to guess at his thoughts. We were all captivated by the setting of Ran Island. We had no motive for moving towards our stated objective other than that it had been the collective reason for us coming together in this spot. Yet we had only ourselves to please. We had no media contract, no grants from any exploration fund to satisfy. We were too old to need to be seen to be successful; we already enjoyed that reputation. As Smart put it we were playboys of the Western world. But when a group is gathered together for a stated objective such as robbing a bank or climbing a mountain, somehow the objective takes over even if it begins to seem unwise. And so, with our leader's mind far away, we put-putted our way at five knots along the superhighway of fjords, a most beautiful and memorable journey the like of which none of us had ever experienced. The last section within Kejser Franz Josephs Fjord itself had us spellbound and put our nerves on edge. Fifteen miles inwards from Kap Payer the sides rose 5,000 feet, sheer out of the water, literally sheer – the first step ashore would have been a rock climb; there was not a hint of refuge anywhere. We prayed that there would be no glacier calving sending down a tidal wave, nor a katabatic wind to create a dangerous sea, for we were sorely overloaded. In fact we experienced both events on the way back.

The great fjord ends (or more correctly starts) where the Nordenskiölds Glacier, draining the ice cap, enters. Its history is told in hundreds of icebergs great and small jostling for space in the confined waters of the inner fjord. Four miles from the snout we set up our base camp at the mouth of the arid and dreary Knæk Elven. Here the five of us fissioned into two camps, two to one tent, three to the other and, with little communication, ferried loads up the valley, crossed the river and continued up Knæk Dalen until we had a sufficient dump of food, fuel and gear at the foot of the Gregory Glacier that led to the base of Peterman. We were under Gog and Magog, claimed by N.E. Odell of Everest fame, though no cairn was found on the summit.

This far north the Greenland Arctic is a desert in which a sandy surface can lie undisturbed for years. I was intrigued by paw marks which looked to be those of wolves. I resolved to protect our camp, since they might eat our supplies while we were up on the hill. I had recently read Farley Mowat's *Never Cry Wolf* in which he used the Inuit trick of making a ring of urine around the camp. Apparently the wolves understand that this territory is out of bounds to them. This idea was greeted with mirth and derision by my companions, and I was left to fill my bladder with litres of tea and pee away on my own.

The Gregory Glacier proved my undoing. The dry ice surface soon gave way to breakable crust. We had heavy sacks and in an involuntary movement my back gave way, leaving me in great pain. A tent was pitched and I lay down inside. Outside, my four companions could be heard indulging in a heartless discussion, of which I had difficulty in distinguishing between serious suggestions and a tendency to tease me. After some hours I needed a pee and with help managed to get to my feet. To my surprise I found the pain much diminished. Roland Zeyen, my Luxembourger friend with whom I shared a tent, nobly took a huge chunk of my load. He was 25 years younger than me. There comes a time for older mountaineers when it is wise to have some younger strength in the party! I was left to hirple on behind the others, who rapidly disappeared up the glacier.

Two days later we camped at the base of the peak at 5,500 feet. It was a pyramid 4,500 feet above us, rising from the plinth of a flat glacier. The younger pair would try a new line, the north-east ridge. Iain and Pat would take the known, easy south-east ridge as Pat was not a climber. I morosely watched them set off. An hour later, desperate again for a pee, I rolled over on my stomach, got onto all fours, crept of out the tent as if I was about to say my prayers at Mecca and with the support of my ice axe managed, like an ageing dromedary, to get off my knees and onto my feet. As I watched their progress up the lower ice slopes, very slow in the case of Iain and Pat, my ego was sorely afflicted. My mind turned back to the last time my back had so tortured me and how I had been cured. I had been returning to my base in Italy with my family via the San Bernardino pass on a winter's day. The children wanted to ski at Splügen, a very plain, but delightful, resort frequented by working-class Swiss. Its simple facilities made it Switzerland's answer to Meall a'Bhuridh. I ached miserably sitting in the car. It was snowing gently. In desperation I put skins on my skis and gingerly slid up through the woods. To my amazement, after about ten minutes my back began to loosen up. The pain subsided little by little. At the end of an hour it felt no worse than it might have after carrying a heavy rucksack all day. Recovery was so complete that I was able to ski down in good style. It's a recovery technique that has worked every time since! The key is to walk uphill – never on the flat. Now was the time to put it to use again. Methodically, I assembled my gear. Bending to lace my boots and strap on crampons was pure hell. Iain and Pat were now up the initial ice slope and out of sight. With ski pole and ice axe I turned myself into the quadruped hillwalker now to be seen everywhere on our native hills. To my joy each uphill step seemed to ease my back. The end of the tale is that I caught up with the others and made the summit.

Once back at base, unmolested by wolves thanks, I argued, to my circle of urine, the party which had briefly coalesced upon the summit fissioned into its component parts. Quoting Smart again:

> Phil was wont to tootle endlessly on his penny whistle as he
> worked out in his mind the next decisions in his life. The
> tootlings were semi-competent renderings of folk tunes. One
> day Roland picked up the whistle and played exquisitely a
> fragment of Mozart with all the twiddly bits. He then put the

whistle down and made no further comment. Phil seemed to miss the point and continued tootling unabashed.

Leading an expedition with Slesser in it is a complicated business. Things have to be stratified into several levels with minimal intermixing. Occasionally leaks occur . . . At one time I heard him remark with some irritation: 'There are decisions being taken in this expedition that I don't know about.'

The mountain was worthy only in terms of its height and the superb Arctic environment. The ridge we climbed was a crappy moderate. But on its summit we were the highest point for 600 miles to the south and nothing higher stood between us and the North Pole. The view over the undulating ice cap to scattered nunataks was limited only by the curvature of the earth. The very banality of the mountaineering was possibly why the esprit de corps of the expedition had not cemented. It was the price one paid for undertaking a climb where the outcome was virtually preordained. It was not a real adventure. Only some stupid error or far-fetched bit of bad luck could have prevented a successful ascent. Moreover it was a second-hand peak. Each of us had an aesthetic appreciation of the setting and journey, but we should have been making it at our own pace unencumbered by the minds of others.

CHAPTER 13

Skiing Rough

Once, in his early days, Dougal Haston set off to climb the north face of the Grands Jorasses in winter. He never even got to the foot of the face because he couldn't ski. For a long time, skiing was regarded as degenerate by the mountaineering fraternity – something for your old age, like boating or golf. It is now accepted that away from the manicured slopes of a resort, skiing can offer a new and exciting dimension to mountaineering. Just as the climber seeks a rock face of technical difficulty and character, so the mountaineer turned skier is drawn to a summit, the ascent and descent of which couples the skill of the skier with that of the Alpinist with the added thrill of speed. Here is one domain where the individual is free to move at his or her desired pace, unrestricted by signs, regulations and speed cameras.

Controlling planks attached to your feet is not a technique that comes naturally to the body, for the essence of the craft is to be able to transfer the kinetic energy of your moving body to the two skis in such a way as to make them go where you want them to, carrying you with them. It takes time to learn. Whereas from the time we start walking as infants we learn to cope with a huge variety of surfaces, snow challenges us with an even greater variety. It may be a dream-like surface, as when there is a veneer of dry powder snow on a hard surface which almost any beginner can cope with, to, at other extremes, crusted snow, wet snow, deep snow, heavy snow, frozen névé, snow on grass, steep snow, rutted snow or, worst of all, sastrugi. The variation is tremendous and each type calls for its own specific technique. Indeed recognising the nature of snow texture as one is moving swiftly is a further necessary skill development. So let's not be too hard on the young Haston, who later became a very accomplished skier.

I was chewing over this topic with Bill Wallace as we stood in the queue for the Aiguille des Grands Montets *télécabine* at Argentière. Like many mountaineers, he and I had taken up skiing when we became family men, our long-suffering offspring goaded into sliding down the slippery slopes in all weathers, poor little things, so that we could still enjoy our mountains while pretending to be responsible fathers. Bill had developed his skills in tandem with expanding his mountaineering experience, becoming a very respectable ski racer. Built like a rugby forward, he was an elegant but aggressive skier: I have broken ski sticks to prove it.

In front of us in the queue was a French guide with his English client. 'With modern equipment,' explained the guide, 'anyone can cope on the piste. It's skiing off-piste that separates the men from the boys.'

'A bit like investing,' said the Englishman. 'Any fool can make money in a bull market.'

The guide nodded, smiling. Unlike his client he had no money to invest. He took each day as it came and like the stockbroker charged steeply for his services.

Like us, the guide and his client were taking the lazy way to the Argentière glacier by skiing off the back of the Montets. It's the way the penniless young Haston might have taken had he had the skill and the price of a ticket. The Argentière is a great setting and the starting point for some delightful and not too demanding Alpine ski ascents like the Tour Noir, the Aiguille Argentière or the Trient plateau by the '*trois cols*'. The most popular route is to climb on skins to the Col du Passon from which there is a superb 5,000-foot descent of the Glacier de Tour to the hamlet of Le Tour. It is steep in places and crevassed enough to require caution. If you are young, fit, brave and able, you can turn the other way and crampon up the Couturier Couloir on the Aiguille Verte with skis strapped to your back before skiing back down its 50° slope.

The guide would have had more to say. Deep, cold, powder snow with firm downhill boots and the broad 'fat boy' skis is magical and, for the experienced piste skier, not much more demanding than an early morning piste manicured to velvet by the overnight pistie-beastie. But up on the raw mountainside within the space of a few metres snow can vary enormously; crust, wind-slab, ice, powder, névé, sog, porridge, even treacle. And since the steeper the slope the greater the thrill, there is the abiding risk of avalanche to be considered and, on glaciers, the insidious snare of lightly bridged crevasses. All this adds up to make ski-mountaineering every bit as intellectually and physically demanding as high-level mountaineering. The brothers Claude and Phillipe Traynard, who wrote one of the earliest and best ski-mountaineering guides to the Alps, classified ski-mountaineering routes from *facile* to *trés bon skier Alpin*. In this latter category one must be able to turn where the terrain demands, handle any snow texture, descend 50° slopes and not fall. Those who are lured by the initial gentle slopes of the popular Vallée Blanche from the top station of the Aiguille du Midi find themselves suddenly in *tres bon skier Alpin* territory as they grapple with the gaping crevasses and ice bosses of the Géant Iccfall.

Visibility plays an enormous role, for if the eye cannot read the texture of the snow, the body cannot play its part. Worst of all is mist, especially after snowfall. Sky and snow merge, indistinguishably. One loses all sense of location. It is blindman's-buff. One cannot tell up from down. It is quite common to fall over thinking one has stopped. It's an eerie feeling and potentially dangerous. I know of an experienced guide who broke an ankle under such circumstances. On a big snowfield or glacier in mist without a single rock in sight the disorientation is utterly bewildering. Making a compass course is almost impossible since one has to watch both compass and the ground in front of the ski tips. The procedure if there are two or more in the party is for one person to move forward probing the snow, while the second remains stationary with compass in hand and by shouted instruction guides the leader in the appropriate direction. At the limit of the stationary person's visibility the leader is told to stop. The person behind then skis past and takes over the lead. By such alternation a measure of safety and a correct direction can be maintained. The more skiers in the party the better this works, especially on the downhill. Say there are four. When the rear person comes to ski, he or she has three 'posts' to relate to before passing to the lead.

Let me tell you two true tales.

Two of us were skiing off the summit of Tom a'Choinich above Glen Affric in the West Highlands of Scotland. It was flattering spring snow, but a mist had drifted in. However, we knew there were no crags, so we boldly slalomed down what we thought was our uphill track. I was in front, my friend behind, followed by my dog Fergus. I felt an unusual and sustained lightening of my skis. I did not realise I was airborne until with a massive thump I hit a steep slope, turned into the hill and fell, unharmed. Glancing up I saw my companion in mid-air. Such faith in my route-finding! She badly wrenched her ankle. As we collected ourselves the mist cleared to reveal that a cornice had built up on a steep edge. We must have flown 50 feet at least due to the speed with which we had taken off. The black nose of the hound peered over the cornice and quickly withdrew. He refused to join us.

I witnessed the consequences of a much grimmer event in the Maritime Alps of France. Our party of three, consisting of myself, Allan Petit and Bill Wallace, all dedicated salvationists, were making a ski tour from the south to the north, hut to hut, taking in peaks. These hills are a wonderful ski touring terrain with rugged peaks but with no glaciers and therefore no crevasses to worry about. We had left the Refuge des Merveilles in doubtful conditions; high clouds, settling lower. A damp *föhn* wind funnelled up the valley and already there was dew forming on the spiculae of the snow crystals. Bad sign. Our objective was the little hamlet of Boréon where there was reputedly a comfortable gîte. Our proposed route would take us over the modest peak of the Cîme de l'Agnellière at 8,852 ft (2699 m). It was a steep climb on skins, but without any technical difficulty. Soon the clouds were down around us. The thaw penetrated upwards faster than we ascended making for heavy going on increasingly soggy snow. Our ridge narrowed and the perspective diminished. Eventually there were no more rocks to give a sense of location. We were uncharted objects in space–time, like charcoal drawings without a frame. We knew that the slope to our right fell steeply towards the valley of the Madonna de Fenêstre, to which we planned to descend. What with the narrow ridge, the big drop and zero visibility we roped up for safety – just as well, for a little later Bill, in the lead, stepped into space. We hauled him back onto terra firma, and with minimal discussion strapped our skis to our sacks and retreated to the valley to find a nice little gîte with a roaring fire and abundant grog.

Next day it was still warm and humid. We telephoned for a taxi to meet us at the bottom of the valley and took it round to Boréon. The place was alive with police, *pompiers* and ambulances. We were told that six Swiss students had descended the very route we had intended and had been avalanched. All six had perished. This is an unimaginably awful death. If your face is buried, you cannot breathe – the wet snow congeals to grip you like setting concrete. One is as surely wrapped up in a cocoon of snow as the fly in the spider's web. Since there were no survivors it was not certain whether they themselves had triggered the avalanche or whether it had silently descended upon them from above. Whatever the case, had they chosen to ski widely apart, as they should have, some would have survived and others would have been there to dig them out.

So what's the lure of ski-mountaineering when there is so much potential danger? In the first place snow-covered mountains have an irresistible picture postcard appeal, impelling you to get in amongst them. In deep snow, skis make access more feasible. One can get there faster than a walker on the way up and very, very much faster on the way down. I once took my teenage children, Morag and Calum, up the Piz Albigna in the Italian Engadine on a June morning, rising before dawn. The 3,000-foot ascent took 3 hours from the hut. We reached the top just as the sun had started to thaw the névé. The descent on glorious spring snow took ten minutes! But what a ten minutes!

On a prolonged ski tour there is also the delicious sense of travelling, of constantly meeting fresh vistas. And then there is the technical satisfaction of dealing with varied snow conditions, of making fine judgements, of performing something difficult with aplomb, of leaving one's own unique track in the virgin snow. A touch of hubris there. It may be thought that plodding uphill with the weight of skis on one's feet is a fearful drag, but this is more than compensated for by the rhythm of the slide, slide, slide of the ski.

Today one can be taken to the top of such virgin slopes by helicopter in the USA, Canada, Switzerland and Italy, but not in France. This kind of extreme skiing, where a fall will almost certainly be fatal, has recently become popular. Martin Burrows-Smith has skied Hayfork Gully on An Teallach. Even I (with Bill Wallace) have skied No. 4 Gully on Nevis. Davo Karnicar, a Slovenian, skied down from the south summit of Everest to base camp in five hours! Mt McKinlay (now Denali) has also been descended on ski (carrying the skis up!). Every ski film show now depicts incredible descents, much to be admired. French skiers like Anselme Baud and Patrick Vallençant make a living out of such daredevil acts. I once attended Patrick's video show when he described how he introduced clients to steep skiing. In the video one noviciate was seen to fall, to be swept away by an avalanche out of the picture. Afterwards someone in the audience asked him what had happened to the poor fellow. He shrugged his shoulders in Gallic indifference. These extreme performances have little to do with the adventure of climbing summits on ski as a mountaineer – the satisfaction of getting there under your own steam.

The equipment for ski-mountaineering is inevitably a compromise.

Those skiers you see on film plunging down 55° slopes (the maxium angle at which snow can lie) and creaming off small avalanches, are wearing the best downhill boots that money can buy, broad carving skis and rigid bindings. The slightest nuance of the leg or foot is instantly transmitted to the ski. But you cannot travel through the mountains with such equipment. Flexibility is needed. Nowadays there are step-in bindings, in which the heel can be freed to allow the foot to rise and fall for uphill climbing, and held firm for the descent. The Fritschli Diamir model has virtually cornered the market. The boot is where the compromise mostly lies – it must be flexible and light enough to walk on snowless terrain. Any resort visitor will be familiar with the end-of-the-day scenes of downhill-only skiers hobbling painfully back to their chalets in boots apparently designed for deep-sea diving. Yet the ski-mountaineering boot must be adjustable so as to give adequate support on the descent. Fashions have fluctuated from lightweight floppy boots comfortable to walk in to versions not far different from a regular downhill boot – but heavy. The fact is that a good skier can manage on poor boots, but will do better on good ones. Try walking off the hill wearing those heavy boots! Some of them come so far up the leg that a serious fall can easily cause a tibia fracture. A new class of skier has recently evolved adopting the Norwegian Telemark turn with heel-lift bindings: it's not for the faint-hearted and it requires great suppleness. It is beautiful to watch, but it has its limitations, both as an uphill device and when skiing on very steep hard snow.

Skis have continually evolved as new materials like carbon fibres and kevlar have been developed and new turning techniques have emerged. The compromise here is between a ski that is rigid enough to hold on ice, but flexible enough to handle the deep soft. It took a while for carving skis to make their way into this market, but they are now available, and well worth the money.

The sheer variety of snow surface on the mountain calls for a range of techniques. The elegant short swing will come off – sometimes. Confidence and good technique helps. For those taking up ski-mountaineering for the first time three essential skills must be mastered. The first – to be able to sideslip with full control, both forwards and backwards, on steep hard snow: this can be practised on the piste. You can get out of all sorts of difficult or dangerous situations with a controlled sideslip. Once coming off the Glacier de Trient onto the moraine I had no choice but to sideslip continuously downward for 700 feet. When such a movement gets out of control the lower shoulder slips forward. Never let this happen. Always peer down the slope, with 90 per cent of the weight on the lower ski.

There was one occasion in Scotland when I thought I had overplayed my hand. Three of us had ascended Stob a'Choire Claurigh in the Grey Corries, south of Spean Bridge. This is one of the best ski-mountaineering areas in Scotland, with the famous Vallée Blanche that runs north-west from the summit. The previous day's thaw had been followed by hard frost, providing frozen névé and on the summit ridge a carapace of ice. Nonetheless we elected, on my advice I have to say, to return to the valley by the east ridge and so down to the Larig Leacach. This is a lovely, dramatic route that involves traversing the south-east slopes of Stob Coire na Ceanain just above a cliff. Thus a fall is simply not to be contemplated. The safest way to handle the traverse is by a long controlled forward-moving sideslip. My two companions, though experienced mountaineers, were not yet highly proficient skiers. As we were poised to make the move across, I rehearsed with them the right body position. I crossed over first, finding myself alarmed at how tenuous was my ski's grip on the snow and how difficult it was to maintain control. Once on safe ground I was about to shout, 'Don't come!' when one man launched himself, followed soon by the other. I prayed as I have never prayed before and sent out the strongest telepathic message I could muster. They arrived safely, if, like me, a little pale. I would not like to have had their falls on my conscience.

Incidentally, it was just beyond this point that I once encountered the largest avalanche I have ever seen in Scotland. The whole east face of Stob Coire na Ceanain had slipped down. The resulting avalanche had actually crossed the river and ridden up to the dirt road beyond. There were blocks of ice and snow as large as a car.

The second essential skill is to be able to kick-turn. To bring off such a conversion on a steep slope requires a degree of confidence that only comes with practice. It requires, too, a certain suppleness. I have two skiing friends with hip replacements. They are forbidden on doctor's orders to kick-turn! But then they are told not to ski anyhow.

Thirdly, *never* adopt a stem turn (often called a snowplough turn) in deep snow. It is the one manoeuvre most likely to result in a broken leg; not good news on a remote mountain. The safest way is feet always together, though a stem-christie is permissible. I have never known anyone to break a leg while parallel skiing. The snow plough manoeuvre as a means of slowing down is useful on a narrow path, but can be extremely tiring.

But there are conditions when the parallel turn just doesn't come off; crust for example, or heavy, dense snow. Here I adopt what I call the 'Wallace Loup', invented, so far as I can determine, by Bill Wallace. He leans forward, plants both poles in the snow, leaps forward, turns in the air, and lands with his body facing down the slope while his skis are across it. If such a manoeuvre won't get you out of your predicament, it's time to take the skis off and walk. Also it is an ideal turn when you are so tired that your judgement and technique are failing you. One caveat: don't do it on a wind-slab surface. It might just split the surface.

Wind slab is the least predictable and most dangerous snow state. It forms on the lee side of slopes, where, driven by the wind, snow accumulates. If the wind carries any significant degree of moisture, the surface hardens. Tap such a surface and it has a hollow feel to it. An experiment done in one's home can help in understanding real-life situations. Lay one sheet of glass upon another. Holding the bottom sheet, raise the angle until the top sheet starts to slide off. Note the angle. Now add a little fine sand between the two sheets and repeat the experiment. The top now slides off at a shallower angle. Repeat again, but this time as you raise the sheets lightly tap the surface. The top sheet now slides off at an even lower angle. The vibrations created by a skier or walker crossing a slope of wind slab have the same effect.

If you go on a ski-mountaineering course you will be asked to dig a pit to reveal the profile of the snow. The 'sand' between the 'plates of glass' are obvious if wind slab is present. The trouble with this approach is that no one ever has time, or inclination, to proceed on the basis of constantly digging pits. Here's an example of wind slab in action.

Wallace and I had been holed up in the Refuge des Drayères at the head of the Nevache valley in France for two days during a blizzard. On the third day we ventured out to find that about a foot of snow had fallen. The wind had dropped. The sun was out. It was time to continue our traverse to Modane. But first we had to get over the Col de Nevache. We also had Mont Thabor in our sights.

The beautiful French IGN 1:25,000 map showed in purple the recommended ski route, but it would have been suicide in the prevailing conditions with the virtual certainty of wind slab in our path. For safety, then, we approached the col by the crest of the adjoining ridge known as the Crête de Madeleine. At one point, forced by rocks to step a foot or so onto the east-facing (wind-slab prone) slope, I watched in wonder and then in awe as the cutting action of my ski edge triggered a split in the snow slope. In ultra-slow motion a crack ran away from me just below and along the crest. It took a few seconds to widen, revealing a wedge of snow two feet deep and several hundred feet long that then commenced to slide majestically down hill. As it fell away it broke into massive blocks that would have pulverised a human body. Gathering momentum, it bore down onto the lower slopes, raising a cloud of snowdust that obliterated the valley from view. Bill grabbed my ski stick and held me firm. Yes, we had made the right decision to keep high!

We could have turned back, but logic prevailed. The west-facing slope should be all right. From the Col de Nevache at 9,164 ft (2,794 m) the route descends 700 feet to a basin from which the next and final col for Modane can be reached. We were now again on a recognised ski route, but ominously marked with crosses, implying that it was too steep to ski up.

After checking again that our avalanche transceivers were transmitting, Bill, bold as ever, swooped down the steep slope, on a traverse line in case the slope gave way. When at a safe distance from any possible avalanche, he called me to follow. The ascent to the next and final col was without risk. But the slope beyond gave us concern. It was steep and showed signs of slab. Roping up and belayed by me, Bill sideslipped the slope for about ten feet, then proceeded to jump up and down as if bitten by a train of soldier ants. The slope didn't budge. He descended a further ten feet, and repeated the exercise. No wind-hardened surface. No telltale crack. Untying the rope, he did a Wallace Loup and whistled down the remaining slope to safety, obliging me to follow. Mt Thabor was clearly out of countenance. We skied the gentle valley to Valmenier and so to Modane, food and wine. It should be mentioned that this approach to testing a slope is not foolproof. I know of at least one case (in Corsica) where the slab broke off and the skier (guide, Jean-Louis George) was carried away as the rope broke under the strain.

You would imagine that ski-mountaineering with a guide would be the safest way to get around. You can certainly learn from a guide, as from any experienced friend, but in my view all a guide offers you is local knowledge, which is safety of a kind, but they do seem to take risks. Perhaps familiarity breeds contempt. The record of accidents to guided parties is not encouraging. If you do use a guide, make sure he is an old one. If he has lived that long he is probably safe and wise. Here are a couple of tales.

With a young French guide, Claude Rey, a friend, I was making a three-day ski traverse of the Vanoise hills. This is a great area in France lying adjacent to the Italian border, with many huts and heaps of options in the way of peaks and passes. This particular day our objective was Pointe Alberon 11,968 ft (3,649 m) from the Refuge des Evettes. We had clumped up the glacier, crossed an icefall and were now on the steep north face 2,000 feet below the summit. Claude led. First upwards, then across the slope above a yawning crevasse. As he progressed, he ran onto a hard snow surface and was forced to stamp his skis to get purchase. As he did so, the snow fractured, broke into blocks and slid into the crevasse 30 feet below him. All the ingredients for an avalanche were there. Had I been making my own judgement I would have turned back. I stopped and watched anxiously. Indeed, I expected him to turn back. Eventually he gained gentler ground and looking back seemed surprised not to find me at his heels like any well-behaved client. With beating heart I eventually followed. There is something about being with a guide which robs you of your own judgement.

This follow-my-leader syndrome is dangerous. In 1995 a group of 11 doctors, attending a medical conference at Val-d'Isère, hired a guide to take them on an off-piste ski traverse from Val-d'Isère to La Plagne. It was the usual crocodile, with skiers close behind each other, sliding in martial order to the rhythm of the leader. The guide took them across a virgin snow slope. It broke away. Not one survived. This was crass foolishness. At the very least the crocodile ought to have been stretched out. If there is any doubt about a slope only one person should cross at a time. If the slope does go, then the rest of the party are at hand to dig out the unfortunate guinea pig. Blind obedience to a leader is dangerous. It's best to be your own man or woman, even if it means being a coward.

The best-known ski traverse in the Alps is the so-called 'Haute Route' from Zermatt to Chamonix or vice versa. The going is easy and the route safe, except for the section on the Grand Combin, which is often omitted. The scenery is magnificent, but such is its popularity that the huts are disagreeably crowded and the trail a deep trench. However, the Alps offer many traverses where one can be alone, find empty huts and virgin snow slopes. My best experience is a route called the 'Via alta Ticinese'. Ticino, which is part of Switzerland, lies on the south side of the main Alpine chain. While its mountains barely touch 10,000 feet, the terrain is incredibly rugged and diverse, offering a subtlety of landform not found in the higher hills. Part of the route lies in Italy. This traverse also offers the opportunity every second night to stay in a place providing food, showers, bed and drink, and facilities to re-supply, yet without losing the sense of wilderness so essential to the whole undertaking. I've included a detailed description of the Via alta Ticinese in the appendices.

Ski-mountaineering brings together more potential dangers and requires the application of more skills than straightforward rock climbing. Gaining experience little by little is the way to proceed. Nobody should start skiing the way I did. It was in 1947, during that great winter when Scotland was wall-to-wall snow for weeks on end. I had taken the night train to Aviemore and using borrowed ex-Army hickory skis from the University Sports Union, had put them on outside the station. My boots were for hillwalking and were strapped to the skis by a spring-tensioned cable. I immediately liked the sensation of gliding along at a speed a good bit faster than walking. The road to Glenmore was a dirt track, unploughed. No one was about. I swished through Rothiemurchus forest towards the Larig Ghru, grateful that I was not trying to walk, so deep was the snow. I had climbing skins. Though the attachments were primitive they had the merit of being real seal skins, the *peaux de phoque* by which the French describe skins to this day, even though all are now made of artificial fibres.

As I took to the snow-covered heather to gain the slopes of Creag an Leth-choin, the going became more arduous, but then eased as I traversed the wind-scoured escarpment and onto the plateau leading to Beinn Macdhui. By now I was in mist, following a compass course. As I slid, slid, slid towards the summit, I became conscious that each of my steps was being echoed. I had recently read about *Fear Liath Mor*, the Great Grey Man of Beinn Macdhui, who is said to reveal himself from time to time. Since no less a person than the venerable and totally rational Professor Norman Collie, Victorian veteran of many climbs, had encountered the beast, the idea got lodged in my mind that this could only be him. I had recently read that an Aberdeen climber, Sandy Tewnion, while on leave from the Army, had had a 'terrrifying encounter' with the Grey Man and had fired three shots from his revolver into the mist to scare him off. A terrible panic overtook me: I hastened. The steps behind me quickened: I stopped. Nothing. I repeated this experiment several times, then with beating heart I turned to face the ghost: nothing but mist. Feeling very foolish I sat down to eat and while tightening my rucksack straps realised what I had been hearing was the flip-flap of a loose strap.

I learnt that day that it is quite one thing to climb on skis, it is another to descend. I had never in my life made a ski turn and though

I had read up the theory of the snowplough turn, I was unable to put it into practice and had to make long traverses of the hillside changing direction by kick-turning. Practice makes perfect. It was one of the two skills I mastered that day that have since stood me in good stead. Such a turn is normally used when changing direction on a steep slope. Many people are crucified by this manoeuvre. It requires technique, suppleness and conviction. It is not as easy as it looks. I also learnt that day, through innumerable falls, that it is essential to fall sideways and not forwards. Not a bad first day's training!

My best ski-mountaineering has not been in the great ranges of the Alps, nor even in Scotland, which has much to offer, but in Greenland. Round about the end of the winter, before the spring thaw, conditions can be ideal. North-east Greenland does not get a lot of snow, but what falls stays and is not subject to intense sunlight. The avalanche risk is much diminished compared to the Alps. Powder on a firm base is normal. This, coupled to continuous daylight from April onwards, makes for the most marvellous ambience. Two areas are particularly worthy of recommendation: the Staunings Alps and the Roscoe Bjaerg just north of Ittoqqortoormiit. This tiny range whose core of granite mountains rises little higher than Ben Nevis (but straight from the sea) offers such variety, and such summits, as to eclipse the Alps for satisfaction and thrills. Of course, you must camp. In early April the temperature will be about -20°C, but with such dry air that it does not feel cold. The thaw will come at the end of the month or in early May. Such a trip, self-organised, need cost little more than £1,000 for a fortnight.

CHAPTER 14

An Expedition Climbs on its Stomach

It is a simple physical calculation to arrive at how much energy it takes to raise a human body up a hill. Add to that one's clothing and a heavy rucksack and you find that to sustain 3,000 feet of uphill work, day after day, calls for a food intake of about 3,000 kilo-calories, unless you want to lose weight. If the objectives are more ambitious or it is very cold, then an intake of 4,000 kilo-calories may be called for. Of course, a day's hillwalking doesn't immediately call for such an increase. But you can only live on your fat for so long.

It's not easy to switch from a typical urban intake of about 2,000 kilo-calories to 4,000 without provoking some objections from your stomach. The problem, however, really surfaces on high mountain trips, where digestion is usually difficult, yet the required energy output huge. Moreover, lack of hygiene in the primitive environment of a high mountain camp, especially if climbers are too tired to keep their hands clean, can easily lead to food poisoning and violently upset stomachs. On the Pamir expedition (related in Chapter 7), four out of six members of the British summit team succumbed to food poisoning. The fact that three of them reached the top of Pik Kommunizma is a tribute to their persistence in the face of great personal discomfort. All four ate insufficiently and felt utterly weak.

Calories are not the only issue. One's electrolytic balance is also critical. Drinking snow water, which is devoid of any electrolytes, can reduce tigers to kittens. During an exceptionally hot spell in Zinal I climbed the Besso by way of limbering up for a traverse of the 13,000-foot Zinal

Rothorn by the Weiss Fluh and so to the Zermatt side. I drank copious quantities of meltwater. That evening in the Cabane des Montets, aware of the problem, I ate well and added lots of salt to my food. Yet next day I could scarcely put one foot in front of the other. Bill Wallace, my companion, dragged me over the top and down to the Rothorn hut where I collapsed. The problem was a simple potassium deficiency.

In brief, energy out must be balanced by energy in. The food must be palatable and digestible. I noted that on the Pamir expedition the Russian climbers had no stomach problems. Unlike our carefully prepared mix of dried foods and pasta, they lived off tins of caviar, chicken, a porridge made of wheat flour and lashings of tea. It was heavy, but it worked. Ours was lightweight, but it did not.

So, echoing Napoleon, it is my belief that an expedition literally climbs on its stomach. I have been on numerous expeditions where food, sooner or later, became a bone of contention and induced much backbiting. Pity the poor guy whose responsibility it is to assemble the expedition's food ration. Every expedition organiser knows the critical importance of food to the welfare and good spirits of the party. The problem is to square the equation between palatability, digestibility and weight. What you are going to eat you have to carry uphill. The food we buy at home contains a huge proportion of water, so it is natural to seek to eliminate this. There is plenty of water on the hill. Unfortunately, even in these days of advanced food technology, most dried foods are boring as they nearly all contain added glutamic acid – palates very quickly become jaded.

Whatever you do, don't let a young climber arrange the food. Most of them are fast-food junkies, who live off all-day breakfasts. Cooking (as opposed to re-hydrating) is considered to be a bore and uses too much fuel. Eric Shipton and Bill Tilman were typical bachelor hard men who satisfied their energy needs with a kilo of biltong a day, or half a pound of pemmican mixed with margarine (to taste), or a porridge of tsampa. Their only concession was to their thirst; tea with lashings of sugar and dried milk stirred into a vile concoction known to the British armed forces as 'char' and readily available at most Indian bazaars as *chai*. I avoid travelling with such primitive eaters. Sooner or later your stomach and palate will cry out for refreshment and you will be prematurely drawn back to the flesh pots. This is daft. Good tasty food is easily arranged these days, so bring it.

Mike Thompson, who organised the food for Bonnington's expedition up the south-west face of Everest, invited suggestions, as we all do, from the expedition members. It is a hopeless quest to find any common denominator. One revealed a craving for granola and French nougat; another for hot pickles and chutney. Even marmite and anchovies have been requested. I favour oatmeal porridge; Joe Brown favours curries – in such circumstances it is best to camp upwind! Anyway, making up ration packs capable of appealing to the diverse and recherché tastes of the bunch of egoists that usually comprise a high-altitude expedition is an impossibility. Thompson was an anthropologist, not a nutritionist. Here is what he came up with as a four-man day pack for the higher camps:

sugarcubes	vitamin tablets
coffee whitener	salt
instant coffee	tea bags
fruit drink crystals	margarine
stock cubes	instant porridge
dried soup	dehydrated potatoes
mint cake	surprise peas
chocolate	high-fat biscuits
cream (in a tin)	chocolate digestive biscuits
honey	Irish stew (tinned)

It is partly a credit to him that they got to the top, but you would have to be in pretty good fig to want to eat surprise peas and Irish stew at 27,000 feet.

My first experience of eating a diet designed by someone else (apart from my dear mother) was when I travelled with Harold Drever to west Greenland, an experience related in Chapter 2. Whether through laziness or indifference he provided case after case of tinned steak and kidney pudding, but little else. Perhaps Crosse & Blackwell had sponsored him. These concoctions, nice in their way as occasional snacks, quickly palled after the third successive meal. When he wasn't looking we flogged as much as we could to the Inuits at Uummannaq, in return for seal steaks and whale meat. These proved hard to cook and for a while you would have seen us chewing and chewing and chewing. But in the end we found out how to render them edible, however cooking them consumed an awful lot of fuel.

Happily the trip was coastal: the seas were so full of cod they could be caught by foul-hooking – simply pull up the line quickly enough and you were bound to impale a fish. Sad to say we had no fat with which to cook them. Even fresh cod boiled in water palls after a time. Our diet was close to that of a lower deckhand on a naval ship in Nelson's time. Incidentally, the Inuit have committed the same folly as European fishermen – through using larger ships and more advanced technology they too have fished their seas dry.

In the '50s, with the Second World War behind it, the Army found itself with warehouses stacked with rations called 'compo' – Army speak for comprehensive. These could be cheaply bought. On breaking open a case one would find a nippy tin-opener (valuable and hoarded), a tin of soup, tinned margarine and an anonymous tin containing some proteinaceous material, often steak and kidney pudding. There were also biscuits so hard and unappetising that without water they could scarcely be eaten and would have made perfectly good beer mats in the officers' mess. And these were served to soldiers fighting in the arid North African deserts, poor devils!

Compo rations finally caught up with me on the British North Greenland Expedition. For those of us prone to constipation these rations were hellish. I recall the expedition doctor, John Masterton, rushing into camp to say that he had found evidence of sheep grazing! As the autumn gave way to the 24-hour polar night, food should have been one source of variety in our lives. Instead the monotonous diet of dehydrated food dulled our palates. We were organised into a cooking rota in which each cubicle housing four people cooked for one week, followed by four weeks off. Being cooks was the best part of the cycle. Cooks did not have to bring in ice (to be melted into water) and they did not have to wash up. My group consisted of four scientists. We were high up on the scale of inventiveness. During the days of preparation in London I was told to learn to cook, so I popped into the Good Housekeeping Institute in Oxford Street and asked the director if she could help us. 'Well,' she said appraising my shaggy looks, 'there is a brides' course starting next week.' I spent a happy fortnight in the company of a covey of blushing brides-to-be wondering why I was about to deprive myself of female company for a whole year. My quiche lorraine was sold to the public at lunchtime – today Health and Safety regulations would probably have something to say about that!

Then out of the night, which was forty below, there stumbled a musk ox. To say that we shot it is to imply an orderly procedure. In fact, the poor beast fell to its knees with the sheer weight of lead that we pumped into it in our desperation to make sure this source of fresh meat didn't get away. We spun out the flesh and bones for a couple of months. What a difference it made to our appetites.

But there's more to food than content. How it is cooked and where eaten plays a vital role in one's welfare. My worst experience was on a trip to the Cordillera Blanca in Peru led by the famous and highly likeable editor of the American *Alpine Journal*, H. Adams (Ad) Carter. He had led more expeditions to the Andes than anyone could count and was fixed in his ways, so I knuckled under his regime. Ad's system was that he slept in a large mother tent, while we clustered around in satellite tents. He cooked breakfast for us all. It consisted of a processed oatmeal mash whose sludge-like consistency would have constipated an elephant. You can't turn flax into gold. When this was ready, if one can use such an allusion to describe its final state, we were expected to leap from our sleeping bags and join him. He had by now turned off his stove so that his tent was barely warmer than the sub-zero Andean morning outside. Unlike Oliver Twist, none of us ever asked for a second helping. Ad also made a tea brew and as every Briton knows, no American can make tea. Shivering in our sleeping bags, this was our breakfast. No wonder we never made the summit of Chacralaju.

On Himalayan treks the torture is more refined because one is paying for it. At first light the porters and Sherpas reignite the previous evening's fire and sit around enjoying its heat, bringing huge vessels of water to the boil and having a thoroughly good time. Their frequent laughter encourages you to think they are picking over your Western foibles. Then with a cheery 'good morning, sahib' a mug of rapidly cooling tea and a basin of warm water is left at the tent door. Nobody seems to have had the courage to explain to them that modern European climbers (I cannot speak for anyone else) rarely wash, and certainly not first thing in the morning. It must be some hangover from the days of the Raj. Here, too, you are expected to get out of your sleeping bag, huddle miserably in the communal tent eating – yes, you've guessed – porridge, but Indian-style. This concoction was certainly one star better than Carter's, but three stars below acceptable. Turn to the appendices to see how this nectar of the gods should be made!

Any fool can suffer, but it takes a good mountaineer to be comfortable. Here are my rules:

- Rule 1: Have your own stove.
- Rule 2: Know how to light it without burning the tent down. This is both literally and emotionally a searing experience. I know. I've done it! Never leave an unguarded stove alight – I have seen a stove blown over by the wind getting under the groundsheet.

- Rule 3: Have two billies (pans) filled with water (or ice, if no water) at the tent door together with the ingredients for breakfast at hand before you go to sleep. Then you won't have to get out of your sleeping bag. This is the last thing you should ever do, in my view. A sleeping bag is man's best friend, followed by his dog. A wife is said to come third: whoever said that is on dangerous ground.
- Rule 4: Always cook your own breakfast and do it in the tent so that you may enjoy the warmth of the stove.

Now for the diet. The issues are weight, energy, palatability and digestibility. I believe there is another key requirement: variety. It is perfectly possible to achieve all of these features with a ration pack that weighs no more than 1 kg per person per day, while providing 4,000 kilo-calories of food energy. My own approach to solving this simultaneous equation, one which has proved successful on winter Arctic trips and has been copied by others, is included in the appendices.

I was astonished to read in Maurice Herzog's account of the ascent of Annapurna, the first 8,000-metre peak to be climbed, that the French climbers let the Sherpas cook their food, even on high camps. Throughout the expedition story, one reads of frozen fingers and boots and of desperate measures to warm up. Yet there was a simple solution. Each tent should have had its own stove and its own food pack. Heating and cooking go together with drying boots and gloves.

Now for fuel. The modern climber can choose from a variety of lightweight portable stoves:

> GAS: On the face of it a stove fuelled by a canister appears the handiest. Open the valve and light. There are three downsides. First: disposal. Environmental regulations nowadays require expeditions to bring back all metal containers – no more chucking out of the tent door! Second: weight. The weight of the container is a significant proportion of the weight of the contents, so if weight matters then this is inefficient. Third: lack of pressure. This disadvantage arises only in really cold conditions, -20°C and below. Such temperatures are not uncommon on high mountains and in the Polar regions. As the temperature falls there comes a point at which the vapour pressure of the liquid within is less than

the atmospheric pressure without. At this point the effect of opening the tap is to let in air! In the Pamirs in 1962 I experienced this effect. Making such a stove produce heat was a long-drawn-out process. To begin with, I put a fresh canister inside my duvet as close to the skin as I could tolerate. In due course this warmed up the gas within sufficiently for it to have a vapour pressure greater than atmospheric pressure. With a burner affixed, this was lit, whereupon it delivered a puny flame. Since the liquid within is boiling, the latent heat of vaporisation quickly cools it down. This rapidly waning source of heat was then used to heat the canister of a second stove (very dangerous!) which once warmed would provide a decent flame. Once there was a pan on top, the downward radiant heat kept it going. I found that the only way to get breakfast reasonably fast was to sleep with the stove next to my shirt.

PETROL: This and other high-volatility fuels, such as Coleman fuel sold in the USA, are easy to light – in fact too easy. If any spills, its vapour spreads fast and readily ignites. After several bad experiences I will never again allow such a stove in my tent. It is too dangerous.

PARAFFIN: Also known as kerosene, this is a much safer higher-boiling fraction of petroleum than petrol – a lighted match dipped into kerosene goes out! The wonderful thing is that it is available at any airport. Ask for Jet A1. Burning paraffin requires a heat-exchanger type pressure stove such as was invented a century ago by a Swede, who called it the 'Primus'. It has stood the test of time. He deserves a Nobel prize. It emanates a delightful purring sound, particularly soothing if there is wild weather outside. It is used all over the world from Bedouins in the desert to Inuit hunters in their igloos, from Indian tea-shops to Mongolian *yourts*.

Inefficient lighting of such stoves can result in smoky flames for a short while. Until you master the process of lighting you will have to accept that the roof of your tent may soot-darken somewhat with time. Bill Wallace tells the story of how he took his tent back to the makers – Benjamin and Edginton – for repair after a lapse of 20 years: 'This cannot be our tent, sir. Our tents at that time were white.'

Weight for weight, petrol, paraffin and gas give the same amount of heat (but they have different densities). In the Arctic winter I allow one litre of paraffin per tent per day. With that amount of fuel, one can centrally heat a tent for as much as eight hours. This is important because boots and socks can be hung from the roof to dry out. Reading becomes comfortable. A one-pint Primus can be pumped up to give as much as one kilowatt of heat, valuable for fast heating and drying out the tent. Such an intensity of heat cannot be got from a gas stove.

There is a fourth alternative, much used in present times: the MSR stove. Primus owners allege that MSR stands for 'My Stove is Rotten'. Small lightweight stoves are invaluable for one-night stands on some mountain wall, but otherwise leave them at home.

After years of complaining about expedition food I was eventually hoist by my own petard and manoeuvred into organising an expedition food ration for a spring trip to the Arctic where temperatures would be as low as -20°C. I enquired of my companions what were their likes and dislikes. One summed it up thus: 'You are such a fussy bugger if it suits you it will suit anyone.' This, as it turned out, was not the case. Being too lazy to wash a porridge pot, and therefore unable to cook with it, he deprived himself of many calories.

How could I meet the criteria of palatability, digestibility, weight and variety? I considered variety very important and since we would be tent-bound for at least 12 hours a day, cooking becomes an agreeable way of passing the time. The tent space is warm and conducive to conversation. I wanted to create the environment of a well-stocked kitchen where the choice of meal depends on the whim of the moment; in other words, a ration which could be cut many ways. For this reason alone pre-prepared meals were out.

I found everything I sought could be had from a big supermarket. Once the surplus packing was stripped off (thus losing about 10 per cent of unnecessary weight and about 30 per cent of the volume) it is possible to create a food pack for 12 days with 3,750 kilo-calories a day that would fit into a typical cardboard wine case and weigh 12 kg: 1 kg per person per day. A 12 man-day box is ideal as it can be cut many ways: 6 persons for 2 days, 4 for 3 days, 1 for 12 days.

I was so impressed by the Russians' use of ground wheat to make kasha during the Pamir expedition described in Chapter 7, I included some. In the UK it is known as semolina. It can be cooked like porridge (Russian style) for those with wobbly stomachs, or mixed to a paste and baked on a hot pan surface to make a chappati, to be eaten with jam or marmite, or even fried.

Those who mix with native peoples in remote areas must adapt to their eating habits. I particularly admire Marie Herbert's efforts to integrate with her neighbours when she and her husband Wally and their one-year-old infant spent a year with the polar Inuit in north-west Greenland. How about this little vignette from *The Snow People – Life Among the Polar Eskimos*:

> That afternoon I worked on the tusks (of a walrus), boiling them for a while to get the meat off the base, and then scraping to get the thick gristle off. I sat outside with Maria (an Inuit neighbour) and followed her instructions. She gave me a wing from a bird she had boiled. It was delicious. Avatak came in later with some seal. The children stood round her as she cut one open and handed them each a piece of raw liver. The twins wanted an eye. Maria cut them out and handed them to the children who sucked them as if they were sweets – almost the size of a golf ball. After a while they handed them back to her and she cut the ball open. The children squeezed out the almost colourless liquid which they sucked and swallowed. They turned the black fleshy cast inside out and chewed it, and rolled a small colourless ball, like a small marble, round in their hands for me to see before popping it into their mouths.
>
> Later in the summer I noticed Martha flip a tiny red jellyfish out of the water. She turned it inside out, sucked it, and threw the skin back in the water. I sometimes wondered if there were any living thing the children would not eat.

August in the Arctic tundra provides a variety of food. Summer is already on the wane and the night frosts that kill off irritating mosquitoes also turn the dwarf birch and willow herb into every imaginable shade of green and russet. The tundra is a veritable tartan carpet, more a Farquharson or Buchanan than Royal Stewart. Now is the time to look for free food. There are mountain cranberries, crowberries, bilberries and cloudberries as well as the occasional clump of sorrel to add to your vitamin C intake.

Notwithstanding all this free food, in 1958 when Iain Smart and I arrived at Syd Kap on Scoresby Sund we were seriously hungry. We had traversed the Staunings and then walked down a 40-mile strath, known by the Danish name Schuichart. At the summer hunting settlement we found three Inuit hunters and their families stocking up for the winter, shooting seals, walrus and narwhal, and drying them on

215

racks. There was a shout of 'Narwhal!' and the hunters rushed into their kayaks and sped out to sea. We lost sight of them, but in due course they reappeared towing a dead narwhal. Everyone was very excited and a party spirit descended upon us. The outer layer of the narwhal's two-inch-thick blubber (called *mattaq*) is regarded as a delicacy, and as visitors we were offered first bite, in much the same way as I would offer the first plate of my porridge to a visiting Inuit. To convey the sensation of chewing this mattaq try to imagine biting a soft pencil eraser permeated with rancid fish oil lightly flavoured with a touch of Brazilian whisky (which is reputedly flavoured with urine). I did my best but gave up as the urge to vomit overcame my good manners. Iain, to his eternal credit, manfully chewed away with an expression on his face as if he had seen his mother's ghost. Finally, with a gigantic swallow, he downed the lump, and clamping down as his stomach muscles convulsed gave a gracious nod of thanks. He declined a second helping. I was inevitably regarded with some disfavour.

Fortunately there was a government store at Syd Kap, however we had no money. I persuaded the local chap in charge to give us credit. To organise payment I wrote out the following document:

> I, Malcolm Slesser, being the leader of the Scottish East Greenland Expedition of 1958, being in need of food under circumstances beyond my control, hereby authorise the Danish Government to request payment from the United Kingdom Foreign Office through its embassy in Copenhagen.

We raided the store. It took six months for this piece of *lèse-majesté* to percolate through the system. I received a stern letter from the UK Foreign Office together with a bill for £4.

Travellers from the more developed countries rightly worry about picking up infections, particularly from drinks. Perhaps one of the most worrying sources are native brews. Like any beer, these are made from malted cereals, the difference being that human spit is used in lieu of yeast to set the fermentation going. Unfortunately the final product, being unfiltered and with a frothy top, looks for all the world like a jug of spit. Not easy to drink if you have a fertile imagination. In Greenland such brews are known as *imiaq*, in Peru *chicha* and in Nepal *chang*.

It is a sad commentary on the destruction of many pristine environments, particularly in North America, that even water from a spring may be contaminated with guardia. This can give rise to very unpleasant consequences and stomach pains. Ad Carter used to lace his water with iodine; it was unbelievably foul. Personally I keep to tea from well-boiled water, with a bottle of Scotch at hand for tummy troubles. Not many bacteria can stand up to cask strength whisky!

CHAPTER 15

The Mountaineer's Footprint

It is spring in the high Arctic. The temperature is -15 °C. A light wind blows in from the Barents Sea. At three in the morning with five companions I reach the top of one of the highest unclimbed peaks of the Roscoe Bjaerg, a jagged group of rose-tinted granite mountains lying against the Liverpool coast of east Greenland, so named by the English whaler, William Scoresby, after his native town. We experience an uncanny sensation of height, many times more than our mere 4,230-foot altitude, partly because we are surrounded by lesser peaks that each carry their own rugged alpine aura, but mainly because of the extraordinary clarity of the air. This perception of height is accentuated by the ice pack that presses against the coast, extending seemingly forever and ever into the polar sea. The sun in the north-east is but 2° above the horizon, casting a vivid lemon light on the peaks to our south. Incredibly, it seems we have found a place in the northern hemisphere where there is no air pollution, indeed no pollution at all. Here the sun's rays are not attenuated by dust or moisture. This is truly a pristine wilderness undefiled by the footprint of man. The next snowfall will obliterate our crampon marks. Not even the migrating Inuit of the past have left any sign of their passage, whether on mountain or coast. It is the habitat only of the polar bear, the walrus, the fox, the seal, the raven, the lemming and birds like the snow bunting.

But that is not all. We have the mountain to ourselves. Indeed we have an entire mountain range to ourselves. Awed by the majesty of the scene, aware of how privileged we are, it even seems bad taste to chatter. The mood evoked by such an environment is superbly articulated in a poem by Malcolm McMillan, a past member of the Edinburgh University Mountaineering Club. It was inspired by his first visit to the Arctic as he sat in the lee of Mt Shackleton in north-east Greenland:

> Staring beauty;
> me staring at it, helplessly moved,
> it staring through me, unmoved.
> Fish-scaled sky sliding into quiet, distant ice.
> No separation or boundaries –
> just one single spectrum through snow and sky.
> Want to step into the spectrum; squeeze under the sky –
> be part of that beauty, that rests in my eye.
> But I can't.
> So I sit, silently watching
> silently crying
> not understanding
> inside.

Words like ambience and aesthetics seemed inadequate. You could say this was the world as nature had intended. It offers us a benchmark against which to judge the rest of the world's so-called wild places. And it raises an interesting question. Can there truly be such a thing as eco-tourism?

A recollection crossed my mind of another day upon another summit, this time on the Italian border with Switzerland. It was summer and not long after dawn. I was at 13,000 feet on the top of the Lagginhorn looking south towards the valley of the Po, from which rose a grey pollution haze. Only those summits exceeding 10,000 feet were visible. The scene had, of course, a certain magic to it; these snowy triangles poking through the smog and we enjoyed a certain smugness at not being down there. Turning round 180° towards the giant peaks of the Swiss Alps, there, too, it was the same. This was human-made pollution. The sparkling snow may have been pristine, but little else.

There was a time when we accepted pollution as the inevitable price of economic progress. We, the mountaineers, had the ability to escape to our high-level sanctuaries, to our clean and clear air, though to do so we used all the machinery of economic development – planes, cars, téléphériques, karabiners, nuts, synthetic fibres, weatherproof clothing requiring advanced manufacturing techniques and so forth. We were no less guilty of the damage to the environment than the very factories that produced the essential materials of our calling or the entrepreneurs who ran them.

As I looked down from that pristine Arctic summit, left unsullied, let me tell you, by any human-made cairn or sardine can with our names on it, over to the frozen ocean, my thoughts turned to global warming and its possible effect on the Atlantic Conveyor, and thus its role in the changing state of the frozen polar sea. We had flown from the British Isles and helicoptered into our base camp. Our contribution of carbon dioxide and nitrogen oxides to global warming was probably in excess of that of the average urban citizen back home. Our Green credentials, if we ever flaunted them, were blown. If anyone thought of this as eco-tourism, then they were fooling themselves.

It is a chemical fact that burning fossil fuels creates carbon dioxide, and often a little carbon monoxide and oxides of nitrogen. The consensus amongst climatoligists is that the rate of humankind's combustion of these fuels is exacerbating global warming. However, there is a strong counter lobby. The verdict is much like a jury making a judgement on circumstantial evidence. The fact of global warming is not in dispute, only whether we humans have a hand in it. The Norwegian Polar Institute has studied the logs of hundreds of ships that have penetrated the Arctic during the last 500 years. From these they have been able to map the changing margins of the polar ice front. Up to 135 years ago it touched the north coasts of Iceland and the Kola Peninsula to the west of Murmansk. Today satellite pictures show it has retreated more than halfway back towards east Greenland across the Denmark Strait. There is even ice-free water on the west side of Spitspergen at latitude 78°N in the dead of winter. Only the east of the Barents Sea shows little change. Here is one of the last pristine ocean environments in the northern hemisphere.

We can take it that if governments (or their advisors) believe human-made carbon dioxide is responsible for global warming then the evidence must be pretty strong, for the measures required to reduce such emissions are not easy to administer for governments always seeking enhanced economic growth. So what should we do about it? Reduce fossil fuel consumption, as was agreed by most nations at Kyoto in 1998, or move away from fossil fuels to sources that produce no greenhouse gas emissions? Here we have to shift gears to engage one or both of two realistic options and reconsider one idealistic one.

This latter option is widely pushed by governments. It is to achieve more with less energy: so-called energy conservation. But as energy is unrationed, we are limited in our consumption only by what we are prepared to pay for it. Energy is embodied in every good or service we buy. Thus though we are exhorted to use less energy, in fact we do not, for it is too cheap to really hit our pockets and what we save by conservation we simply spend elsewhere. In Europe (including the UK) motor fuels have never been cheaper in terms of consumer buying power. This is reflected, I find, in how we go to the mountains: 20 years ago one arranged with friends to share transport to the hills; now we meet at the car park.

The two realistic options are sun and nuclear power. Solar energy beams down upon earth a flux 1,000 times greater than the rate at which we earthlings consume fossil fuels. The sun drives the wind and so the waves. To many minds, therefore, the answer is staring us in the face – switch to solar energy, for not only is it renewable, but it produces no greenhouse gases. Unfortunately capturing solar energy and delivering it in a form our modern economies can use is not all that easy. It comes to earth as a weak flux. Even in the Nubian Desert it amounts to no more than one kilowatt (kW) per square metre. So, for example, the area of ground required to produce the same amount of electricity as a typical 660 MW (660,000 kW) nuclear reactor is 660,000 square metres at 100 per cent efficiency (which is impossible), and in practical terms at least 5 times this, or 3.3 square kilometres. Relocate that in Europe and it becomes more like ten square kilometres. The cost of the physical structures for such solar capture delivered as useful fuel is of the same order as a nuclear power station. And there is a further problem. The sun does not always shine, nor the wind always blow, so that on average, over a year, one can only harness about a third of the potential capacity of these devices. So we are now talking about 30 square kilometres, the area of a small city, to deliver the equivalent output of a nuclear power station. In other words area is a significant factor in deploying renewable energies, with the one exception of tidal currents. And where does one find spare land area? Why, on the coasts, the moors and amongst the mountains! In other words, where we go for our recreation.

The abiding problem with renewable energy is storing it, so that on days of surplus it can, like rainfall, be squirrelled away for a future time of deficit in a dam. One of the neatest ways of storing energy is to use any temporary surplus to pump water uphill to a high-altitude reservoir, to be later used in a hydro-electric station when needed. This is called 'pumped storage'. And it means building dams and flooding valleys. Older readers may remember the campaign to save the Nevis Gorge from obliteration by a dam. Yet, without them, we have to engage a higher technological gear and generate hydrogen by the electrolysis of water, which then becomes the fuel for not only generating electricity again, but for powering engines, even vehicle engines. They are already doing this in Iceland.

The issue, then, is not technological. All the answers are known, and better ones may be round the corner. The costs, however, of changing to such an energy infrastructure are enormous and will take several decades to implement, much of it over the mutilated psyches of opposing hill-lovers. Moreover, not every country is well placed. Some areas, like Scotland, have the potential capacity to be totally driven by renewable energy systems if all possible sites are deployed – heaven forbid! To give some impression of the magnitude of such a development, it would be the equivalent of having sixty 100 kW wind turbines every mile along the coast. It needs this much because as oil and gas are depleted we will have to use electricity to make hydrogen with which we can synthesise liquid and gaseous fuels. This increases the required electricity-generating capacity enormously from beyond their frontiers or by embracing nuclear energy.

There have been some exaggerated assessments of Scotland's potential, such as the report compiled by the architectural consultants Garrad Hassan for the Scottish Executive which goes so far as to suggest that Scottish renewable energy potential could also provide enough electricity to meet demand in England. Naturally it caught the attention of the media, but it is a false prospectus. Some areas like England, Belgium and the Netherlands are too densely populated to be able to meet their requirements without additional energy from beyond their frontiers.

Today the critical issue is not technological but aesthetic. There is no question but that wind-driven renewable energy structures are obtrusive. They do not add to the aesthetic background in the way of a traditional Dutch windmill housing animals and people. Perched on its canal bank it makes an engaging creaking sound as its canvas sails slowly revolve, pumping water out of the lowest country in Europe. Anyway, the Netherlands is essentially an urban country with no wild land at all. Very few people seem to want a wind farm on their doorstep and even those not immediately affected object to the visual blight they impose on rural scenery. Wind turbine location also has an impact on land values; down if your home is near a wind farm, up if you own some land where a farm will be situated. Greed, as ever, is flourishing.

The debate has now reached a fine pitch. On the one side we have governments encouraging the expansion of renewable energy systems with subsidies, supported by the Green parties and their kin. The objective at one time attracted wide support, though realists kept pointing out that the renewable energies are no good without storage or back-up systems.

Now enter the mountaineers, the hillwalkers and the devotees of wild places like members of the John Muir Trust, The National Trust, the Royal Society for the Protection of Birds, the British Mountaineering Council, the Mountaineering Council of Scotland, the International Mountain Wilderness Association, etc. Adherents to these bodies are a significant, though not large, proportion of the population. They do not want these visual obtrusions, whether on wild land or upland terrain. Though willing to yield a moor or two, like the Black Bog of Lewis, they do not wish to see anything built which might detract from the aesthetic sense of wildness, of which there is only too little left in the British Isles or elsewhere in Europe.

So how are such people, amongst whom must be counted myself, to square their consciences? As citizens of the world we have a duty to help diminish greenhouse gas emissions. Not one of my mountaineering associates, not one of my friends, disagrees with this aim. Yet we do nothing about it, not even those whose consciences are as tender as a sunburned neck. It is a textbook demonstration of a primary tenet of economic theory; that homus œconomicus instinctively acts in his or her self-interest. Thus when (or if) we (as individuals) invest in energy conservation, we may successfully reduce energy use in that sphere of our activities, only to find that we now have more cash to spare and spend it in other ways. I have a friend who in the interests of conserving energy lives in a house which I teasingly call a 'modified refrigerator', but he drives 30,000 miles a year in his car. It is a catch-22 which economists call the 'rebound effect'. The bottom line is that if you want to save energy the best way is to be poor. This is not a vote-winner!

So what are we to do to salve our consciences? Yield wild land to the renewable energy merchants, or go for nuclear? How this choice makes us squirm. Nuclear is a potentially dangerous technology, though not as dangerous as the car – in 2002, 1.26 million people were killed in traffic accidents worldwide.[1] The main problem is long-term storage of highly radioactive waste and preventing it getting in the hands of terrorists. The ordinary citizen can be forgiven for indecision, for even the Government cannot bring itself to spell out the issue in words of two syllables, as was evident in its recent energy White Paper (2003) – like a vampire at a crucifix, it flinches from telling it like it is. Instead it has set about financially ruining the UK nuclear industry. This White Paper has been branded as intellectually indefensible by practically every competent authority on energy. None of this affects France, for example, a country which uses nuclear power for the majority of its electricity generation. When a British journalist asked the French Energy Minister how he got away with it, he replied: 'If one is draining the swamp, do you tell the frogs first?'

Let us put aside nuclear energy – like a match it will always be there if or when we get tired of rubbing two sticks together. How much of what we love are we willing to sacrifice in order to bring into being a renewable energy-driven economy, one where homes are warm, industry has enough energy and we mountaineers have enough motor fuel to get to our hills? Not much it would seem. You might think that in Iceland, a country with the lowest population density in the developed world, they would happily tolerate a hydro-scheme which would create a new aluminium smelting industry and secure substantial economic benefit to a country which has seen its main industry – fishing – decline as stocks have withered. But the outcry has been enormous and the scheme been whittled down. Let's look at the details. The proposed dam is on the north east side of the Vatnajökull, a massive ice cap in the south-east of the country. The dam would create a huge reservoir 57 square kilometres in area, dwarfing anything in the whole of Europe. It would drown the superb Dimmugljúfur Canyon as well as breeding grounds for pink-footed geese and reindeer. Iceland has a population of 250,000 people – about the same as that of the city of Aberdeen or Zurich – and an area of 103,000 square kilometres: 3 times the area of the Netherlands; 45 per cent of the area of the UK; bigger than Austria; bigger than Ireland and Switzerland combined. It works out at an average population density of about 2.4 people per square kilometre, lower than the Outer Hebrides. The area under threat is about one thirtieth of the national land area and will affect no rural activities. There will be dams, roads and generating stations.

Iceland is wild, much of it untamed. Even with this development, 97 per cent will be unchanged and the area of wild land remaining will exceed that of the whole of Europe. How would you vote on this issue if you were Icelandic?[2] If we compare it to the pristine Arctic environment of east Greenland this area is already demoted. There are farms and roads, though not many. There are power cables and telephone lines.

Let's move now to an entirely different scale. One of the finest areas of wild land in temperate Europe is the Flowerdale Forest[3] in Wester Ross, in Scotland: there, 3 stark, lonely lochs, separated by the brooding mass of Baos Bheinn, are fed waters from the 3,000-foot-high western slopes of some of the wilder peaks of Wester Ross. From these tops the view is sublime, especially westwards down into the dark coires, sweeping over the lochs to the moor beyond and so to the wooded fringes of the Gairloch. Further still are the Quirang and Storr in the north of the Isle of Skye, and just visible one of the Summer Isles west of Ullapool. There is a proposal to use these lochs as a source of hydro-electricity.

From below, at the habitation level, we see these grand summits forming a magnificent backdrop to the wild oaks and birches of the natural forest. Two paths penetrate this area, one of them able to take a vehicle. It eventually becomes a walker's path and ends at the head of the furthest loch at a primitive bothy. The other is a rough track in appalling condition. At two spots one has to ford a river. Notwithstanding these tracks it is as wild as it gets in Europe, and that's saying quite a lot. It's not pristine wilderness, but it's worth keeping for all that.

Now the developers propose two weirs, which will raise the lochs by six feet, and due to the periodic withdrawal of water, will leave a tidemark of that height at certain times. Below the weirs there will be a pipeline. The scheme will have a capacity of a mere 3.5 MW, a tiny fraction of the Icelandic proposal, but nevertheless able to produce about 28 million kW per year, enough to supply 3,000 homes. All this equipment will be located no higher than the altitude of lochs, namely 1,200 feet above sea level. With the hills beyond rising to 3,300 feet, the greater part of the wildness is retained. No pink-footed geese or deer are going to lose their breeding grounds. A local community will gain a royalty of £15,000 a year. The visual impact is negligible. Yet the mountaineering community and wild-land organisations like the John Muir Trust are up in arms. A responsible organisation can only do this if it offers an alternative, because energy is necessarily embodied in every good or service we use, and without it we would slip back into the Middle Ages. Do objectors propose we tighten our belts and engage in a sharp reduction in energy consumption? Why not? I am all for it if it is carried out at national level. But if not, what then? Are objectors content to let electricity be generated by the visually less intrusive, but technologically more risky nuclear energy? If not, then objection may simply be self-indulgence. Much, much worse could have been proposed; two massive dams and a giant pumped storage scheme. These will inevitably come elsewhere if we choose the renewable route in its entirety.

One wonders whether in Europe that which we call wilderness is anything more than the after effects of rural depopulation. One would have to go back 4,000 years to the times of the first occupation of Skara Brae to find pristine land. The human footprint has long been here. Much of what we seek to preserve as wild land, such as in the West Highlands of Scotland, looks wild because it is the present end-point of centuries of ecological vandalism. And it's still going on, though thanks to many conservation and environmental bodies the decline is slowing. The problem is that we humans are many and the land is finite. There are about two and half hectares of land area in the world for each inhabitant. In the European Union (before its recent enlargement) it was 1.07 hectares per inhabitant. In the UK it is 0.42 and in Scotland it is 1.6, the lowest density in the EU after Finland. The more land area per inhabitant the easier it is to locate systems of renewable energy without damaging the best bits.

Nonetheless, these residual spaces represent something as near to wilderness as we can find in our overpopulated Europe. Many do have a real sense of remoteness. Ecologically they please us because we are ignorant of what was once there. They give us lungfuls of clean air and refresh the mind and body. So if we are minded to expand renewable energy systems we have to consider where we are willing to forego some of this quasi-wilderness, or to what degree, recognising that it is not now pristine anyway. What a choice, what a difficult choice! We come up with different answers depending on our priorities, and also on the extent to which we fully understand the issues and quantities implied. I have heard it said that we can surely put wind turbines at sea off North Sea coasts, which lack the charm of the Atlantic coasts of Europe and will not attract opposition. Try the fishermen for a start. Can you imagine the interaction of a whirling blade with the mast of a boat? The Royal Yacht Association is also in this battle.

What is it we men and women of the hills seek when we sally forth? Environment is obviously an important factor. But also adventure? My definition argues that we should not know the outcome in advance, except in so far as we intend to stay alive, unharmed, and able to return to our homes and jobs in time to meet our obligations. Here one might be talking about a day, a weekend, a week or months. A huge number of options are open: one could go forth, spy a promising piece of terrain and without map or guidebook go for it. That's adventure. Since safety is awareness, we should not do so unless we have the navigational skills to cope with such a foray and, at least, a compass. However, most of us find we cannot resist being forewarned, so we have a map, some ideas, perhaps imparted by a friend or read in a magazine article or guidebook. We can still add to adventure by avoiding paths and treating each penetration as if we were the first-ever explorers. In this way we may probe their mysteries sequentially. One of my most satisfying walks was leaving Kinlochewe to meet some friends at the Fionn Loch. I had no map and knew only that my route lay north and west. I not only encountered the most lovely north shore of Loch Maree, but was engaged in a trackless passage along the edge of the magnificent Loch Fhada. The mountains revealed themselves bit by bit and the feeling of entering wilderness was strengthened.

Guidebooks, of course, are death to adventure, but good for achieving objectives. Personally I find it more interesting to read the guidebook on my return. I have written a number of them myself and with hindsight I feel a little ashamed. Most guidebooks are little more than a verbal description of a good contour map. There is, of course, one excuse for using a guidebook: to shorten the day in order to reach some key point of departure, such as a cliff face upon which one plans to climb.

The current deluge of guidebooks and pathfinder guides is simply due to people cashing in on the market. Beginners need them. Tourists need them. Climbers like them, as they point to the exact spot on the cliff where the routes lie. How much fun they miss using these. Much more fun and adventure is to be had on a cliff without a guidebook. It offers the excitement of a first ascent. The trouble is that we are all to one extent or another driven by competition: to be able to say we have done such and such a route grades us more than the route and affects our standing – indeed to join certain clubs you need to be able to detail your successes.

Paths are good for getting places and reducing effort, and as a conventional way of approach or return. But the moment one puts in a path in a wilderness area it is by definition no longer pristine. Such is the case with Flowerdale as with the Cairngorms and the entire Alpine chain. A better example is the peak of Schiehallion in Perthshire where no less than half a million pounds is being spent to build a path to its summit. It is done for good reasons – a popular hill, the hillside has become braided and disfigured as each successive walker seeks to avoid the degraded boggy original path. Unfortunately, by suburbanising the hill, we are removing all sense of wildness. It is just another elevated tourist walk.

Though it is now considered a fundamental human right in Europe to have access to nature and wild land, the rigorous application of this will destroy the ambience we seek. The best procedure is a granny-stopper at the margins. When Percy Unna and his friends got the cash together to buy the south side of Glencoe for The National Trust for Scotland, they laid down rules – that no paths would be made and no access made easier. In my youth one could only access the Lost Valley in Glencoe by negotiating the river, which if in a spate was impossible. Then came a single pole bridge. It stopped the insecure tourist, but let the sure-footed walker go by. Now there is a broad bridge and the coire is never free of people. The single wire bridge at Steal in Glen Nevis is extremely successful in curbing numbers.

The fact is that the future of wild land cannot be divorced from the future of ourselves:

> Ah, love! Could thou and I with Fate conspire
> to grasp this sorry scheme of things entire,
> Would not we shatter it to bits – and then
> remould it nearer to the Heart's desire?

From the Rubaiyat of Omar Khayyam

NOTES

[1] This was gleaned from an article in *TIME* magazine, 15 May 2003.

[2] In spite of objections from many environmental organisations, the Icelandic Government has given the Kàrahnjúkar dam project the green light. Construction began in 2003.

[3] In the tradition of the Scottish Highlands, a deer forest implies wild land where you can expect to find deer.

CHAPTER 16

2003 – 50 Years On

Things ain't what they used to be – and that goes for the weather too. Scotland used to have winters. Not now. For the climber, the winter of 1947 was a memorable one, the best I can recall in the past 56 years! There was some snow, not a lot, but frost! The Highlands lay in the steely grip of unrelenting frost for weeks on end. It was enough to make any ice climber salivate. One's job certainly came second, for opportunities like this don't come every year. Bill McKenzie, who worked for a bank and was one of the best ice climbers in Scotland at that time, is said to have suffered a severe bout of flu lasting two weeks. Every river was coated with a carapace of ice under which tinkled the much reduced water flow. Every hillside burn was a silver streak. The sun shone brightly, burning snow off the ridges. As some rocks emerged from their earlier snow covering and the snow settled into its crevices, the gullies became safe from avalanche and eminently climbable.

Bill Murray, released from his prisoner of war camp and with his book, *Mountaineering in Scotland*, on the verge of publication, was having a ball. He had taken a young climber, Donald McIntyre, under his wing and the two of them made good use of this great winter. It is described in Murray's autobiography *Evidence of Things Unseen*, published in 2002 after his death.

McIntyre was a postgraduate research student in the geology department of Edinburgh University. I was likewise pursuing chemical research for a doctorate. Our two laboratories were but five minutes apart and as we were both mountaineers, we met and climbed together frequently. He expounded preposterous theories to explain the evolution of rocks – I have never ceased to be amazed at the confidence with which geologists will tell you what happened several tens of millions of years ago. Anyway, Donald arranged for me to join him and Murray on a sortie to Glencoe to climb Crowberry Gully under winter conditions. At this time, 1947, only a handful of winter ascents had been made: Douglas Scott and Rob Anderson had made the one post-war ascent; Bill McKenzie and Kenneth Dunn had climbed it first (as they thought) in February 1936. It later transpired that the legendary Harold Raeburn had knocked it off in 1909. Naturally I was greatly honoured by the invitation and sat mutely in the back of Murray's dilapidated car as he negotiated the tricky bends and icy surface of the Loch Lomond road and onto the moor of Rannoch.

The car had no heating. Our combined exhalations quickly condensed on the inside of the windows. Donald's role was continuously to wipe the windscreen in front of Murray's aquiline nose, maintaining a small circle of visibility. Donald's exuberant vitality interacted well with Murray's restrained and monastic approach. I listened and slowly froze in the back seat.

We stayed at Lagangarbh, recently taken over from The National Trust: though now an SMC club hut, it was little better than an abandoned bothy. Getting water meant first breaking the ice in the nearby burn. There was no sink. The sole source of heat was a Primus that may well have been passed on from some pre-First World War Everest expedition. Some grubby pans and a miscellany of cutlery such as one can buy from a charity shop more or less completed the fittings.

We were up at first light – it was February – and I was glad to be moving as I had never managed to warm up after that dreadful car journey. The Buachaille Etive Mor was looking magnificent as the first blush of sunrise touched its summit. By 8 a.m. we were at the gully's foot, roping up. I could scarcely believe that there was a feasible route up there. Like the pages of an enormous book, the two sides of the gully, the Crowberry Ridge to the left and North Buttress to the right, seemed ready to snap shut on us like some Venus flytrap. The route took the tenuous seam between the pages.

Murray's purpose in climbing the route was to note details for the guide to Glencoe climbs that he had been commissioned to prepare. It came out two years later. This is how he describes it in that first-ever guidebook description:

There are usually five pitches, of which the last is either clear ice or black, and the others snow ice . . . It is not safe to allow less than three hours for the last two pitches. Six hours is a very fast time for the whole climb, and normal time is between 8 and 10 hours. A full 12 hours has been taken more than once by parties of 4 . . . The crux is the Crowberry Junction, where the gully forks. The best winter route is across the slabs on the right. But a coating of snow ice is required for the traverse . . .

If there is powder snow keep a sharp look out for avalanches – the risk is especially great around the junction . . . The last cave pitch is always clear of ice, is always likely to be very hard – often harder than the crux [*sic*].

Incidentally, after a heavy March blizzard in 1937 the gully was so full of snow that all the pitches were eliminated in a steep ribbon of snow.

Climbing in winter bears little resemblance to the delicate manoeuvres of a well-tuned body flowing up a vertical rock face – at least in those days. Facing us was a steepening slope of snow partly turned to névé ending in a bulge covered with blue ice. In summer this is a cave created by a huge boulder jammed in the gully like a champagne cork half out of a bottle. The cave was now filled with snow. Donald plunged his ice axe into the névé, wiggled it about a bit to penetrate deeper, wound a couple of turns of the rope around it and informed Bill that he was belayed: such was the state of the art in those days. Bill then took his shortened axe and, with a superb rhythm, cut a series of steps up the snow until below the bulge. There he rested. It's tiring stuff cutting hard snow. Now the problem was to overcome the bulge. Making use of his considerable height, he cut both foot and handholds in the ice as high as he could reach, then stepping up on one toe, grasped the highest hold with his free hand and used his other free hand to cut a further couple of holds above, pulled up and was over. A shower of ice and snow descended upon us as he cut a large stance for his feet, along with a space where Donald could also stand when he arrived.

I was highly impressed by this masterful execution, in particular the rhythm with which Bill plied his axe. Bill later offered me some instruction, which I was able to put to good use in the years to come before crampons and ice picks took over. Donald joined him and I was left to continue contemplating the strengthening sun illuminating the lochs and crests of the Moor of Rannoch and the shapely cone of distant Schiehallion. My problem was that as Bill continued up the climb, a never-ceasing shower of ice chips and snow rained upon my head and collected around my feet. The idea of wearing crash helmets had yet to catch on. Once Bill had climbed the second pitch, I was called upon to join Donald at the top of the first. I would not have liked to have led over that bulge.

In due course we all assembled at the foot of the junction pitch: to the left a slit oozing icicles rose to the neck where the Crowberry Tower joins the main mountain. Its very sight made me shiver. Bill led across the slabs, delicately cutting shallow steps, as there was no great depth of snow-ice. It was a masterful performance. Donald's meagre belay (as I now appreciate with hindsight) would never have been sufficient to hold him had Murray slipped and fallen, doubtless taking both of us with him.

It was a great climb and a privilege to watch the master at work. At 2 p.m. – after six hours of climbing – we were exiting the final slopes and a few minutes later we were basking not only in the satisfaction of our ascent, but in a warm sun and enjoying the staggeringly beautiful views offered by this isolated mountain.

I never had another opportunity to climb with Murray, but Donald and I made many exhilarating sorties to the hills and had fierce arguments about the physics of rock flow. And so it came about that, 53 years later, it occurred to me that I had never repeated this climb in winter. My memories of it were still quite vivid. At the time it had seemed very hard, but in the intervening years the technology of climbing and the philosophy of belaying had developed out of all recognition. We now had lightweight step-in crampons with front points, banana-shaped picks that were beautifully balanced and short and effective ice pitons and screws made of such hi-tech materials that each one cost a day's wages. Braided nylon ropes had replaced the hemp that we used in 1947. It was now perfectly thinkable to fall off, for the fall would be short, and it would be easily held. This aspect alone reduced the seriousness of the climb. However my problem was that I was now over 70 years of age. Did I have the stamina to climb a 1,000-foot ice climb of 6 pitches, even though it had now been downgraded to a Grade III climb?

Keith Anderson, a younger climber who had led me up several routes that were now beyond my abilities to lead had no doubts. In my comfortably heated car we drove to Laggangarbh, now a luxurious hut in the style of Habitat. The conditions were adequate. Though the winter had been poor, with little snow, a fresh fall a few days ago and a firm frost boded well enough. There was just one problem – other climbers. Whereas in 1947 it would have been unusual to see anyone else on the hill in winter, even one as alluring as the Buachaile Etive Mor, climbing was now so popular and transport so easy and cheap that climbers flocked in from all parts, even abroad. The one thing I did not want to experience was to be below another party slowly scrabbling up the Crowberry, under falling loosened ice chips and, who knows, falling bodies. Some parties tend to be very, very slow.

We were up before dawn and it was just after first light as we roped up. The day promised well: clear skies and a frost, albeit a light one. Keith is a determined climber; having fallen twice and broken his ankle, he still soldiers on, in spite of the pain. He climbs neatly, indeed quite effortlessly, and has a pleasing habit of flattering his older companions, something those peers of my own age never do and never did.

I looked up at the bulge at the top of the first pitch. It looked no easier than 53 years ago. I cannot recall Keith even slowing down as he smoothly swam over the bulge, using front points on his feet and expertly placed pick holds. This type of climbing falls into the 'shit or bust' school of ascent. When it holds it holds. When it doesn't you come off. My first experience of this method of ascent on ice was at the hands of Doug Lang who felt that before I grew too old I should be brought up to date. We stood at the foot of Green Gully on Ben Nevis on a cold winter's day, as he uncoiled a 200-foot rope, his trademark. He led the first pitch with his usual aplomb and I, with my first set of modern ice picks in my hands, found myself climbing with such speed that I had to pause to draw breath. It was an utterly new sensation! Pitch two, at a gentle angle, he offered to me. I revelled in the ease of the ascent. Pitch three he took and then generously offered me the last pitch. It was just less than vertical. Age diminishes one's strength-to-weight ratio. Halfway up the pitch, my strength ran out. My only recourse, short of falling off, was to hook my rope over the one axe that seemed decently rooted in the ice and ask Doug to lower me. The axe held. Doug then led. I followed. End of climb.

So, now a little more skilled in the art, I followed Keith up the various pitches without difficulty. Keith protected the junction pitch so well that a fall would have been no more than an inconvenience. I could not but think back to my earlier ascent with Murray and McIntyre, and McIntyre's totally inadequate belay. The awareness of safety has enormously improved. Yet, in the last resort, safety lies in the mind of the adventurer.

Even as we started climbing, the first of several climbing teams were racing each other to be the next in line. We had just beaten the first of them by half an hour. Our ascent took a little under three hours. More time was taken up with placing protection than in actual climbing. The climb was without risk, but not without pleasure and not without an appreciation of the wonderful ambience of that narrow slit in one of Britain's finest mountains.

Three days later winter virtually disappeared and it was back to rock climbing. And how things have changed in those 50-odd years. By now, in the UK, virtually every acre of vertical or quasi-vertical rock has been climbed. New routes are only to be found on tiny walls, often sea cliffs. The routes are short, sometimes as little as 30 feet, yet they are recorded and given names. They are usually very hard, otherwise what is the point of them? For me, for whom an E1 (extreme) is now beyond my strength, to read of the recent ascent of an E9 move on Dumbarton Rock, as described by Dave McLeod, is sobering indeed. McLeod was safely belayed and had practised this move many times, but he fell off every time (to be held), until finally he worked out the exact and appropriate sequence of body moves. He led it before an admiring audience. Britain's hardest move on rock.

So you see, the urge to explore and discover is alive and well, it's just that the focus has had to narrow. My generation was lucky to start climbing when horizons were wide and there were places on some maps marked 'unsurveyed'. Yet even my generation could not match the excitement of the early explorers venturing into regions where the charts offered the cautionary words: 'Here be dragons.' My generation was also lucky in that political correctness had not then run amok. It was quite acceptable for a single competent mountaineer to lead a group of lads and lassies on the hill and to camp with them. Unstructured adventure was the norm. This has all gone, under the baleful ordinances of nervous, do-gooding and uncomprehending authorities, to the detriment of future generations of young people who now have no chance to learn by experience that safety is awareness. My one fervent hope for the future is that mountaineering by individuals remains beyond the reach of politicians and regulating authorities. It seems to be the last sport or activity where decisions and conventions are left to the good judgement of its practitioners. Long may it so remain.

APPENDIX 1

A Scale of Risk

Just how risky is it to wander among the mountains or to go climbing? If some of the very best climbers perish, what hope is there for the rest of us? It is, however, an awareness of danger, rather than skill, that seems to be what keeps most of us alive long enough to die in our beds. There are no reliable statistics, but we can get some impression from the reaction of insurance companies, who specifically exclude 'roped climbing'. There are collective insurances, such as those negotiated by the British Mountaineering Council, the Austrian Alpine Club or the French Alpine Club, to name but a few. In the case of the French Alpine Club, one's annual subscription is enough to cover all contingencies anywhere, if you live in France. In the case of the Austrian Alpine Club, the modest annual subscription, which is less than the cost of a typical ten days' holiday travel insurance policy, will not only compensate for death and injury, but provide 30,000 Euros towards rescue costs. So clearly perceptions of risk vary greatly. Another way to judge risk is to compare it with the risks we run into in our normal day-to-day lives.

The table below was compiled by the Department of Health (UK) and called 'A Richter Scale of Risk' by John Adams. Some impression of risk for Scottish climbers was assembled by Eleanor Steiner in an unpublished doctorate thesis.

(D) is risk of dying in any one year; (A) is risk of developing an adverse response.

TERM USED	RISK RANGE	EXAMPLE	RISK ESTIMATE
High	Greater than 1:100	A. Transmission of susceptible household contacts of measles	1:1–1:2
		A. Transmission of HIV from mother to child (Europe)	1:6
		A. Gastro-intestinal effects of antibiotics	1:10–1:20
Moderate	Between 1:100 & 1:1000	D. Smoking 10 cigarettes/day	1:200
		D. All natural causes, age 40 years	1:850
Low	Between 1:1000 & 1:9999	D. All kinds of violence & poisoning	1:3300
		D. Influenza	1:5000
		D. Accident on road	1:8000
Very low	Between 1:10,000 & 1:100,000	D. Climber falling (source: Steiner)	1:10,000
		D. Leukaemia	1:12,000
		D. Playing soccer	1:25,000
		D. Accident at home	1:26,000
		D. Accident at work	1:43,000
		D. Homicide	1:100,000
Minimal	1:100,000 & 1:1,000,000	D. Accident on railway	1:500,000
		A. Vaccination-associated polio	1:1,000,000
Negligible	Less than 1:1,000,000	D. Hit by lightning	1: 10,000,000
		D. Release of radiation by nuclear power station	1:10,000,000

(Source: Department of Health, 1996)

APPENDIX 2

Via Alta Ticinese

The maps required for the Via alta Ticinese are Swiss National 1:50,000 Nufenen Pass (265), Val Antigorio (275) and Visp (274). Metric measurements have been used in this appendix to correspond with those featured on the recommended maps.

Each person should take a sleeping bag and prussiks loops (for crevasses). The party should be equipped with one rope and some ice axes. Whether from the north (Zurich) or the south (Milan) take the train to Airolo, on the south side of the Gottard Pass. From here one of the most beautiful valleys in the Alps runs westwards – the Val Bedretto. Take a taxi to the hamlet of Ossaco (café, 1,320 m) and skin up to the Cristallina hut (2,439 m, telephone: 094-881-081) through deciduous woodland, then at 1,800 m into a narrowing treeless valley. At its head you will find bed, food and wine. Incredibly this hut, which had stood for half a century, was destroyed by an avalanche in 1998. This serves to emphasise the unpredictability of snow. A new and more magnificent edifice was opened on 27 December 2002.

Above, soars the narrow crest of the Cristallina (2,912 m). You can dump your sack at 2,500 m, and pick it up on the way down since the route now continues over the Passo Cristallina (2,568 m). The view south from here is of a wild and empty mountainscape beyond which lie the Italian Lakes and the purple pollution haze arising from the motor traffic of the Piedmont. Work your way through highly dissected terrain to a loch, Lago Sfundau. Beware of tide cracks, because it has no surface overflow: it is part of a hydro-scheme which draws off water.

From the south end find a way west-south-west through complicated micro-terrain, which in less than a mile brings you to a tiny sheet of frozen water: Lago Bionic (2,076 m). You may even see signs of a metalled road on the way: it is a facility used in summer by the network of hydro-stations and has no connection to the valley. If you find it, follow it round. It goes first south-east, then south. Soon you can see Lago de Robei (1,906 m) below you. About 50 metres below its dam is the Capanna Robei (1,856 m), also known as the Refugio Basodino. This is inaccessible in winter from below and in season is served by a téléphérique owned by the hydro company. Enter. The hut will be unlocked and it is all electric, supplied by the grid. Turn on the heating!

Next day, head for Basodino (3,273 m). The simplest way on leaving Robei is to take the gallery that leads to the Lago de Zott. If not attractive, then climb to the téléphérique top station, and follow the streambed to the sheiling of Radinascia. The summit is ahead and the route obvious as the glacier leads to the summit. It is lightly crevassed. From the summit descend to about 2,900 m, then traverse north-east to the Kastelücke, a pass at 2,784 m. From there descend to the dam on the Lago Castel. Beyond may be visible, according to season, the hairpins of the road that leads from Val Formazza. Up to the end of March this should be skiable, right down to the village of Valdo (1,273 m) where there is a delightful, modestly priced hotel. This is a good place to re-stock – you will need two days' provisions for the next stage.

From Valdo take the chairlift to 1,900 m on the Torrente Vannino, and follow this river valley to the Vannino (Eugenio Margaroli) hut (2,194 m, telephone: 0324-63-118). It should be guarded and offer restaurant facilities: check at Valdo. From this hut, perhaps on the same day if you are energetic, you can readily ascend the Punta D'Arbola – or Offenhorn, according to the Swiss (3,235 m). The route is very beautiful and subtle. A short ascent takes one to the Lago Sruer (2,351 m) which will be frozen. Cross it heading for the gap between the Terre del Vannino and the Punta Lebendum. In due course this slope leads to the Sabbione Glacier which falls directly from the summit. This glacier is unique in the Alps in that its snout ends in the waters of Lago de Sabbione, where it behaves just like a polar glacier, casting off little icebergs from time to time.

From the summit you look down upon the most beautiful Alp in the entire Alpine chain – Alpe Devero. For the bold, in good conditions, it is possible to ski directly down the south face of Punta d'Arbola to Alpe Devero. This seductive route has one serious drawback: at 2,800 m a hidden 50-metre cliff runs the width of the glacier. This can be circumvented at each end, but coming from above the route-finding would be tricky: a rope is advisable. The alternative is to return to the Vannino hut for another night.

The easy route to Alpe Devero from Vannino is by the Scatta Minoia Pass (2,599 m). Ski to the head of Lago Vannina and on steepening slopes make for the pass. This should not be undertaken unless conditions are free of avalanche danger.

Once with Bill Wallace I crossed this pass in the other direction – towards Vannino. The conditions were very soft, and we had much reason to doubt the safety of the snow on the Vaninno side. Roping up, I descended a few feet and leapt about as if I had a ferret in my breeks. Slowly the wet snow started to slide away. I fell, held by the rope. As the slide gathered momentum, its bow wave widened, taking in more and more snow. Soon a slope hundreds of metres wide was gracefully sliding down. It was quite undramatic. No noise. No powder snow plumes filling the valley. It stopped well before the bottom of the slope, which was now safe to ski down.

Returning to the route, from the Scatta Minoia take one of the easy west-facing slopes down to a small loch at the sheiling of Pianboglio, then by following the river you arrive at the dammed waters of Lago de Devero (1,597 m) in its lovely woodland setting. This can be negotiated on either side but the loch will almost certainly be frozen and can be crossed safely. About 150 m below the dam is the charming little *pensione* known as the Locanda Fizzi at the hamlet of Crampiolo (1,797 m, telephone: 0324-619-108). Here Mario and his wife will offer you cheap accommodation and excellent food, accompanied by two-litre bottles of a very acceptable coarse Barbera d'Asti at a ridiculously low price – you are, after all, now in Italy.

The next stage is to Alpe Veglia. First ski down about half a mile to the hamlet of Devero (1,680 m) and take the drag-lift system to its highest point. Then skin up in a south-west direction to the crest beyond, called the Scatta d'Origna. Below you, to the south, the land falls away precipitously. A bold sweeping traverse downwards brings you to gentler slopes. Do not fall, there are cliffs below – shades of Stob Coire na Cennain! Traverse to the Passo Valtendra and then down easy slopes to the second most beautiful Alp in all the Alps – Alpe Veglia. This is a particularly hallowed spot since for most of the winter access from below is impossible due to avalanche danger on the approach road. You are almost certain to have it to yourself. You will have to bivouac here, finding shelter amongst the woodstores. Above rises the hugely impressive Monte Leone (3,553 m). Your way now is towards the Chaltwasserpass (2,770 m), via the Glacier

241

d'Aurona. If you have energy after the 1,000-metre climb from Veglia, another 800-metre will take you to the summit of Monte Leone, a truly magnificent summit and viewpoint. But you can just as well keep this pleasure for the morrow.

Descend to the Simplon Pass, where the brothers at the Simplon Hospice (1,997 m, telephone: 028-291-322) will welcome you with a warm dormitory, a restaurant, cheap (by Swiss standards) wine and a climbing wall! You are now in Switzerland again.

The route to Monte Leone rises directly behind the hospice. Ascend in a south-easterly direction under the north-east wall of the adjacent Hübschhorn. This leads to the Domattug Glacier. At about 3,300 m this abuts onto a shallow snow saddle from which the gentle upper snows of the Alpjerg Glacier lead across to the summit ridge of Monte Leone. It is best to make somewhat south of the summit and then, once on the crest, head north to the top.

Arriving at the Simplon need not signal the end of the Via Alta Ticinese, though from here a bus will take you south to Domodossola and so to Milan, or north to Brig and so to Geneva or Zurich. There is an *embarras de richesse* on your doorstep at the Simplon monastery. The Rauthorn (3,267 m), the Böshorn (3,233 m) and even the mighty Fletschorn (3,905 m) are all accessible from here if you have the energy for a 1,800-metre climb. Alternatively the Sass Valley is accessible via the Sirrvolter Sattel (2,621 m). From it, traverse north to Gamslag Glacier up to about 3,000 m, from which the ground opens out to the west. Easy slopes lead down to the Sass Valley and so to Sass Fee via Sass Grund, and eventually on to Zermatt via the Britannia hut and Adler Pass, perhaps taking in Strahlhorn (4,000 m) en passant.

APPENDIX 3

Mountain Rations

The following outlines my successful 4,000 kilo-calorie-per-day food ration for 12 man-days. Every item in the ration is available from a decent supermarket.

In 1992, it cost about £3 per person per day, and 10 years later about £4. Air-freight to your destination and it costs about £8 per person per day.

ITEM	WEIGHT (GRAMS)	K.-CAL./ BOX
sugar, brown	500	2,500
fruit crystals	120	600
corned beef (tinned)	454	980
savoury mince (soya)	240	520
saucisson (whole)	300	750
cheese (hard Cheddar, sealed)	1,000	5,000
corn pasta (tagliatelle)	300	630
semolina	200	550
pasta	120	350
tomato paste in tube	100	70
sun-dried tomato	20	70
garlic/pesto paste in tubes	100	70
Marmite (2 oz jar, every 2nd box)	50	
tuna fish in oil	2,200	840
potato powder	240	480

rice (boil in bag)	500	1,700
oatmeal (medium ground)	750	2,800
dried milk powder (5 pints)	283	1,360
soups of the world (instant)	4	660
Abernethy shortcake	200	900
whole bran	200	860
oatcakes	225	1,020
digestive	250	2,485
chocolate-coated digestive biscuits	200	1,020
crispbread	200	800
chocolate (milk)	200	1,020
chocolate (plain)	200	1,020
boiled sweets	100	500
bacon – dry cured	900	2,600
butter	500	3,500
margarine (Flora)	250	1,800
jam/marmalade (in plastic containers)	900	3,600
dried apricots, mixed fruits	500	1,200
dried sauces (bolognaise, curry etc.)		negligible
sardines in oil	200	1,440
mackerel in curry sauce	240	1,200
anchovies (great taste!)	100	600
roasted peanuts	400	2,320
tea bag, salt	30	
toilet paper, pot scrubber, cloth		
TOTAL	13.3kg	47,815 k.-cal. 3,985/day

APPENDIX 4

Nectar of the Gods

Oatmeal has the highest protein content of any cereal. It is the perfect breakfast food, being easy on the stomach. Cooked properly it can be delicious – cooked as it usually is in hotels it is unattractive; cooked by the ignorant it is vile. To the real porridge buff, there is only one form of oats – pinhead oatmeal (a coarsely ground meal). This needs overnight soaking and a fair bit of cooking and is not suitable for expedition camping. Then there are rolled oats, available under various brand names. Their apparent attraction is that they cook quickly, but they don't cook as quickly as medium-ground oatmeal and the taste is nothing like as good. This is the stuff to go for: moreover, it's dirt cheap.

THE TRUE RECIPE
The ingredients are water, medium-ground oatmeal and salt. The oatmeal must be packed in such a way as to retain its freshness. Place in a pan an amount of water equal to 80 per cent of the volume of porridge you wish to prepare. Place this upon a briskly burning stove. Before the water gets hot add the medium ground oatmeal, immediately stirring vigorously so that no lumps persist. The ratio of oatmeal to water is learnt by experience, but the thing to look for is a light slurry before it starts to cook. Immediately add salt, about a good pinch per spoonful of meal – this is a matter of taste, but some salt is essential. Turn down the heat and stir more or less continuously until it comes to the boil. Thereafter it needs only about two to three

245

minutes. If you have got the water-to-meal proportions right the porridge will have a consistency of a thick vegetable soup. If it is too thick it is not too late to add a bit of water. If too thin, then reduce by evaporation, stirring the while.

Two things will alert you to when the porridge is ready. Firstly, it will have the right consistency. Secondly, a beguiling odour will emanate from the pot, initiating a surge of gastric juices.

Eating this delicacy also merits a specific approach. After pouring the porridge into a bowl, leave it for two minutes. It will set ever so slightly. Do not spread sugar on it. If you do, you might as well eat junk food like cornflakes. Pour milk carefully into the side of the plate, so that a moat surrounds the porridge. This allows you to bring in some milk with each spoonful of porridge. Delicious!

And then, for the hardy or those without a stove, there is the old Highlander's mainstay used when the Duke of Cumberland was marauding Scotland: brose. This is simply oatmeal stirred with a little cold water and salt, and eaten directly. It will swell in your stomach and keep you going all day long. Atholl brose is with the addition of honey and whisky. It was Bonnie Prince Charlie's sustenance during his flight from the English.

Glossary

BELAYING: Where one climber, preferably firmly attached to the mountain, handles the rope as the lead climber ascends. This should be done in such a way that were the lead climber to fall, the belayer can sustain the fall. Various techniques are adopted to make this possible. Absorbing the energy of a falling body is no easy matter. The methods of 50 years ago were virtually futile. Today, with stretchable ropes to absorb the energy, and sophisticated techniques, there is a very good chance of arresting a fall. Nonetheless a fall is a fall, and can be serious.

BILTONG: sun-dried strips of meat.

BJAERG: the Danish word for 'mountain range'.

BRAE: the Danish word for 'glacier'.

BURRO: the Spanish word for 'mule' or 'donkey'.

COL: the lowest point between two higher points on a mountain ridge

CORRIE OR COIRE (Gaelic): a landform sculpted by ice, creating a bowl with a steep upper face, often a precipice. In England, the word Cwm (from the Welsh) is often used. There is no international synonym.

COULOIR: a commonly used French term indicating a gully, often snow- or ice-filled.

DORY: a small, flat-bottomed boat with a pointed prow and stern.

FRONT-POINTING: an ice climbing technique that evolved in the 1960s and has since been highly developed. A climber ascends by kicking the two front-pointing spikes of the crampon, strapped to the sole of the boot, into the ice. Balance is secured by swinging a short axe with a sharp point into the ice above one's head. The design of these axes has evolved tremendously. Hamish MacInnes is credited with its early development. A recent development called 'dry-tooling' uses such axes for climbing steep rock.

PEMMICAN: meat and fat concentrate in brick form.

PITCH: If a lead climber is attached by a rope to a belayer (q.v.) the maximum length he or she can go is the length of the rope between them. This distance between belay points is called a pitch.

PITON: a high, tensile metal peg of varied design which can be hammered into a crack or ice to provide a point of security.

RAPPEL: (German term for abseil) – where a rope, attached to a fixed point, is used for descent.

SASTRUGI: an Inuit word describing a snow surface that has been blown into furrows, up to two feet deep, often with sharp edges to the crests.

TSAMPA: roasted grain.

TINDE: the word for 'peak' in Danish.

TWO-PICK TECHNIQUE: *see* front-pointing.

CONVERSION TABLE

Imperial measurements have been used throughout the book, except where a metric height represents something symbolic, for example a 4,000 m summit in the Alps.

The following calculation can be used to convert feet to metres, and vice versa.

1 foot = 0.305 metres
1 metre = 3.281 feet

Bibliography

Adams, J. 'A Richter Scale of Risk' in *Re-thinking Risk*, ed. Julian Morris, Butterworth-Heinemann, London, 2000

Banks, Mike *Commando Climber*

Bennet, D. *Staunings Alps*, The Expedition Library, Blackwell, Oxford, 1972

Benuzzi, F. and Loomis, C. *No Picnic on Mount Kenya*, Wm. Kimber, London, 1952

Bonnington, C. *Quest for Adventure*, Book Club Associates, London, 1982

Bonnington, C. *Everest the Hard Way*, Random House, London, 1977

Boysen, Marten 'The fissure Boysen', *Mountain*, 1976

Brooks, R. 'Yerupaja', *Illustrated London News*, 5 November 1966

Brown, J. *The Hard Years*, Mountaineers Books, 2001

Byrd, R.E. *Alone*, Putnam, New York, 1939

Campbell, R. 'The Angry Corrie', *Scotland's Heritage Hillzine*, 55, (November 2002)

Carson, Rachel *Silent Spring*, Mariner Books, 2002

Connor, J. *Dougal Haston: The Philosophy of Risk*, Canongate, 2002

Crocket, K.V. *Ben Nevis*, Scottish Mountaineering Club & Trust, Edinburgh, 1986

Department of Health, 'On the State of the Public Health: the Annual Report of the Chief Medical Officer of the Department of Health for the Year 1995', HMSO, London, 1996

Halliday, G, Kliim-Nielsen, L. and Smart, I.H.M. 'Studies on the flora of the north Blosseville Kyst and on the hot springs of Greenland', in *Meddelser øm Grønland,* 199, no. 2, 1974

Hamilton, R.A. *et al.* 'British North Greenland Expedition 1952–4: Scientific Results', *Geographical Journal,* CXXII, Part 2, (June 1956)

Hansen, Kjeld 'Farvel til Gronlands Natur' (*A Farewell to Greenland's Nature*), Gads Forlag, Copenhagen, 2001

Haston, D, 'Reflections on the Eiger direct', *Mountain World,* Allen & Unwin, London (1968)

Herbert, Marie *The Snow People – Life Among the Polar Eskimos,* Pan, 1973

Herzog, Maurice *Annapurna,* Jonathan Cape, London, 1952

Kosterlitz, M. 'Yerupaja', *Alpine Journal* (1967)

McNaught-Davis, I. 'Hjørnespids', *Alpine Journal,* 66, No. 303 (1961)

Mikkelsen, Ejnar *Two Against the Ice,* Steerforth Press, 2003

Minchietti, L. and Slesser, M. 'Mountains of Brazil', *Mountain World,* Allen & Unwin, London (1967)

Murray, A. *Evidence of Things Unseen,* Burton Wicks, London 2002

Noyce, Wilfred *They Survived,* Heinemann, London, 1962

Ovchinnikov, Anatole *Alpinists of the Moscow School,* MGTU, N.E. Bauman, Moscow, 1998

Paterson, W.B., 'Altitudes on the Inland Ice of Greenland', *Meddelser øm Grønland,* 137, Nr 1, 1955

Patey, Tom *One Man's Mountains,* Gollancz, London, 1971

Radcliffe, P. *Land of Mountains,* Methuen, New Zealand, 1979

Simpson, C.J.W. (ed.) *North Ice,* Hodder & Stoughton, London, 1957

Simpson, Joe *Touching the Void,* Vintage, London, 1998

Simpson, John *Strange Places, Questionable People,* Pan, London, 2001

Slesser, M. *The Andes are Prickly,* Gollancz, London, 1966

Slesser, M. *Brazil: Land Without Limit,* Allen & Unwin, London, 1969

Slesser, M. 'The Staunings Alps of East Greenland', in *Mountain World,* Allen & Unwin, London (1962)

Slesser, M. 'Dedo de Deus', *SMC Journal,* XXIX (1968) including Henley's account. Also published in *The Best of Ascent,* eds. Roper, S. and Steck, A Sierra Club Books, San Francisco, 1993

Slesser, M. 'Peterman Peak', *SMC Journal,* XXXIII (1986)

Smart, I.H.M. 'Pushing the boat out', *SMC Journal,* CLXXXXII (2001)

Smart, I.H.M. 'Miscellaneous notes', *SMC Journal,* XXXV (1995)

Smith, R. 'The Bat and the Wicked', *SMC Journal,* XXVII (1960)

Tennent, N. 'The primitive approach', *SMC Journal,* XXVII (1962)

Tennent, N. 'Missing the last post', *SMC Journal,* XXVII (1960)

Wilson, K. *Games Climbers Play,* Diadem Books, 1978

Index